REGULATION AND DEREGULATION IN EUROPEAN FINANCIAL SERVICES

The **European Science Foundation** is an association of its 56 member research councils, academies and institutions devoted to basic scientific research in 20 countries. The ESF assists its Member Organizations in two main ways: by bringing scientists together in its Scientific Programmes, Networks and European Research Conferences, to work on topics of common concern; and through the joint study of issues of strategic importance in European science policy.

The scientific work sponsored by ESF includes basic research in the natural and technical sciences, the medical and biosciences, the humanities and social sciences.

The ESF maintains close relations with other scientific institutions within and outside Europe. By its activities, ESF adds value by cooperation and coordination across national frontiers and endeavours, offers expert scientific advice on strategic issues, and provides the European forum for fundamental science.

This volume arises from the work of the ESF Scientific Programme on European Management and Organizations in Transition (EMOT).

Further information on ESF activities can be obtained from:

European Science Foundation
1 quai Lezay-Marnésia
F-67080 Strasbourg Cedex
France
Tel. (+33) 88 76 71 00
Fax (+33) 88 37 05 32

Regulation and Deregulation in European Financial Services

Edited by

Glenn Morgan and David Knights

MACMILLAN
Business

First published 1997 by
MACMILLAN PRESS LTD
Houndmills, Basingstoke, Hampshire RG21 6XS
and London
Companies and representatives
throughout the world

ISBN 0–333–65542–7

A catalogue record for this book is available
from the British Library.

10   9   8   7   6   5   4   3   2   1
06   05   04   03   02   01   00   99   98   97

Typeset by EXPO Holdings, Malaysia

Printed in Great Britain by
Antony Rowe Ltd
Chippenham, Wiltshire

Contents

v

List of Tables and Figures

Tables

Figures

Preface

This collection derives from a series of papers presented at a workshop financially supported by the European Science Foundation's Programme on European Management and Organizations in Transition (ESF EMOT). Richard Whitley as Co-Director of the ESF EMOT Programme played a significant role in securing the funding for the workshop and encouraging the production of a book deriving from it. Jean-Pierre Daniel acted as host to the original workshop. He provided us with excellent facilities at the Centre de Recherche sur L'Epargne which included an impressive view over the magnificent roof of the Paris Opéra. Lesley Gilchrist has had the major task of producing all the chapters in the appropriate format and deserves our sincere thanks for her patient help and forbearance in the completion of this book. Finally, our thanks are due to the contributors and the other participants in the workshop for helping us to produce this volume.

Manchester

GLENN MORGAN
DAVID KNIGHTS

Notes on the Contributors

David Courpasson is a researcher at the Management Research Institute, Groupe ESC Lyon, France. He has published widely in French sociology journals such as *Revue Française de Sociologie* on professional identities amongst bank employees. His latest book is entitled *L'Identité, entre enterprise et marché: Les Transformations de la Profession Bancaire* (1994).

Nestor D'Alessio has taught Sociology in Latin America and Germany. He is currently researching European financial services at SOFI, the University of Göttingen.

Jean-Pierre Daniel is Coordinator of International Research at the Centre de Recherche sur L'Epargne, Paris. He has recently published two books on *bancassurance*.

Lars Engwall is Professor of Business Administration at Uppsala University, Sweden. He has recently acted as Adviser to the Swedish Commission on the Banking Crisis as well as publishing a number of articles in books and journals such as the *Scandinavian Journal of Management* on banks as organizations. His books include *Newspapers as Organization* (1978) and *Mercury Meets Minerva: Business Administration in Academia* (1992).

Swen Hildebrandt is a research student at the Wissenschaftszentrum, Berlin. He is currently completing his dissertation on French and German banks.

James Høpner is a researcher at Copenhagen Business School, Denmark. He is currently completing a thesis on banking in the Danish banking system.

David Knights is Professor of Organizational Analysis and Director of the Financial Services Research Centre at the Manchester School of Management, UMIST. His books include *Managing to Discriminate* (with D. Collinson and M. Collinson) (1990) and *Managers Divided* (with F. Murray) (1994). He is a joint editor of a series of books arising from the

UMIST/Aston Labour Process Conferences including most recently *Resistance and Power* (with J. Jermier and W. Nord) (1994).

Kari Lilja is Professor of Business Administration and Head of Department at the Helsinki School of Economics. Professor Lilja has written extensively on the Finnish business system and the paper and pulp industry in Finland.

Glenn Morgan is a Lecturer in Management, Manchester Business School, the University of Manchester, UK. He is author of *Organizations in Society* (Macmillan, 1990); *Dynamics of Organizational Change* (with A. Sturdy) (Macmillan, forthcoming).

Herbert Oberbeck is Co-Director of the Soziologisches Forschungsinstitut (SOFI) at the University of Gottingen, Germany. SOFI is one of the foremost research institutes in the field of the sociology of work and industry in Germany. Dr Oberbeck's publications include *Die Zukunft der Angestellten* (with M. Baethge) (1986) and *Changes in Work Patterns and their Educational Implications* (with M. Baethge) (OECD Report, 1987).

Sigrid Quack holds a research position in the Labour Markets and Employment Group at the Wissenschafszentrum, Berlin, Germany. She has published articles on employment and training patterns in European banking industries.

Danielle Salomon is a researcher at the CNRS Groupe d'Analyse des Politiques Publiques based at the Ecole Normale Supérieure, Paris. She has recently completed her thesis on the public policy implications of bank restructuring.

Timo Santalainen is a researcher at the Helsinki School of Economics, studying developments in the Finnish banking industry.

Andrew Sturdy is a Lecturer in Management at Bath University School of Management. His book publications include *Skill and Consent* (edited with D. Knights and H. Willmott) (Macmillan, 1993) and *The Dynamics of Organizational Change* (with G. Morgan) (Macmillan, forthcoming).

Risto Tainio is Professor of Business Administration and Vice Rector at Helsinki School of Economics, Finland. He has held visiting professorships at Stanford University and the European Institute for the Advanced Study of Management, Brussels. Professor Tainio has published widely on management in Finnish banking and the Finnish business system.

Introduction

Glenn Morgan and David Knights

During the 1980s and into the 1990s, the world economy has been fundamentally affected by a process of deregulation. The proponents of deregulation argue that releasing markets and economic actors from regulatory constraints can generate the levels of economic growth and productivity that seemed to have deserted Western economies during the 1970s and early 1980s. Led by the free market enthusiasms of Reagan in the USA and Thatcher in the UK, a range of initiatives were taken throughout the world to remove the hand of government from direct intervention in the market system and replace state control with various forms of indirect regulation.

The financial services industry was at the heart of these changes. More and more states began to allow free movement of capital across their boundaries. Controls on lending limits and conditions for credit were loosened and often removed. Companies were allowed to develop new products for both corporate and personal customers that incorporated and managed risk in new ways. Prohibitions which restricted organizations' ability to diversify from one area of financial services into another were reduced and often removed. Whilst often this deregulation necessitated the state to withdraw controls, it also sometimes needed state action in order to force companies out of long-standing cartels and restrictive practices where forms of self-regulation had operated to sustain high profits.

Deregulation in financial services was part of a wider movement but it attracted particular attention. Partly this was due to a recognition that in many countries banks and insurance companies were 'sleeping giants' that had been protected from competition for too long and would therefore be particularly hard hit by deregulation. Partly it was due to the growing belief that service employment and earnings from service exports (particularly in financial services) was going to be the answer to the loss of manufacturing capacity that occurred in the early 1980s in the USA and the UK. By the mid-1980s, the boom in financial services employment in Sassen's 'global cities' – London, New York and Tokyo (Sassen, 1991) – and the rise of a new cultural phenomenon in those cities – the Yuppie, invariably identified as a young, highly paid trader in one of the many burgeoning sectors of the finance industry – seemed to reinforce the centrality of financial services deregulation to the new economic order.

Most of all, changes in financial services seemed to represent the clearest expression of the emergence of a global market and the relative weakness of national governments in responding to these changes. The creation of Euro-dollar markets, spurred on in the 1970s by the petro-dollars recirculated from the oil-rich OPEC countries, threatened the ability of national governments to control internal credit expansion and squeeze through traditional measures. Companies could now go directly to international markets for funding. These changes created a pool of credit that was available beyond national controls. The largest multinational companies no longer had to rely on their home banking institutions. In the event of requiring new capital, they could go direct to these money markets. The financial institutions operating in these markets gradually developed many new ways of providing finance depending on the needs of their customers. At first, the Euro-dollar markets were mainly based on the creation of large syndicated loans, where financial institutions joined together to provide capital to both nations and companies. As the markets developed and the floating of exchange rates offered new possibilities both for matching needs and risk more exactly and for extending the range for speculative trading and gains, new products emerged. Securitized bonds and floating rate notes as well as the whole range of futures, options, swaps and derivatives enabled companies to draw on credit in different currencies as and when they desired. In these markets, the credit rating of the borrower was a crucial element in determining the level of interest. Thus the large multinationals were by the mid-1980s often given a credit rating superior to that of some of the major banks, making it even more advantageous for them to borrow directly from the money markets rather than via their banks. Even the most speculative ventures such as the leveraged buy-outs of the 1980s could be funded from these markets so long as interest rates reflected the risk level (though as became clear by the end of the decade, there was a massive underestimation of the risk involved).

The growth of the money markets prompted the large multinationals to deal in them on their own behalf. Thus corporate treasury departments were set up that lent to the markets and engaged in speculative behaviour on the company's behalf as well as managing the company's more orthodox borrowing and currency requirements. Once again, traditional banking institutions were circumvented (Meerschwam, 1991).

The classic intermediation role of the banking system was being undermined by these changes. Traditional bank lending was becoming less profitable. As the largest multinationals were able to raise their own funds, banks were forced into looking for new markets. Some of these new markets proved to be highly risky, particularly lending to less developed countries, property investment and junk bond funding. Over the 1980s, each of these areas of lending returned to haunt those banks most closely involved. Other markets were less risky but more competitive. In particular, banks refocused on lending to medium and small enterprizes in their home markets and expanding their services for personal customers. Margins in these areas of business had typically been wide due to low competition and cartel-like agreements which operated in many countries. However, the pressure to find new business arising from disintermediation forced banks out of their traditional agreements and into aggressive competition. Thus the broader changes at the global level began to impact both directly and indirectly on national institutions and national markets.

Disintermediation, therefore, had the effect of forcing traditional banking institutions into new ways of working. It led to an explosion of demand for new types of financial services both at the global and the national level. At the global level, financial institutions were still able to play a major role in organizing the new forms of credit and managing the emerging markets in foreign exchange, securitized bonds. This type of work, however, was much more competitive than previously. Profitability was based on either fee-based work or on taking a position for oneself (in currencies, stocks or bonds). Both were more short-term and risky than traditional banking business. They also necessitated worldwide presence (to maximize opportunities and match the multinational client base) and high amounts of capital. In order to gain a global presence in these new markets, therefore, banking institutions had to develop new structures that put their expertize and capital to work in new ways.

Although national markets evolved more slowly, there was a series of intricate ties between the two levels. Those banks wishing to play on the global stage sought to squeeze maximum business out of their home markets, thus pressurizing the local institutions to become more competitive as well. Failure at the global level impacted on national strategies and vice versa. Losses on loans to LDCs, for example, led British banks to work harder to make their personal customer and small and medium sized enterprises (SME) business more profitable in the 1980s.

In order to play a part in these changes, however, financial institutions had to release themselves from the regulatory and organizational structures which limited the nature of the activities which they could undertake. These structures were often deeply embedded in political and economic ideas about the nature and role of financial institutions. In some cases such as the USA, these systems legislated against universal banking (the combination of commercial, retail banking with investment, wholesale banking); in other cases such as Britain, the institutions had developed separately for a variety of reasons and combining them required major organizational and cultural changes; in still other systems such as Germany, universal banking was established but its *modus operandi* was conservative and based on managing relations within a stable national market. Pressures therefore developed within national systems to get rid of legislation and regulation which was restricting banks' abilities to operate in this new environment (Herrig and Litan, 1995; Stubbs and Underhill, 1994; Gardener and Molyneux, 1990). In particular, in Britain and the USA, the Thatcher and Reagan governments sought to respond by opening up their economies and their financial centres to international competition (Moran, 1991), and other countries began to follow (Canals, 1994).

Since the early 1980s, governments and financial institutions have struggled to reshape their national financial systems in ways that meet the challenge of the new international financial system (Dale, 1992). They focused in particular on deregulation, defined broadly as the dismantling of barriers between different markets and institutions. Deregulation would release competitive forces within and between nations that would force financial institutions to become more efficient and in doing so create efficient national and international financial markets. These changes affected different types of financial institutions in different ways though its general impact was to create a major upheaval for all of them. They had often enjoyed many decades of protection from external competition whilst internal competition had often been formally and informally regulated by cartel-like agreements supported by the government, rendering the organizations highly conservative and resistant to change. The advent of new forms of competition and uncertainty posed major challenges to policy-makers in government, regulatory bodies and the financial institutions as they all struggled to respond to these broad global changes (Swary and Topf, 1992).

In much of the popular and academic discourse attempting to analyse these changes, deregulation was treated as an inevitable result and consequence of the underlying economic processes represented by increased international financial markets and disintermediation. Whilst it might be a 'risky experiment' (Dale, 1992, ch. 11), the 'financial revolution' (Hamilton, 1986) was inevitable because regulation had failed. Furthermore, what was occurring was 'global financial deregulation' (Swary and Topf, 1992). National differences were not disregarded but a 'convergence of the financial system globally' (Swary and Topf, 1992, p. 7) was expected to be the outcome of deregulation. These ideas have common currency, superficial attractiveness and widespread legitimacy. Clearly the financial world has changed but the question is whether the language of 'regulatory failure', 'global deregulation' and 'convergence' is the most appropriate way to understand these processes.

From the perspective of the late 1990s, it is becoming increasingly clear that the process of change is not simply unidirectional, from regulation to deregulation, from divergence to convergence, from national systems to a global order of competition. In the late 1990s, the impact of deregulation, for example, appears more complex than was at first expected. Freedom from one set of restraints may require the construction of another form of regulation. Certainly, it appears that initial attempts at deregulation increased the amount of risk which financial institutions took on, leading in some cases to catastrophic losses, which have raised new demands for reregulation. In Britain, the senior management of the major clearing banks have suffered harsh criticism for their lax lending policies in the 1980s. Their counterparts in the wholesale markets have also lost money on a large scale, culminating in the bankruptcy of Barings Bank. In France, major institutions, most notably Crédit Lyonnais, have reported huge losses. In the Scandinavian countries, experiments in deregulation have failed and have shaken the foundations of the whole financial system. The result is that in the 1990s, the key policy issues concern not deregulation *per se* but the reconstruction of regulatory regimes at both the national and the international level in order to bring some sort of order into the complex and fragile interdependencies of the global system. In national and international contexts, governments, regulators and companies are slowly building new regulatory structures. It is not a case of moving 'from regulation to deregulation'; rather there has been a reconstitution of the nature of regulation in financial services.

Similarly, the idea of convergence conceals the fact that national financial systems and their regulatory structures remain distinctive in many respects. The institutional legacies of decades are not wiped out in the space of a few years. Zysman, for example, argues that:

> Institutional history is a function of the country's distinct political and industrial development ... the progressive evolution of these structures defines evolving sets of constraints and incentives... That institutional structure of the economy ... creates a distinct pattern of constraints and incentives. This defines the interests of the actors as well as shaping and channelling their behavior. The interaction of the major players generates a particular 'policy logic' and a 'particular market logic'. Since the national institutional structures are different there are as a consequence many different kinds of market economies. (Zysman, 1994, p. 246)

Zysman's argument is reflected in a range of studies which are emerging that indicate the continued importance of national institutional factors to forms of economic organization (Whitley, 1992a, 1992b; Whitley and Kristensen, 1995; Hollingsworth, Schmitter and Streeck, 1994; Dittrich, Schmidt and Whitley, 1995).

If the impact of changes in the international economic system is going to be understood properly, simplistic conceptions of convergence, modernization and transition need to be jettisoned and replaced by more careful analysis of the levels and types of changes occurring in national and international markets and institutional orders (see, for example, Alexander, 1995). Thus, it is clear that there now operates a global financial market for certain sorts of products, for example, foreign exchange and all its associated phenomena, large corporate loans, stock and bond trading for large companies and national governments, major corporate insurance risks and commodity trading. These markets are global in the sense that financial institutions from any part of the world can participate in them if they meet certain conditions of entry and the prices which are set reflect supply and demand features present on a global scale. They are not global in the sense that they exist simultaneously in every part of the globe. On the contrary, they are local and highly concentrated in a few 'global' cities (Sassen, 1991). This points to the fact that rather than a process of convergence, it may be more appropriate to pay attention to the roles of cities, nations and firms within a new international division of labour (Sassen, 1995; Amin and Thrift, 1995; Knox and Taylor, 1994; Corbridge, Martin, and Thrift, 1994). The creation of global markets and global forms of regulation reinforce certain types of local distinctiveness, whether defined in national, regional or city terms. Within these national contexts, institutions and structures adapt and change in different ways, reflecting the interaction of their own trajectories of development with the changing dynamics of the international economy. This interpenetration and interdependence of the global and the local cannot be captured in the discourse of convergence, globalization and deregulation. It has to be picked out and unravelled in particular contexts.

In this book, the authors present a series of studies of how national financial institutions are changing in this new context. The pressures on banks and financial institutions arise from heightened competition within national contexts and at the global level. However, the way in which national systems, firms and regulators adjust to these pressures is different in each society under consideration. The goal of these studies is not to present a definitive account of how each national system is changing. Rather, the authors focus on a particular element of the system and reveal how this has changed as a result of new forms of competition and deregulation at both the national and the global level. The result is a distinctive approach to the study of regulation and deregulation in financial services. It is an approach which is interdisciplinary, informed by the economics, politics and sociology of banks as organizations evolving and changing in a national context set within an international political economy.

In the first chapter, Morgan examines the interrelationship between national systems of finance and the international political context. His argument is that national institutional distinctiveness is itself a historically constituted phenomenon. The existence of an international trading economy depends on forms of coordination between its constitutive parts. Since the nineteenth century, this coordination has been achieved in a number of ways. Coordination can be achieved through the creation of fixed exchange rates between nation states, policed and controlled by a single dominant power. Where this power declines or fails to maintain coordination, the system either breaks apart into competing blocs (as happened in the interwar years) or is reconstituted on a new basis through floating exchange rates. These forms of coordination have different implications for nation states depending on the role which they play in the international system. Nation states that played a hegemonic role in the world order found that their institutional system was substantially influenced by this requirement and their economy and financial system tended to become open. Nation states that participated on the basis of trade backed up by possession of gold or the dominant currency are able to protect their own financial institutional structures from outside pressures. This helps to explain why financial systems were able to retain their distinctive national structure until the 1980s. However, once the USA was unable to retain its hegemony, national systems were forced to change faster and further than previously.

The distinctiveness of national financial systems arose from the complex interaction between the state, manufacturing industry, the financial institutions and the owners of personal wealth. In his chapter on the Danish banking system, Høpner shows how the financial system in Denmark reflected and reproduced the basic distinction between large firms (based mainly in Copenhagen) and the small and medium-sized enterprizes located outside of the centre. Depositors in small cities and towns developed their own local financial institutions to support local business. Even when the local institutions have been taken over and merged into the national banks, local autonomy remains important. Branches maintain close links with their local clientele which enables them to make a fundamental contribution to the flexibility and responsiveness of small and medium-sized enterprizes in the Danish system (Kristensen, 1995). Thus in spite of the fact that the Danish financial system as a whole has become more centralized and concentrated in response to increasing international competition, elements of the underlying logic of the system continue to be reproduced. It is therefore necessary to distinguish between processes of concentration and centralization at the ownership level and centralization of decision-making. Concentration of ownership may occur in response to a variety of factors such as the need to attain scale in order to compete in global markets either on one's own account or on behalf of large national firms. Failure to achieve profits in these markets weakens banks in their home markets, either making them susceptible to takeover (foreign or otherwise) or allowing new entrants into the market. However, this need not be accompanied by a centralization of decision-making. There may be strong pressures to retain local branch autonomy as part of a broader institutional order linking firms, banks and local communities.

Høpner's study of the social embeddedness of financial systems thereby raises the question of how far institutional structures based on local autonomy will change. Courpasson's study of French retail banking indicates the possibility of other outcomes. Courpasson shows how the French system was also traditionally based on strong local relationships between the banks and the local business and its community. He emphasizes the role which the bank branch manager played in garnering local knowledge and making decisions based on this. However, he shows that French retail banks have undermined this system. In the search for ways of reducing costs and increasing profits, they have adopted new management techniques of market segmentation and automatized credit rating, thus doing away with the special localized expertise of the bank branch manager. On the other hand, the individual employee within the bank is pressured to achieve more detailed performance targets. Thus the system both depersonalizes decision-making whilst at the same time personalizing the work performance of the employees. Courpasson argues that employees in French banks are facing great ambiguity in trying to deal with these pressures.

The German system, on the other hand, stands between the Danish example and the French. Oberbeck and D'Alessio argue that the distinctive structures of the German financial system – the relationship between banks and manufacturing, the conservative nature of financial products, the decentralized structure of the industry split between the private banks, the savings banks (Sparkassen) and the cooperative banks – are evolving rather than fundamentally changing. They show that there are changes beginning to occur at certain levels of the system. The largest German companies are becoming less reliant on a single tie with their 'Hausbank' and are developing more links with other German and non-German banks. In response, the largest German banks are gradually venturing beyond national borders in a search for new clients as well as new ways of serving the old clients. However, the local banks have responded with great vigour to the challenges which have arisen and the savings banks have developed new products and work practices which have helped them survive in a strong position. In their view, it is therefore too soon to talk about the 'end of the German model'. The distinctive institutional characteristics of the system appear resilient and capable of change without destroying the fundamental structures.

Quack and Hildebrandt's study of bank relationships with small and medium-sized enterprizes in France and Germany brings out these contrasts clearly. They argue that the pressures arising from disintermediation in the 1980s impacted differently on the two countries because of their distinctive institutional structures. The German banks have always been integrally involved with their small and medium-sized business clients which in turn constitute a substantial and stable part of the German economy. They attempted to compensate for losing the business of the largest German firms by increasing the profitability of the SME sector. In France, on the other hand, the small and medium-sized firm sector (in distinction to large businesses on one side and very small businesses on the other) has not been very powerful or significant and has certainly not been nurtured by the French banks in the way which occurred in Germany. The French banks were therefore forced into riskier loans at the local, national and international level as they tried to compensate for falling business with their largest clients. Once again, therefore, the way in which financial systems developed and responded to the creation of global markets depended on their own internal 'market logics'.

Salomon's chapter shows that these 'market logics' have complex effects. On the one hand, they reach down into the firm and on the other hand they shape and structure the way in which the state interacts with the financial system. She examines in detail how one major French bank responded to the relaxation of credit controls. She shows how bureaucratic rigidity within the bank led to an expansion of risky lending with very little management control. This derived from the dominant position of the bank within the financial system, which in turn reflected its importance to the French government. The government tried to resolve the crisis of indebtedness caused by reckless overlending by the bank through modifying its own regulations. The state could not, however, directly influence the bank which responded by simply curtailing lending rather than developing a new system. Salomon compares this to a more specialist credit-lending institution in France which operated a more rigorous system of controls. However, the dominant logic set for financial institutions in the French case has derived from the handful of nationalized and private large banks which have, throughout most of the postwar period, been integrally involved in the French system of state-directed credit allocation (Zysman, 1983). Salomon's analysis indicates the importance of linking processes of change within the financial system to that of the role of the state.

Sturdy, Daniel and Morgan examine the relationship between the state and the financial system through comparing the development of *bancassurance* in Britain and France. In both countries, *bancassurance* (the sale of insurance products manufactured by subsidiaries of banks through their bank branch system) was stimulated by deregulation and increasing competition between the different financial institutions. However, the authors show that beneath these similarities, the nature of *bancassurance* differs considerably and this can be related both to distinctive institutional histories and the role of the state. In France, *bancassurance* developed as a means of providing cheap and standardized savings products to the mass of the population. The French state aimed to halt the rise in its pension payments by encouraging individuals to save for their own retirement. French insurance companies were highly conservative, bound by existing distribution channels which were traditionally expensive. The banks, on the other hand, saw this as a crucial new market, enabling them to boost their profitability in the personal sector when, as Quack and Hildebrandt show, their corporate business was in difficulty. Thus *bancassurance* in France is a very different entity from old-style insurance companies in France. In Britain, on the other hand, whilst government stimulus for personal pensions was, if anything, stronger than in France, the banks' sales forces, products and expenses structure took on many of the features of the insurance companies. Although there were rivalries and competition between the bancassurers and other financial institutions, these were not as deeply institutionalized as in France, where there has been great hostility between the two. Once again, therefore, the institutional structure of the two societies shaped the way in which firms and their management responded to similar types of deregulation and competition.

The role which managers play in interpreting and implementing deregulation is demonstrated by Engwall's chapter. He shows that Swedish banks adopted new recruitment strategies in order to meet what they saw as the opportunities arising from deregulation. Banks took on experts in marketing and sales and reduced their numbers in traditional occupations that were responsible for control inside the banks such as auditors and accountants. The banks were eager to gain more business in the new deregulated environment and therefore concentrated on expanding numbers in those jobs closest to the customers and the market. The consequence was that control systems in the banks declined in significance and strength. As a result the banks took on loans that turned out to be risky and insecure in the long term. Within a few years, the whole Swedish banking system was in crisis due to the non-performance of these loans. As a result, banks and the government have had to look at new ways of reregulating the system.

Tainio and his colleagues show a similar process occurring in the Finnish context, though they emphasize the role of top managers. In their view, the over-expansion of lending which occurred in Finland following deregulation resulted from a series of traps into which management fell. In particular, top managers in one of the major banks identified their initial successes in the deregulated environment with a particular strategy. They fell into what the authors term an 'internal' trap, that is, a particular strategy from which it was difficult to escape. They continued to pursue this strategy even when economic conditions were changing. The result of this was that they fell into an 'external trap'; they were uncompetitive and unsuccessful because of their strategy.

In the final chapter, David Knights looks more broadly at the significance of financial services and deregulation in the British context. Building on his previous work (Knights, 1988), he develops the concept of financial self-discipline and argues that current moves towards deregulation and the privatization of welfare are part of a broader process of change in which individuals are made responsible for their own financial security and well-being. However, he notes that in modern societies where governments have to balance a wide range of interests and the administrative apparatus becomes highly complex and differentiated, it is impossible to implement such changes without there also being contradictions and conflicts in the process. He shows how the goal of financial self-discipline is both promoted and inhibited by government action and its unanticipated consequences. Knights's chapter therefore provides a further link to broader debates in social theory concerned with how financial institutions and financial security are managed in modern societies.

In conclusion, this book offers a new approach to the study of regulation and deregulation in financial services. Such an approach can be said to link to other studies which emphasize the distinctive institutional structure of particular societies and the impact which they have on firms, economic actors and forms of economic coordination. Applying these insights to financial services, one can identify the following elements:

- Financial systems and their regulatory regimes have deep historical roots which shape the ways in which actors formulate and implement their strategies for change
- Competitive forces which appear to drive change take shape within specific social contexts; how they are interpreted and managed by actors varies between contexts
- The outcome of change processes is uncertain; it depends on the resources and powers brought to particular contexts by a range of actors, including the state, regulators, the organizations, their employees and their customers
- The opening up of the international economy has a range of effects on national systems depending on the level which one is examining and the processes which are being considered

In terms of empirical research, the studies in this book represent only the beginning of what is necessary in order to move beyond simplistic concepts such as convergence, deregulation and globalization. In order to go further, it is clear that a multidisciplinary approach is necessary. Political economy, sociology, geography, economics and politics will all need to be considered if we are to understand the trajectory of financial systems. This is a major challenge to scholars as it also requires an openness and familiarity with comparative research that is daunting. Nevertheless, such a challenge is being taken up in many places and we hope that the readers of this book will be at least convinced of its validity and interest in relation to understanding financial services in Europe.

References

J. Alexander, 'Modern, Anti, Post and Neo', *New Left Review*, 210 (1995) pp. 63–101.

A. Amin and N. Thrift (eds), *Globalisation, Institutions and Regional Development in Europe.* (Oxford: Oxford University Press, 1995).

J. Canals, *Competitive Strategies in European Banking.* (Oxford: Oxford University Press, 1994).

S. Corbridge, R. Martin and N. Thrift (eds), *Money, Power and Space.* (Oxford: Blackwell, 1994).

R. Dale, *International Banking Deregulation.* (Oxford: Blackwell, 1992).

E.J. Dittrich, G. Schmidt and R. Whitley (eds), *Industrial Transformation in Europe.* (London: Sage, 1995).

E.P.M. Gardener and P. Molyneux (eds), *Changes in Western European Banking.* (London: Routledge, 1990).

A. Hamilton, *The Financial Services Revolution*. (Harmondsworth: Penguin Books, 1986).

R.J. Herrig and R.E. Litan, *Financial Regulation in the Global Order*. (Washington, DC: Brookings Institute, 1995).

J.R. Hollingsworth, P.C. Schmitter and W. Streeck, *Governing Capitalist Economies*. (Oxford: Oxford University Press, 1994).

D. Knights, 'Risk, Financial Self-Discipline and Commodity Relations', *Advances in Public Interest Accounting*, 2 (1988) pp. 47–69.

P.L. Knox and P.J. Taylor (eds), *World Cities in a World-System*. (Cambridge: Cambridge University Press, 1994).

P.H. Kristensen, 'On the Constitution of Economic Actors in Denmark', in R. Whitley and P.H. Kristensen (eds), *The Changing European Firm: The Limits to Covergence*. (London: Routledge, 1995) pp. 118–58.

D. Meerschwam *Breaking Financial Boundaries: Global Capital, National Deregulation and Financial Services Firms*. (Boston, Mass.: Harvard Business School Press, 1991).

M. Moran, *The Politics of the Financial Services Revolution*. (London: Macmillan, 1991).

S. Sassen, *The Global City*. (Princeton, NJ: Princeton University Press, 1991).

S. Sassen, 'The State and the Global City: Notes Towards a Conception of Place-Centered Governance', *Competition and Change*, 1, 1 (1995) pp. 31–50.

R. Stubbs and G. Underhill (eds), *Political Economy and the Changing Global Order*. (London: Macmillan, 1994).

I. Swary and B. Topf, *Global Financial Deregulation*. (Oxford: Blackwell, 1992).

R. Whitley, *Business Systems in East Asia*. (London: Sage, 1992a).

R. Whitley (ed), *European Business Systems*. (London: Sage, 1992b).

J. Zysman, *Governments, Markets and Growth*. (Ithaca, NY: Cornell University Press, 1983).

J. Zysman, 'How Institutions Create Historically Rooted Trajectories of Growth', *Industrial and Corporate Change*, 3, 1 (1994) pp. 243–283.

1 The Global Context of Financial Services: National Systems and the International Political Economy

Glenn Morgan

INTRODUCTION

During the 1980s, it became common to speak of the 'global revolution' in financial services and the processes of 'convergence' which were being set in train as a result of this revolution. However, the link between national systems and the international political economy goes back much further than the 1980s. The creation and maintenance of the world capitalist economy has from its earliest origins depended upon financial institutions which can manage the transfer of value across national boundaries and different systems of currency.[1] The development of these institutions[2] has occurred over various phases. The purpose of this chapter is to identify those phases and in doing so make clear the distinctive character of the 1980s and 1990s. Emphasis is placed on the interaction and mutually constitutive nature of the national and international systems for regulating[3] financial services markets. The argument is that the form and nature of internal national systems are interdependent with the international context in which they exist.

It is argued that the period of the 1980s and 1990s is the latest stage in a long series of economic and social developments in the integration and management of national and international financial institutions. It is not a unique turning point from regulation to deregulation, from national to global, from stability to uncertainty. It carries aspects of continuity and discontinuity from the past.

INTERNATIONAL POLITICAL ECONOMY AND NATIONAL FINANCIAL SYSTEMS

In a recent discussion, Ingham has argued for the need for a 'clear... distinction between state and market power in the production and management of world money' (Ingham, 1994, p. 30). He goes on to note that according to Weber 'valid and effective forms of money are the outcome of the interplay of market-based and state interests' (p. 31). Financial systems evolve as a means of managing the interplay between markets and states in the production, distribution and consumption of money. This interplay occurs within national borders; the production of money and financial systems is the *sine qua non* of a modern nation state.[4] It is simultaneously a condition and outcome of the maintenance of a modern nation state.

However, modern nation states are involved in complex trading relationships with each other. An international system of money must therefore also be organized. Any form of trade beyond barter is dependent on the existence of what Dodd has termed 'monetary networks' (Dodd, 1994). Dodd describes monetary networks in terms of particular social relationships which are necessary in order for trading to be based on money rather than barter. These include a standardized accounting system, expectations about the value of money over time and space, its legal foundations and enforceability as well as its acceptance for use by others. Monetary networks *within* nation states are sustained and reproduced within the context of the regulatory regime governing financial services. These regimes define what is to count as money, the conditions under which money can be invested and lent, and the returns to money in the form of interests and dividends. They also define the types of organizations which can deal with money, such as banks and insurance companies. Finally, these regimes consist of systems for monitoring and supervising the use of money both by financial institutions and individuals. Regulatory regimes are backed by the power of the state.

Yet clearly in all trading economies, monetary networks must extend beyond the national boundary. By definition, there is no longer a state which can act as final arbiter of interests and disputes; nor is there a central bank which can act as lender of last resort. Within national boundaries, certain guarantees exist that are absent once trading starts to cross them. However, like trade within national boundaries, trade[5] across these boundaries requires the existence of a standard and store of value which is accepted by the multiple parties involved. Creating these standards and stores is the key to understanding the international financial system of regulation and how it relates to national systems of regulation.

Traditionally this standard and store consisted of precious metals. In seventeenth- and eighteenth-century Europe, the possession of bullion *per se* rather than its use as a means of managing trade became the central objective of state policy. Mercantilism 'encouraged the export of goods, while banning exports of bullion or coins, in the belief that there was a fixed quantity of commerce and wealth in the world' (Anderson, 1974, p. 35). States aimed to hoard bullion in order to increase their power and weaken that of their enemies. Thus their internal regulatory regime (which forbade bullion export) was built upon their conception of the international political economy – one in which political power flowed to the most powerful economy. By the nineteenth century, mercantilism, 'the ruling doctrine of the Absolutist epoch' (Anderson, 1974) was as dead in most of Europe as was absolutism itself. However, the intricate relationship between bullion (mainly gold by the late nineteenth century, although debates on the role of silver and bimetallism continued particularly in the USA (Foreman-Peck, 1995, pp. 158–60)), paper money and state power remained important. What system emerged to manage international trade and how did this relate to internal financial and monetary systems?

REGULATING INTERNATIONAL TRADE

The Gold Standard and Sterling

Foreman-Peck states that:

> An expanding international division of labour was only possible because of the corresponding development of the international monetary system. (Foreman-Peck, 1995, p. 66)

From the eighteenth century states entered this system at different rates and at different times. Mathias writes that 'the process of industrialization in Britain was to become more integral with international trade than virtually all other countries' (Mathias, 1969, p. 103). In the case of textiles in the early nineteenth century, 'probably more than 50 per cent of total production was exported' (p. 104). From the early part of the nineteenth century, the British also began to export capital, first in overseas government stock, then in railway stocks. In 1856, foreign investment constituted 9 per cent of total UK assets and by 1913, this had risen to 34 per cent (Michie, 1992, p. 108). Few other countries had such a high dependence on international trade, yet most of the industrializing nations became increasingly involved. France, for example, was dependent on British capital for the financing of their railway system in the 1840s; according to Pollard, 'in 1847–48 ... allegedly half the French railway capital was in British hands' (Pollard, 1981, p. 155), though this flow soon reversed and France itself became a major exporter of capital to support railway building in the rest of Europe. French exports, which had equalled British exports in the pre-Napoleonic period, lagged behind throughout the nineteenth century yet specialist French products such as wine and silk were highly valued on world markets. Germany on the other hand was self-sufficient in capital throughout most of the nineteenth century, though by the end of the century it was making substantial exports in chemicals, engineering and textiles.

The web of international trade grew throughout the nineteenth century. Manufactured goods, raw materials and capital flowed to an increasing extent across national borders around the world. World trade grew at an annual rate of 3.5 per cent in the period 1870–1913 (Kitson and Michie, 1995, p. 7). In order for this to happen those people who participated in the trade needed to know that they would receive the value of their part of the transaction, that is, it would not be reduced or destroyed because of unexpected changes in the value of the currencies which were the units of the exchange. This was achieved through extending and developing the gold standard.

Gold (and silver, to a lesser extent) was traditionally the means whereby value had been transferred between societies. As trade between states increased, so did the importance of gold as the medium of exchange. Currencies measured their value against the amount of gold which could be bought per local unit of currency. Even though the discovery of new sources of gold in the mid-nineteenth century increased its supply, this did not lead to a decline in gold's value. Rather, it 'provided the opportunity for the major industrial powers to move to gold standards whether de jure or de facto' (Foreman-Peck, 1995, p. 87). On the other hand, whilst gold could be the ultimate arbiter of the international system, the extent of trade internationally as well as nationally meant that, as with domestic banking systems, it was the existence of a *gold standard* rather than gold *per se* that was crucial. The gold standard constituted a promise to pay the bearer of paper money a certain quantity of gold. From the point of view of the issuers of currency, the risk lay primarily in the potential for currency-holders to demand gold.

Once a country went on to the gold standard, it automatically placed itself in a situation where its currency could be converted to that of another through the medium of gold. Thus Foreman-Peck shows how the amount of gold embodied in British 1869 sovereigns related to the amount of gold in French Napoleon coins (worth 20 francs) and enabled the calculation of an exchange rate of 25.2215 francs to the pound in 1870 (Foreman-Peck, 1995, p. 71). The gold standard therefore offered a means whereby it was possible to transact and close out positions between different currencies. The system was based on fixed exchange rates both to gold and to different currencies participating in the system. The discipline which the international system imposed was the need for countries to balance their accounts. In theory, failure to balance (usually because of an excess of imports over exports) would lead to an exodus of gold which would be passed on internally as a reduction in the money supply, thus deflating the economy, reducing demand for imports and thereby balancing the national accounts again. Alternatively, in the case of creditworthy nations, there would be an inflow of credit to enable the shortfall to be overcome without excessive deflation. There was very little in the way of exchange rate risk that could not be managed by small changes in interest rates where countries were on the gold standard.[6] The 'dominant and overriding objective of monetary policy was the maintenance of gold parity' according to Ruggie (1982, p. 389). Furthermore:

> Insofar as the adjustment process ultimately was geared to securing external stability, state abstinence was prescribed so as not to undermine the equilibrating linkages between the balance of payments, changes in gold reserves and in domestic credit supply. (Ruggie, 1982, p. 389)

However, in the same way that domestic systems cannot be based entirely on gold but use gold as the base with paper money as the means of transaction, international systems also need an alternative to gold itself. There had to be a currency which all parties would be willing to treat for all practical purposes as though it were 'as good as gold'. Thus institutions and individuals, no matter what their nationality, would be willing to leave their wealth in a certain currency rather than convert it into gold or back into their own currency. As a result, that paper currency becomes the medium of exchange on the international markets and the central element in maintaining a system of fixed exchange rates between currencies and gold. The other countries in the system may devalue or revalue without undermining the system as a whole but if the central currency threatens to do this, the whole system crashes. In the nineteenth century, the pound sterling took on this role and 'benefitted most of all' from this monetary order (Gilpin, 1987, p. 127).

The Dollar and Embedded Liberalism

The 'Pax Britannica' was based on processes of automatic adjustment between countries that were determined by the inflow and outflow of goods and capital. In the period from 1945 to 1971, a similar system was eventually established under the domination of the American dollar.[7] In principle, all the currencies of the major trading countries were fixed against gold and against each other. However, unlike in the period up to the First World War, adjustment would not occur automatically through the operation of the market. Gilpin states that 'the conflict between domestic economic autonomy and international economic stability has become the fundamental dilemma of monetary relations' (Gilpin, 1987, p. 122) and the experience of the interwar years led many to emphasize the need to give the national state a more active role in the management of the economy than had been possible under the gold standard. However, this could lead to the threat of 'national capitalisms', that is, systems which were effectively closed off from each other, and trade which was organized on a bilateral basis rather than open markets. This in turn would damage international trade. In such systems there would be severe exchange controls and external trade would be controlled by the state. However, the USA as the dominant economy of the period was committed to free international trade; it required a system which would keep other societies in the international trading system whilst still leaving them leeway to pursue their own economic objectives of full employment. This was to be achieved by the creation of a set of international institutions which would 'cushion the domestic economy against the strictures of the balance of payments' (Ruggie, 1982, p. 395). There would be created a 'double screen' between the domestic and the international.

The double screen would consist of short-term assistance to finance payments deficits on current account, provided by the International Monetary Fund, and, so as to correct 'fundamental disequilibrium,' the ability to change exchange rates with Fund concurrence. Governments would be permitted to maintain capital controls. (Ruggie, 1982, p. 395)

In the postwar period, there was explicit recognition that there might need to be adjustments between countries. However in order to minimize these adjustments, the IMF offered loans to countries to enable them to overcome short-term difficulties. In the event that these proved insufficient, devaluation was an option open to any particular country so long as it sought IMF approval first. In both cases, the IMF could make its agreement conditional on certain requirements for internal restructuring.

THE NATIONAL IMPLICATIONS OF THE INTERNATIONAL POLITICAL ECONOMY UNDER FIXED EXCHANGE RATES

During these two phases of the world economy, the major currencies were in principle (if not always in fact – European currencies did not in reality become convertible again after 1945 until 1958, though they were treated as such for the purposes of the trading system and the international institutions) convertible into one another at fixed rates. In theory, traders and any others holding paper from these currencies knew that the value of the paper was not just conventional or confined to the particular issuing country. It was recognized by and convertible in other countries. Whilst such traders had to be careful of holding some currencies which might devalue or occasionally revalue, they expected that the dominant currency (the pound or the dollar) would not lose value.

However, such a system has within it its own seeds of destruction. Simply because it is so much in demand as a substitute for gold, the government which manages the hegemonic currency might be tempted to print more money without extending the gold base, thus generating inflation and undermining the real value of the currency. This in turn causes other countries to look elsewhere for the store of value, perhaps to other currencies but mainly to gold, converting its holdings of the hegemonic currency gradually to gold. This was what happened increasingly in the postwar era. The institutions of embedded liberalism were run to support American power so whilst other countries were subject to IMF and World Bank strictures on their budgetary deficits and growing inflation (since these would pull underlying currency values out of line and lead to demands for devaluation or revaluation with consequent knock-on effects for other participants), the USA had no such discipline exerted on it (Panić, 1995). Such a system will eventually crack, partly because the other participants will lose faith in the standard currency. The French under de Gaulle for example began to shift out of dollars into gold as they began to suspect (correctly) that the value of the dollar against gold was unsustainable (Hirsch, 1969, ch. 14).

Changes in underlying levels of productivity and competitiveness between countries also undermine the system. Where the hegemonic currency increasingly has to fund a balance of trade deficit (as well as a budgetary deficit) by borrowing, the whole system is placed in jeopardy. Thus a 'good as gold' currency is never as 'good as gold'; it might be sustainable in the short and medium term, but there is always political and economic risk of devaluation. In the case of the USA and the dollar, these changes took place gradually through the 1960s as other countries, weakened by war, began to catch up and challenge American domination of world markets. In the case of the pound sterling, it was the impact of the First World War and the need to sell off overseas investment and borrow to fund war activities that fatally weakened the economy and meant that in spite of efforts to return it to its former dominant position by restoring convertibility at the prewar level (Pollard, 1970; Moggridge, 1969), it could never regain its previous hegemony (McKercher, 1988).

On the other side, the cost for non-hegemonic currencies of staying in the system at a fixed rate was the reduction of their own capacity to manage the internal economy except in a way that sustained their exchange rate position. Once they had lost their hegemonic position, this was a trap which the British fell into after the first World War, when they sought to restore sterling to its dominance by fixing the pound at its prewar rate against the dollar and gold. This could only be achieved at the expense of manufacturing exports which became totally uncompetitive in world markets, throwing vast numbers of miners, textile workers and engineers into unemployment with consequent effects on the economy as a whole (Pollard, 1970; Moggridge, 1969).

However, what may be considered a trap in one set of circumstances becomes a form of freedom in others. In particular, whatever else happens inside the system is irrelevant as long as the exchange rate is maintained. The result is that under the conditions of the gold standard, the structure of the internal financial system is entirely determined inside the country.[8] There is no pressure from outside for systems to converge. If one country wishes to restrict lending or patterns of business between types of institution in one way and another wishes to do it in another, there is no reason why they should converge. Nor was there much pressure for states to open up their financial systems to foreign competition. Financial institutions were an integral part of the governance mechanisms within particular societies. In general, states tried to protect them from foreign competition through fear that this could undermine the systems of control and governance which had been established. Whilst states were pressured to open their borders to manufacturing imports, both by other states and, in the era of embedded liberalism, by the institutions of the IMF and the World Bank, there was little such pressure operating on financial systems. From the point of view of individual states, the main concern was to ensure internal monetary arrangements as managed by the financial institutions did not undermine the exchange rate. In the period of the 'Pax Britannica', the flow of gold in and out of states was supposed to ensure this. During the 'Pax Americana', the institutional mechanisms were more complicated though the principle remained the same. In both cases, the financial system itself, its governance mechanisms and its institutional structure, was predominantly determined by internal national developments. Within the gold standard system, the diversity that came from different social systems could continue to exist even though the world economy as a whole was becoming more integrated.

The only participant in the system which did not have this freedom was the dominant power. It had to keep its doors open, allowing its currency to move around the global system acting as the global currency. For the dominant powers (Britain in the nineteenth century and the USA between 1945 and 1971), this was not a decision which had to be made; it had already become part of their way of functioning. Effectively, this way of being was both a cause of their dominance and a consequence of reproducing it. No other country needed to act in a similar way. Diversity at the national level was sustained by a universally applicable standard of interchange managed by a single dominant power.

However, this combination of universalism and particularism is unsustainable in the long run. Allowing particularism to be maintained and sustained generates a series of centrifugal forces that eventually undermine the system. These forces are of two sorts. First, the continued existence of particularism generates winners and losers. Some societies have resources that enable them to compete successfully in the world market, whilst others fail to do so. The winners gain trade surpluses; in effect, their currency becomes stronger but because its value remains the same in the fixed exchange system, its advantage is in fact further multiplied. As Ruggie notes about the Bretton Woods system, 'there existed no means to compel surplus countries to appreciate' (Ruggie, 1982, p. 408). The same process works in reverse for the losers in the system; their position becomes worse over time and in their efforts to win back markets, they place intense pressure on their internal social cohesion. Thus divisions between and within the participants increase as the system continues.

This is exacerbated by the second centrifugal force. This concerns the dominant state which sustains the fixed exchange system by providing its currency to the world as a whole. At first, this provides the dominant power with a huge advantage. It does not have to worry as much as other participants in the system about having a gold-backing to its currency issue. It is literally in charge of printing the world's money and from this comes an increase in its economic power which was already far superior to others in the system, otherwise its currency would never have emerged as 'good as gold' in the first place. However, over the medium to long term, its willingness to become a debtor to the rest of the world creates a huge risk. What if the world as a whole begins to doubt the currency? Moreover, given that the system is already generating significant centrifugal processes and in particular some economies are becoming stronger, how long will the hegemonic state's power survive? Once these doubts begin to arise, they are almost impossible to overcome. For those powers that are successful in the system and are gradually accumulating the currency of the dominant power, this becomes particularly significant. If the currency is no longer as 'good as gold' they do not want to be left holding devalued pieces of paper. They therefore become active in looking for a new system.

A paper money system based on fixed exchange rates therefore creates two sorts of risks. First, it creates the risk that the whole system may collapse because ultimately it is founded on the dominance of one particular currency and if that dominance begins to decline, the system cannot be sustained. Since the political and economic conditions of dominance cannot be guaranteed in the medium to long term, there will always be a point when the system moves towards collapse. Second, it creates risk by sustaining particularism and difference, thus ensuring that some participants will be winners and others losers; by exacerbating these divides it undermines both the political and economic conditions of its own survival. In effect, then, it creates exactly the conditions of political and economic instability which it is aiming to control. It is an inexorable contradiction that will always trap fixed exchange systems.

FROM FIXED RATES TO FLOATING AND UNSTABLE EXCHANGE RATES[9]

The previous section showed that there was an unexpected relationship between the emergence of a universal market system and the maintenance of distinctive national financial systems. The fixed exchange rate was the mechanism whereby international trade was managed. Whilst this had many implications for wealth, employment and growth within particular societies, it had no direct impact on the organization of financial systems. They were distinct, separate, protected and unthreatened by the universalism of the system.

However, there are limits to the ability of the system to sustain itself. The fixed rate system collapsed dramatically and devastatingly in the interwar years. It collapsed more gradually from the late 1960s and with less catastrophic effects. In both cases, however, a different set of relationships existed between the external international economic context and the internal regulatory order than had been the case under the fixed rate system.

If fixed exchange rates break down, trust in the conditions that make international trade sustainable may also break down. A transaction conducted in conditions where fixed exchange rates have broken down takes place under high levels of uncertainty. The two sides are uncertain how much value is going to be transferred and who will benefit. Sudden adjustments in exchange rates can wipe out profits immediately, as well as the value of investments. However, it is important to distinguish two forms of breakdown. The first form of breakdown is where there is frequent adjustment of exchange rates. The second is where the exchange rates are continuously floating.

The National Implications of Exchange Rate Breakdown in the Interwar Years

The first type, involves a form of *ad hoc* adjustment of currencies. In other words, there is still adherence to the idea of fixed exchange rates but the frequency and significance of the readjustments is such that the level of trust necessary for international trade declines. This is most damaging where one of the currencies making the adjustments was previously the world's 'good as gold' currency, as with the UK in the 1920s and 1930s. As no one currency is willing to act as a world currency and there are no institutional mechanisms for managing and hedging against currency risk, the global system breaks down and is replaced either by autarky supplemented by bartering (Germany and the Soviet Union in the 1930s) or the creation of small-scale trading blocs based on a lead currency (such as the British imperial sterling area in the 1930s where trading links between the Dominions and the UK were maintained and extended) which manages relations within the bloc and also between the bloc and outside trading partners (McKercher, 1988; Rowland, 1976).

Instability of exchange rates has a devastating effect on international trade and through this on employment and business in economies dependent on imports and exports of capital and goods. Paradoxically, however, it could be argued that these effects offered societies the one opportunity since their original institutionalization to alter fundamental aspects of their financial system. In the USA and a number of countries, this opportunity was taken in the sense that a strict new set of controls was placed on banking as an attempt to reduce risk, especially by separating commercial from investment banking (Benston, 1990). In effect, the breakdown of universalism was also surprisingly a breakdown of the old particularism. Although economies barricaded themselves behind new barriers to prevent the loss of home markets in manufacturing to international competitors and to reduce their vulnerability to further deflations elsewhere, behind those barriers some of them began to restructure their financial institutions, particularly to reduce the chances of instability spreading through the system, following the US example and separating commercial and investment banking. Even in the UK, the decline of the international system led the banks and the City into closer relations with industry than was previously possible (Tolliday, 1987). Where this would have eventually led is unclear because war intervened and by the time it was over, the USA was by far the strongest economic power in the world and unlike in the interwar years was now prepared to participate in managing international trade through fixed exchange rates and the maintenance of the dollar as 'good as gold'.

The National Implications of Exchange Rate Breakdown: Post-1971

The second type of instability is where the system moves to permanently floating exchange rates. In principle, this allows for adjustments between economies to be made on a continuous basis rather than differences being stored up and intensified until major readjustments become necessary. Ideally, currencies appreciate to the degree to which they are wanted on the market; this reflects underlying economic strength as well as government policy on interest rates. Too great an appreciation undermines competitiveness and therefore is self-correcting since the currency is no longer so popular. The same mechanism works the other way in theory with weak currencies which depreciate so much that their products become competitive again and so their currency climbs. In such a system, central banks may work together either formally or informally to bring order into the system and create a proxy for fixed exchange rates, thus reducing exchange rate fluctuations.

In such a system, the 'systemic' quality arises in a particular way. Under the gold standard and fixed exchange rates, it is the fixity of the rates which provides the stability. Where rates are floating, by definition, this cannot provide any stability. Instead, the potential for stability arises from agreement on 'process', that is, that rates float in markets where liquidity guarantees the ability of traders to reflect changes in underlying economic performance. This was the system which evolved gradually following the dollar coming off the gold standard in 1971. Such a system had, of course, never been tried before so how it was going to evolve and what its consequences would be for the international political and economic order, as well as for the internal financial systems of societies, was really unknown.

If such a system is to work as the basis of an international political economy (rather than just as a means of adjustment between a limited number of countries), it requires a set of financial markets which will provide the liquidity necessary to enable buyers and sellers to purchase foreign exchange as and when they require it. In effect such a system had already begun to develop in the Euro-dollar markets in the 1960s. As international trade had grown, US dollars which had been earned in Europe by US multinationals were no longer returned to the USA where restrictive banking legislation reduced profitable opportunities. Instead, they became the subject of financial innovation based on the London market and were recirculated from London into Europe and elsewhere. They expanded credit beyond the reach of the regulators in both the USA and the UK, creating new markets for loans in foreign currencies. These markets were dramatically expanded by the redistribution of wealth which occurred in the wake of the oil crises of 1973 and 1975. Dollars earned by the oil-exporting nations sought profitable investment opportunities through the London financial markets. Thus simultaneously with and connected to the collapse of the old fixed rate system, there emerged a massive boost to liquidity in the financial markets. These changes meant that both banks and companies could go into the new markets and buy currencies and credit as and when required at rates determined by the market. In particular they could begin to hedge and protect themselves against potential falls in the exchange rate value of particular currencies. Similarly they could buy into appreciating currencies, as well as protect themselves against interest rate changes. Thus, whole new products began to appear – options, futures, swaps, floating rate notes – which enabled companies to continue trading internationally whilst, in theory, removing elements of risk. In spite of efforts made by national regulators, these new markets were moving beyond their control (Hawley, 1994) and starting to create a new sort of international political economy dominated by international banks and transnational corporations.

However, the new system which emerged did not just enable banks and transnationals to resolve their needs for hedging against currency and interest rate changes. The liquidity which was being engendered and reinforced by the actions of the banks and the transnationals was being used to create products which could benefit from liquidity *per se*; in other words, products which were based on the speculative act itself. Buying into futures and options did not have to be linked to any specific need for a particular currency at a particular time; it could on the contrary become effectively a 'bet' on the direction of movement between currencies. Such a system changes foreign exchange trading from its original function of facilitating trade and adjusting currency values to reflect underlying strength to one where the highest rewards derive from speculation. The uncertainty over where the rate will be between two currencies at a particular time encourages dealers to speculate and bet on outcomes. It also encourages others to hedge against unfavourable outcomes, thus creating markets for swaps, futures and options. These markets in turn change from being a means of protection against the unexpected effects of speculation into being themselves a means of speculation.

Clearly, there is a technological element to a system based on 'process'. It requires that market participants can respond rapidly to changes in the value of currencies in order to reduce risk or gain speculative profits. Floating rates could not work unless 24-hour trading is possible to provide the liquidity that is necessary to establish trust and confidence in the market process. However, once the system is established, exchange rates become less predictable and less determined by underlying economic performance. The speculative dynamics of the system become its drivers rather than the requirements of international trading *per se*. Thus more hedging becomes necessary to hedge against the threat to the previous hedge and more speculation becomes necessary to offset previous speculative losses.

The establishment of these markets around London, New York and Tokyo began to change the whole way in which the international political economy worked *and* the way in which national financial systems linked into that level of economic life. Instead of a universal standard of value embodied in gold and fixed exchange rates, there is now theoretically a universalized process of value creation – that of the market – which will adjust between currencies and economies. All countries which participate in the international trading system have to relate to this universal process in two main ways. First, they have to allow their currencies to be traded. This means that the competitiveness of their products on international markets is affected on a continuous basis by the trading process. Second, and more crucial to the considerations here, their internal financial system is no longer insulated from the international political economy. The increase in cross-border flows of capital that derives from the changing structure of financial markets and transnational corporations requires that national financial institutions have the ability to manage these flows on behalf of their clients. Since the flows are becoming transnational, this requires overseas offices and subsidiaries. Permission to enter closed markets is usually based on reciprocal arrangements, thus opening up more and more nationally enclosed systems to foreign competition. Participating in the markets themselves (and thereby participating in the profits which are available from them) requires that financial institutions bring something to the market; where their ability to do so is restricted by foreign exchange and capital controls, they are effectively denied access. Thus the global financial markets become magnets which attract participants, but in order to get into the game, the national institutions of governance have to change. Where firms are allowed to locate, how they can shift deposits about, what risks they can take are all subject to review. In other words, the old institutional structure is no longer sacrosanct or protected. Without the fixed exchange rate system to act as a buffer, the dynamics of the international financial markets penetrate right into the heart of the national financial system.

The creation of the new structure of financial markets constitutes a change which cannot be ignored by national systems. The reasons for this are threefold. First and quite simply, any international trading company or bank has to go into these financial markets in order to have the liquidity to trade (assuming that barter and bilateral trading is a least favoured option for organizations and states). Second, the profits from participation in these global deals are potentially far larger than those available in national systems. Therefore staying away from these markets may reduce risk but it also reduces earnings power and may leave an organization weak *vis-à-vis* competitors which have been successful. Third, the result of the first two factors is that banks and transnationals from whatever country will pressurize their national regulators to let them enter these markets by reducing barriers to capital export and so on. Thus, the new system compels consideration of reform of the internal structure. The previous system was based on a long-standing institutional structure which was only challenged at the point of severest crisis and near breakdown in the 1930s. The rest of the time its structure remained roughly as it had been established in the nineteenth century. The new international system now raises the questions for national financial structures of what does it mean for their system in the 1990s and how should it be reformed. In this sense, it has forced national decision-makers to take a proactive role towards their national systems. Most commentators would argue that there was only one direction to be taken and therefore it did not amount to a real choice for the policy-makers; they had to open up their home systems and let capital flow across borders and institutions until it found its rightful home in its most profitable outlet. But, as the chapters in this book show, this was an argument which had to be actively promoted. Furthermore it could not be assumed that it would win as there would be many losers in such a process and therefore resistance could be expected.

This choice for national institutions was not simply between yes and no to deregulation and convergence. There were many different ways of moving; changes could be fast or slow, they could be partial or complete. These become decisions subject again to national priorities and requirements. Since national regulatory systems were constructed on different bases, the nature and meaning of deregulation in one system would be different from that of another. Thus systems could change at different speeds, in different ways, according to different political, economic and social priorities. A rhetorical commitment to openness could be reconciled with the maintenance of capital controls and protectionism by arguing in terms of the 'national interest' requiring delay. In these terms, then, the opportunities for change opened up by the new system should not be read as pointing towards convergence. On the contrary it can be expected at least in the medium term that diversity between national systems will in fact increase. Previously national systems were diverse but stable. Therefore differences did not increase but remained embedded and reproduced for over a century. In the 1990s, on the other hand financial systems will change but they will change at different rates and in different ways. Therefore diversity within and between these systems is more likely to increase than it is to decrease.

THE NEW DIVISION OF LABOUR IN THE GLOBAL FINANCIAL SYSTEM

From these considerations, an alternative view of the process emerges which identifies the elements of the new system of international political economy in terms of a new division of labour in the global financial system. The elements of this division of labour are as follows.

The Global Market-Places in the Global Cities: New York, London and Tokyo

The new markets which are emerging are dominated by a handful of locations. Sassen's work demonstrates that:

There is a growing concentration of foreign service and financial firms in New York, London and Tokyo handling business on behalf of both host country firms and co-national firms operating in the host country. In this sense we can think of New York, London and increasingly Tokyo as transnational centers of financial and service activity ... New York, London and Tokyo contain the largest concentrations of leading producer service firms, the top twenty four securities houses in the world, sixty three of the top one hundred banks in the world, 84% of global capitalization and the largest concentrations of a variety of commodity and currency markets. (Sassen, 1991, pp. 189–90)

In 1992, London's share of the global trade in international currencies was 30 per cent (up from 25 per cent in 1989). More dollars were traded in London than New York, more Deutschmarks than in Germany (Roberts, 1995, p. 15). In 1991, Tokyo, London and New York were responsible for around 54 per cent of total international bank lending. Although this was down from 58 per cent in 1985, this was primarily due to the problems of the US banks and their losses in lending to South America (Coleman and Porter, 1994, p. 193). Trade in Eurobonds constituted 25 per cent of total borrowings on bond markets in London and Tokyo in the 1980s and London was responsible for 65 per cent of all cross-exchange trading in 1990 (that is, where a firm's stocks are purchased on a foreign exchange; see also Smith, 1992; Cosh *et al.*, 1992).

These global market-places are located in specific national locations. It is the financial systems in these countries (i.e., the USA, the UK and Japan) which have had to change fastest and perhaps furthest since the 1970s. These countries have taken both the burden and the benefits from managing the transition to the new system. In the case of London, this was a transition which was building on existing institutions and competences. Except in the interwar years, when the international economy effectively collapsed, London had built itself on its international connections, providing funds and services for economies throughout the world (Ingham, 1984; Michie, 1992). In the 1950s and 1960s, it rebuilt that position through its involvement in the Euro-dollar markets such that when the floating rate system emerged, it was ideally placed to intermediate between currencies. In the case of New York and Tokyo, their central roles have been built upon the power of their internal economies, generating needs for both investment outlets and for support of the multinational activities of their largest companies. In all three countries, adjusting to the new system has meant internal conflict and change as new regulatory structures have had to be built (see, for example, Moran, 1991). In particular, the barriers between types of institutions and markets have come down. Starting with those institutions closest to the new international political economy, there has been a ripple effect through the whole financial system. The vast profits generated through the international markets become a magnet attracting organizations and firms from outside the initial inner circle. Thus retail commercial banks which had previously been predominantly domestic institutions move in this new direction, pulling their competitors along with them – in the USA, the savings and loans associations, in the UK, the building societies and in Japan, the credit unions. The whole national system converges on the global city and each global city becomes linked to the other. Sassen argues that:

> these cities relate to one another in distinct systemic ways ... in the mid 1980s Tokyo was the main exporter of the raw material we call money while New York was the leading processing center in the world. It was in New York that many of the new financial instruments were invented ... London, on the other hand, was a major entrepôt which had the network to centralize and concentrate small amounts of capital available in a large number of smaller financial markets around the world ... These cities do not simply compete with each other for the same business. There is ... an economic system that rests on the three distinct types of locations these cities represent. (Sassen, 1995, p. 46; also Sassen, 1994)

To all the participants in these systems, the advantages from playing a central role are obvious. At the level of firms, fees and commissions earned in global markets are huge and for the individuals working in those firms in a professional capacity, earnings are considerably in advance of those which could be achieved in any other industry (Sassen, 1991, ch. 8). None of the financial institutions within these countries wants to be left out, because to do so is to allow your competitors to grow bigger and stronger. Thus it is in these societies that the impetus towards deregulation and change has been fastest and most powerful. If there is any process of convergence it lies here. Moran refers to this as the 'Americanisation of regulation' (Moran, 1991, p. 132). However, this oversimplifies what is a complex process of change. The three systems are still by no means identical even if they are proceeding in the same direction. Furthermore, there are weaknesses within each system which affect the speed of the transition. There is one form of weakness which is generic; this relates to the impact of acting as a global market on the domestic hinterland. As analyses of Britain have shown (for example, Ingham, 1984), there are dangers in having a financial system that is so outward-facing and global in its orientation that it loses contact with its internal manufacturing base. This can become an argument about protection for home industries against foreign competition (as with some elements in the USA) or more broadly about the need for national governments to control financial institutions (as in the UK). The rift between the global cities and their beneficiaries and national political interests may become increasingly difficult to bridge, resulting in both political and economic uncertainties.

Each global city also has its own particular weaknesses. This is perhaps clearest in the UK. The late arrival of the Big Bang in the Stock Exchange has meant that there has been a historical legacy from the previous era of the small firms which dominated until very recently (Thrift, 1994). This is very apparent in the low level of technology in the London Stock Exchange compared to other competitors (including Paris and Frankfurt). Although screen-based dealing has existed for some time, there are key elements of the system which are still dependent on paper. Simplified forms of dealing based entirely on computerized systems offer speed and cheapness both to corporate and individual customers, yet the London Stock Exchange has failed to deliver this in spite of huge investments. This has led to concerns that London may lose its position to other more advanced and simplified trading systems.[10] In the USA, struggles to repeal the Glass–Steagall Act to ensure universal banking nationwide have been going on for some time and are not yet completely resolved. In Japan, banks have been undermined by the losses incurred in land speculation and this has fundamentally weakened their asset strength. In the medium term, all these problems may not prove fatal, though in the light of the growing number of other centres which are emerging, it may be that the system will become more multipolar than it is at present.

The Claimants to Global Status

There are some countries in which the attraction of becoming a global centre has to compete with strong local regulatory systems.[11] This refers in particular to Paris and Frankfurt, both dominant financial centres within their own country.[12] In these centres, unlike London, Tokyo and New York, the shift towards creating global institutions is fraught with much more difficulty. The attraction for the largest banking institutions of the new order is obvious. It offers higher profits, growth and power. As with the internal dynamics in the USA, the UK and Japan, opting out is not really possible for these large institutions. If they do not compete for the new business, they will not only lose that but they will also lose some of their old business as their largest national clients will go elsewhere to the most powerful institutions. However, the internal structure of these financial systems is not so rapidly or completely affected as in the case of those countries harbouring the global cities. In France, the financial and banking institutions have been used directly as instruments of state policy (Zysman, 1983); loosening them from this grip and enabling them to emerge as independent global financial institutions is a highly complex process and to express this in terms of convergence seems rather naive. In Germany, the linkage between finance and manufacturing is highly developed and the degree to which this will change is still being debated.[13] Furthermore, the German system has been characterized by the maintenance of a large number of local and regional institutions, in particular the Landesbanken and the Sparkassen. These are closely linked in to funding both the *mittelstand* sector of German industry as well as local and regional governments. These institutions may not be so ready and eager to change as in some other countries. The growth of Paris and Frankfurt as international centres may then continue but this is unlikely to cause the collapse of all the financial institutions into the one model. To repeat the point made earlier, the opening up of the regulatory systems to change which is an inevitable concomitant of the shift at the international level may cause divergence rather than convergence. Thus the reforms and changes within the French and German systems may serve to emphasize their distinctiveness rather than reduce it. A related aspect of this is the degree to which these two countries and financial centres could lever themselves into a global position by means of the European Union. If there was a single European currency based on a Franco-German alliance, would this make any difference to the structure of the global cities? During 1995, German scepticism about the single currency appeared to increase as the difficulties of meeting the convergence criteria of the Maastricht Treaty became more apparent and the fear of loss of national control over monetary policy more widespread. The contribution of the single currency to Frankfurt's role as a global city is therefore unknown.

The Offshore Markets

The offshore markets are an integral part of this system as they aid the transmission and distribution of funds around the globe behind the backs of potential government interference. What Roberts terms the 'fictitious spaces' (Roberts, 1994), places like the Bahamas and the Cayman Islands in the Caribbean, Liechtenstein, Luxemburg and the Channel Islands in Europe, Bahrain in the Middle East, and Singapore and Hong Kong in the Far East have little history of involvement in financial markets; all of them have given priority to providing a certain environment for financial institutions:

By operating offshore banking centres international banks could act free of reserve requirements and other regulation. Offshore branches could also be used as profit centres from which profits may be repatriated at the most suitable moment for tax minimization. (Roberts, 1994, p. 99)

These centres do not so much converge with London, Tokyo and New York as offer a complementary set of services based on low taxation and limited supervision:

Compared to the major international financial centers, offshore banking centers offer certain types of additional flexibility: secrecy, openness to 'hot' money and to certain 'legitimate' options not quite allowed in the deregulated markets of major financial centers and tax minimization strategies for international corporations. (Sassen, 1994, p. 26)

The existence of these markets considerably complicates the creation of any new regulatory system as often these centres emerge and develop precisely to avoid regulation. In this sense, they are symbiotic with, though living contradictions of, the more regulated markets. Whilst they are gradually being forced to become more regulated (particularly so far as they are conduits in criminal money-laundering), they continue to perform a useful function for legitimate institutions based in more regulated markets which will continue to support their right to exist.

The Recipients of the Global Order

This refers to those countries which, rather than making the system or aspiring to make it, are simply participants in the rules constructed elsewhere. There are two categories here. First, there are those countries which have very little economic power and are struggling either to maintain themselves in the system or to enter it, that is, the less developed world and the countries of the former Soviet bloc. In almost all cases, these countries are in desperate need of foreign capital; inevitably, access to that capital is dependent upon shaping the financial system in a way which conforms to the demands of institutions such as the World Bank or the IMF. They are being sold an open market model which is not even in operation in those countries where the global cities are located! Whether such institutional changes can be sustained in the particular social and political conditions of these societies is uncertain. Thus they may be given American-style systems of banking but will these survive in such different social conditions? Some recognition of these problems is sometimes apparent in that the opening up of financial services markets has only just been agreed under the Uruguay round of GATT talks. Protection of financial services is still possible and allowable for some countries, at least for the time being.

Second, there are those countries which are successful participants in the system of international trade but have very little autonomous influence over its direction. Often such countries find themselves being absorbed into a particular sphere of influence and their institutional structure changing to match that position, for example, Canada's financial deregulation and its Free Trade Agreement with the USA (Bienefeld, 1992). The other major alternative for at least some of these economies (those in Scandinavia in particular) has been to come into a wider alliance (the European Union) in an attempt to contribute to the shaping of a particular type of financial system. This raises again the question of the role of the European Union in the emerging global order.

These arguments then point to the creation of an intricate division of labour in the new international political economy and the national institutions which make it up. What is occurring is both a division between states and a division within states. States are competing for positions within this new order and whilst the dominance of the global cities seems well-established, others both inside Europe (Paris and Frankfurt) and in Asia (particularly Singapore) are bidding for an increasing share. Alliances of states are also emerging which may make a difference to this structure. Clearly, the European Union represents a potentially new force but the creation of NAFTA as well as the establishment of various forms of economic cooperation around the Pacific Rim may also have an impact. The nature of these global markets is that they also separate the geographical location of these activities from the surrounding national institutions. Divisions between the global cities and their national hinterlands may increase and extend.

The new system is therefore not yet stable, but its outlines can be clearly discerned. They consist of a new international division of labour between financial systems. This does not represent convergence but a more complex phenomenon in which nations and cities compete through developing their own institutional strengths (see Martin, 1994, for a similar argument). The orderly nature of this new system is precarious because it lacks any hegemonic power capable of enforcing rules and institutions. Nor is it likely that one could emerge. Japan, which was often touted as a possible new hegemon in the late 1980s, now appears to have as much difficulty managing its own internal financial system as any other country and therefore no longer seems a likely manager of the world financial system. The new system depends upon market processes and yet in the management of money and finance, any interruptions or breakdowns in the market can have massive systemic consequences. Just as the USA was unable to manage the postwar system without the aid of institutions of regulation (what Ruggie (1982) terms the regime of 'embedded liberalism'),[14] so the new system of global financial markets cannot be managed without appropriate international institutions. However, the complex patterns of competition and cooperation between nations and states make the creation of such international regulatory institutions extremely difficult.

CONCLUSIONS

This chapter has sought to clarify the relationship between the global context of financial systems and their national structure. Although financial systems developed in specific national contexts, these contexts were fundamentally structured by the wider international political economy. In the early phases of the international market, the establishment of the gold standard and its management through the dominant power of the pound sterling acted as a buffer between national institutions and the international context. As long as governments managed their systems in order to maintain exchange rate stability, the peculiar and particular structure of national financial institutions could be maintained. Thus what was becoming a universal system of trading in the nineteenth century allowed for the maintenance and reproduction of distinctive particular national institutions. However, by its very nature, this diversity undermined the system because it meant that the relative economic power of the participants in the system would inevitably change but there was no institutional mechanism capable of managing this change. This process was rapidly speeded up when in the First World War Britain had to liquidate many of its overseas holdings to pay for the war effort. The interwar years saw the breakdown of the previous system. As the universalism of the 'Pax Britannica' disappeared, it was replaced by a series of crises reflecting the uncertainty of the USA, the reluctance of Britain to give up its world role, the breakdown of an open world trading system and its replacement by autarky and restricted trading blocs. In this era, institutional reform of the financial system began to emerge in a number of countries but before this had fully developed, another world war occurred. The outcome of this war was to place the Americans at the centre of the new international political economy. The institutions of embedded liberalism which they developed – the IMF, the World Bank, GATT – created a new framework for financial institutions but it also had strong similarities to the 'Pax Britannica'. In particular, it continued to focus on the exchange rate as the interface between national systems and the international political economy. Managing the exchange rate was now a much more purposive activity on the part of governments than it had been in the Victorian era, but it was still the main form of linkage between trading economies. National institutional arrangements were not threatened under this system. Again, the universalism of the exchange rate system perpetuated particularism at the national level. As with the period of sterling hegemony, however, this created its own contradictions. Thus the growing disparities between economies could not continue to be managed within the system. Indeed the dynamics of multinational enterprises and international trading were leading to the existence of financial markets which were beyond national controls. As the old system disintegrated from the early 1970s, each country in the world trading system faced choices and constraints concerning the direction of its development. Where was it going to be in the new international order? The result has been a period of uncertainty and instability as nations and cities have competed for a role in this new system. A division of labour has emerged within the global financial order that relates to both nations and cities. It is not that this order presages the 'end of geography' (O'Brien, 1992) so much as a restructuring of existing social and economic relations. Equally certainly, expectations of convergence of national financial systems considerably overstate the degree of 'orderliness' of this process. The era when national financial systems could be hermetically sealed off from each other was dependent on a particular structure in the international economy. Now that structure has declined, a new period of uncertainty exists. The chapters in this book address the ways in which national financial institutions are seeking to change and adapt to these new uncertainties.

Notes

1.   How far back we have to go to understand the evolution of an international capitalist trading economy is of fascination to many social scientists, for

example, Arrighi, 1994; Wallerstein, 1974. This chapter takes a more conventional approach in linking international commercial trading relations with the process of industrialization, that is, the crucial period begins in the 1850s as capitalist relations are stabilized in Britain during the 'age of equipoise' (Burn, 1966) and huge flows of industrial goods and capital out of Britain begin, fundamentally altering the geopolitical and economic balance of power throughout the world (see Hobsbawm, 1964; Foreman-Peck, 1995; Gilpin, 1987).

2. The term 'institutions' is used in a dual sense in this context. In one sense, institutions constitute expected and predictable patterns of behaviour – in this case, therefore, it refers to the expectations of actors as to the rules by which international transactions will be conducted. In another sense, institutions refers to the formal organizations which embody, act upon and reproduce the expectations – in this case, banks, governments, regulators, international bodies and so on.

3. Again, the term 'regulation' is being used in a dual sense. In one sense, regulation refers to the rules which are laid down in law and enforced through specific processes of monitoring and supervision (see Ogus, 1994, for an elaboration of this approach). In another sense, regulation refers to the ways in which the different elements of a society (the political, the economic and the social) or, more grandly even, a global system of societies are brought together and 'managed' over space and time (see Boyer, 1990).

4. This point could be developed further. The Weberian view of the state as claiming the monopoly over the legitimate use of force within certain geographical boundaries could be extended. The modern state is characterized by the gradual suppression of other forms of specie and the monopolization of the means of financial transactions, that is, paper money, by the state and/or its licensed agents. States that are incapable of sustaining their paper currency and are overcome by hyperinflation face a huge legitimation deficit, for example, Germany in 1923, that can infect and destroy all other claims to legitimacy. This link between currency and 'statehood' is obviously central to debates about a single European currency.

5. The term 'trade' is being used here in a broad sense. As well as the export of goods and services, it is also being used to refer to capital flows. Labour migration has also been a significant aspect of this pattern of trade since the nineteenth century (see, for example, Sassen, 1988, where the interplay between capital and labour flows is analysed).

6. There were some countries which had inconvertible currencies. In effect, the relative value of these currencies (during the 'Pax Britannica', this meant most of Latin America and Central and Eastern Europe) was determined by demand and they were therefore 'floating'. Mill described this as an '"intolerable evil", because of the disturbance to contracts and expectations caused by the consequent changes in the price level' (Foreman-Peck, 1995, p. 77).

7. Block (1977) shows that there was no inevitability to the formation of this international economic order. It developed gradually as US policy-makers managed through the use of Cold War rhetoric to convince the American voters that an open economic system necessitated substantial USA aid (both in terms of capital and in terms of military presence) to the war-damaged

European economies. Similarly, it necessitated these same US policy-makers to act ruthlessly on the Europeans to close off other options, for example, both by contributing to the destruction of communist-linked labour movements and by undermining efforts towards the creation of 'national capitalisms', that is, refusing to provide aid or help to those politicians contemplating erecting trade barriers against US goods and capital.

8. It may need reemphasizing that this is only where the government can maintain the exchange rate. In the period of embedded liberalism, governments which required IMF help to fund their balance of payments deficit could be subjected to IMF demands to restructure their financial systems, in particular to make them more open.

9. There is a further case which is that of currency inconvertibility. This category is clearly relevant to the analysis both of particular crisis conditions such as wartime and to more general social phenomena such as the way in which the Soviet bloc managed its economic and financial affairs. Eastern European currencies had an official exchange rate which did not reflect any economic reality and led to a huge differential with black market currency traders.

10. Another source of London's traditional strength which is now going into reverse is Lloyds insurance market, where huge losses and concerns about the way the market has been run (to benefit insiders at the expense of outside investors) are rapidly undermining its previously dominant position in large-scale insurance risks.

11. There are, of course, other cities in the USA itself which have a claim to global status such as Chicago (which originated futures trading and still retains a central place in these markets) and Miami, which according to Sassen, 'may have emerged as a site for global city functions' (Sassen, 1994, p. 78) due at least in part to its proximity (in geographical, social and economic terms) to Latin America and therefore its attractiveness to USA, European and Asian banks wishing to enter these markets.

12. It may be that Milan would wish to be included in this group but the instability of the Italian political and economic system would mean that, in this context, it would count more as one of the countries which is a recipient rather than a maker of the international order.

13. On France and Germany, see the contributions in this volume which indicate the complexity of these processes of change.

14. Other might prefer to call this regime 'Fordism'; however this refers to a broader debate on the nature of relations between the international system and national institutions which goes beyond the remit of this chapter (see Boyer, 1990; Amin, 1994).

References

A. Amin (ed.), *Post-Fordism*. (Oxford: Blackwell, 1994).

P. Anderson, *Lineages of the Absolutist State*. (London: New Left Books, 1974).

G. Arrighi, *The Long Twentieth Century*. (London: Verso, 1994).

T. Banuri and J. Schor (eds), *Financial Openness and National Autonomy*. (Oxford: Clarendon Press, 1992).

G.J. Benston, *The Separation of Commercial and Investment Banking.* (London: Macmillan, 1990).

M. Bienefeld, 'Financial De-regulation: Disarming the Nation State', *Studies in Political Economy*, 37 (1992) pp. 31–58.

F. Block, *The Origins of International Economic Disorder.* (Berkeley: University of California Press, 1977).

R. Boyer, *The Regulation School.* (New York: Columbia University Press, 1990).

W.L. Burn, *The Age of Equipoise.* (London: Unwin, 1966).

W.D. Coleman and T. Porter, 'Regulating International Banking and Securities: Emerging Cooperation among National Authorities', in R. Stubbs and G. Underhill (eds), *Political Economy and the Changing Global Order.* (London: Macmillan, 1994) pp. 190–203).

S. Corbridge, R. Martin and N. Thrift (eds), *Money, Power and Space.* (Oxford: Blackwell, 1994).

A. Cosh, A. Hughes and A. Singh, 'Openness, Financial Innovation, Changing Patterns of Ownership and the Structure of Financial Markets', in T. Banuri and J. Schor (eds) *Financial Openness and National Autonomy.* (Oxford: Clarendon Press, 1992) pp. 19–42.

N. Dodd, *The Sociology of Money.* (Oxford: Polity Press, 1994).

J. Foreman-Peck, *A History of the World Economy.* (London: Harvester Wheatsheaf, 1995).

R. Gilpin, *The Political Economy of International Relations.* (Princeton, NJ: Princeton University Press, 1987).

J.P. Hawley, 'Protecting Capital from Itself: U.S. Attempts to Regulate the Eurocurrency System', *International Organization*, 38, 1 (1994) pp. 131–65.

F. Hirsch, *Money International.* (Harmondsworth: Penguin, 1969).

E. Hobsbawm, *The Age of Capital 1848–1875.* (London: Weidenfeld & Nicolson, 1964).

G. Ingham, *Capitalism Divided: The City and Industry in British Social Development.* (London: Macmillan, 1984).

G. Ingham, 'States, Markets and World Money', in Corbridge *et al.* (eds) (1994) pp. 29–48.

M. Kitson and J. Michie, 'Trade and Growth: A Historical Perspective', in Michie and Grieve Smith (eds) (1995) pp. 3–36.

B. McKercher, 'Wealth, Power and the New International Order: Britain and the American Challenge in the 1920s', *Diplomatic History*, 12, 4 (1988) pp. 411–41.

R. Martin, 'Stateless Monies, Global Financial Integration and National Economic Autonomy: The End of Geography?', in Corbridge *et al.* (eds) (1994), pp. 253–78.

P. Mathias, *The First Industrial Nation.* (London: Methuen, 1969).

J. Michie and J. Grieve Smith (eds), *Managing the Global Economy.* (Oxford: Oxford University Press, 1995).

R. Michie, *The City of London: Continuity and Change, 1850–1990.* (London: Macmillan, 1992).

D.E. Moggridge, *The Return to Gold 1925.* (Cambridge: Cambridge University Press, 1969).

M. Moran, *The Politics of the Financial Services Revolution.* (London: Macmillan 1991).

R. O'Brien, *Global Financial Integration: The End of Geography*. (London: RIIA, Pinter Publishers, 1992).

A. Ogus, *Regulation: Legal Theory and Economic Forms*. (Oxford: Oxford University Press, 1994).

M. Panić, 'The Bretton Woods System: Concept and Practice', in Michie and Grieve Smith (eds) *(*1995) pp. 37–54.

S. Pollard (ed.), *The Gold Standard and Employment Policies between the Wars*. (London: Methuen, 1970).

S. Pollard, *Peaceful Conquest: The Industrialization of Europe 1760–1970*. (Oxford: Oxford University Press, 1981).

J. Roberts, *$1000 Billion a Day: Inside the Foreign Exchange Markets*. (London: HarperCollins, 1995).

S. Roberts, 'Fictitious Capital, Fictitious Places: The Geography of Offshore Financial Flows', in Corbridge *et al.* (eds) (1994) pp. 91–115.

B.M. Rowland (ed.), *Balance of Power or Hegemony: The Interwar Monetary System*. (New York: New York University Press, 1976).

J.G. Ruggie, 'International Regimes, Transactions and Change: Embedded Liberalism in the Postwar Economic Order', *International Organization*, 36, 2 (1982) pp. 379–415.

S. Sassen, *The Mobility of Labor and Capital: A Study in International Investment and Labor Flow*. (Cambridge: Cambridge University Press, 1988).

S. Sassen, *The Global City: New York, London, Tokyo*. (Princeton, NJ: Princeton University Press, 1991).

S. Sassen, *Cities in a World Economy*. (London: Pine Forge Press, 1994).

S. Sassen, 'The State and the Global City: Notes Towards a Conception of Place Centred Governance', *Competition and Change*, 1, 1 (1995) pp. 31–50.

A.D. Smith, *International Financial Markets: the Performance of Britain and its Rivals*. (Cambridge: Cambridge University Press, 1992).

N. Thrift, 'On the Social and Cultural Determinants of International Financial Centres: The Case of the City of London', in Corbridge *et al.* (eds) (1994) pp. 327–55.

S. Tolliday, *Business, Banking and Politics: The Case of British Steel 1918–1939*. (Cambridge, Mass.: Harvard University Press, 1987).

I. Wallerstein, *The Modern World System Volume 1: Capitalist Agriculture and the Origins of the European World Economy in the Sixteenth Century*. (London: Academic Press, 1974).

J. Zysman, *Governments, Markets and Growth*. (London: Cornell University Press, 1983).

2 Local Autonomy in Danish Banking: Historical Roots – Persistence and Change*

James Høpner

INTRODUCTION

The central role of small and medium-sized enterprises located outside the national capital of Copenhagen has been increasingly seen as essential to understanding the nature of the Danish business system (Kristensen, 1995). These firms exist alongside and in relation to the large international Danish companies headquartered in Copenhagen. The Danish financial system has historically reflected a similar tension between locally based banks with close connections to local communities and the large national banks headquartered in Copenhagen with their close links to large firms. However, unlike in other countries, processes of concentration and merger in the banking industry and the impact of deregulation do not appear to have destroyed local branch autonomy. Rather, the nature of local autonomy has changed. No longer is autonomy secured by ownership independence; it now relies on two factors, first, the devolution of powers from the centre, and second, the active maintenance by bank branch staff of close relations with the local community.

This chapter develops this argument through an account of the historical origins of the Danish financial system, its transformation since the 1960s and a detailed examination of two bank branches.

HISTORY AND CHANGE IN DANISH BANKING

The history of Danish banking is one of an ongoing battle – a battle between Copenhagen and the provinces, between banks and savings banks, between different kinds of banks and different kinds of savings banks. No single logic has dominated the evolution of the industry.

*For thoughtful comments on an earlier draft, I am grateful to Glenn Morgan, Peer Hull Kristensen, Frank Dobbin, Risto Tainio, Peter Wendt, and Marianne Risberg.

A modern Danish banking system gradually emerged in the early nineteenth century, in the aftermath of the Napoleonic War, when the state bank, Rigsbanken, was reorganized as a semi-private bank and named Nationalbanken.

As well as being a note-issuing institution, the bank financed production and trade nationally. The Nationalbanken was located in Copenhagen, and it was subject to severe criticism from people in the provinces for only supporting industry in and around that area (Hansen, 1960). In the 1820s, Aalborg and Viborg (two large provincial cities in Jutland) tried to persuade the Nationalbanken to set up branches in their cities to support local financial needs, but the first provincial branch was not established until 1837. However, this did not change the provincial population's sceptical attitude towards the Nationalbanken, and in the 1840s local initiatives began to establish independent provincial banks. In 1846 a group of local businessmen succeeded in establishing their own bank, Fyens Disconto Kasse, on a joint-stock basis like the Nationalbanken. This was the first privately owned and provincial bank.

In 1857 another important bank, Privatbanken, was established, inspired by the French Crédit Mobilier banks. This bank was set up by financially wealthy and influential people in Copenhagen. The purpose was to support the expansion of Copenhagen-based industry, and to provide the means to improve its competitiveness *vis-à-vis* foreign industry, especially German. Along the same lines Landmandsbanken and Handelsbanken were established in 1871 and 1873. Being engaged in lending operations, investments, and foreign transactions, these three Copenhagen-based banks were connected to large industrial firms and the government. They occupied a very visible position in the economic development and industrialization of the large firms, especially when the Nationalbanken withdrew from engaging in industrial financing to concentrate on its central bank functions (Svendsen and Hansen, 1968). The three Copenhagen banks fought fierce battles, and their development is characterized by a struggle for political, industrial and economic power (for a more detailed discussion see Kristensen and Sabel, forthcoming). During this period an additional number of provincial banks, such as Fyens Disconto Kasse, were established to meet local financial needs especially amongst the small and medium-sized enterprises (see, for example, Lauridsen, 1968). Between 1847 and 1857, thirteen banks of this type were established by local initiative and with local capital in various parts of Denmark. Two of the three Copenhagen banks, Handelsbanken and Landmandsbanken, established a network of branches outside Copenhagen by taking over some of the provincial banks. Landmandsbanken also established its own savings banks. One of the reasons was that Landmandsbanken was interested in establishing contact with the farmers who held large amounts of money at that time due to increasing success with exports. All three Copenhagen banks started collaborating with some of the local banks and savings banks on deposits, loans, and transactions.

At the beginning of the nineteenth century a number of savings banks were established, but they were not connected to business. Rather they acted as a kind of social organization, their primary purpose being to administer poor and old people's money, that is, to hold their money securely and in rare cases lend them money if they were unable to support their family. At first, the deposits of the savings banks were placed on account at the Nationalbanken. But around 1835, the Nationalbanken put a limit on the deposits from the savings banks, as it did not gain enough profits by lending these to other customers. Savings banks were then more or less forced to find other ways of placing their deposits. In the following years they played an important role in the economic development of the local communities, engaging in the financing of local harbours, gasworks and road works (Clemmensen, 1985). But their financing was selective and besides the public goods, they would only lend capital to private customers, such as smallholders and others, who could provide security in real estate.

Savings banks played a different role from that of the banks, functioning both as financial institutions and as a kind of social organization. In the late nineteenth century this difference became increasingly clear, as savings banks in collaboration with cooperative societies and sickness benefit associations developed a system to allocate local resources for the benefit of local needs. They also gradually started to lend money, and this development increased profoundly during the last part of the nineteenth century, to the extent that the Minister of Domestic Affairs appointed a savings bank commissioner in 1880, viewing this type of bank as a dominating factor in the national economy (Clemmensen, 1985). One of the reasons was that savings banks, to a large extent, were managed by people of little formal financial expertise, working on a voluntary basis.

Many savings banks were connected to the cooperative movement, and served, among others, farmers to whom they granted loans on security in real estate or machines. Thus, they became closely involved in the smallholder economy dominating industrialization and the modernizing agricultural sector (Kristensen, 1995). By the end of the century, various types of savings banks were in existence, focusing their interests on more specific areas, but the overriding policy of the savings bank movement was to be risk-averse and lend only to very secure clients. From 1857 to 1874, the number of savings banks increased by 273 to a total of 320, particularly in Jutland where almost 200 new savings banks were started. Also loans increased rapidly from 37.2 million DKK in 1857 to 138.4 million DKK in 1875. In 1900 the size of loan had grown to 390.9 million DKK (Svendsen and Hansen, 1968; Winding, 1958).

Nineteenth-century banking was then characterized by three types of banks (apart from the state bank, Nationalbanken): (1) three large Copenhagen-based banks that strongly influenced the large industrial firms and whose ties to the provinces were limited; (2) a group of provincial banks with strong local ties; and (3) a large number of different types of local savings banks.

Up to the early twentieth century, Danish banking lacked any strong regulatory framework. However, following a real estate crash in 1907–8, a banking commission was set up. In 1912 the commission advanced a proposal for a comprehensive and restrictive law on the activities of banks and savings banks. These restrictions were particularly aimed at savings banks, despite the fact that it was the private banks that had caused the crisis. The large private banks had invested heavily in industrial firms and when the firms failed, the banks were in crisis. This led to demands that banks should not own shares in firms. However, the situation remained unchanged until after the First World War. In 1919 the first Act on banks and savings banks was passed, primarily increasing the state's role in supervising the sector regularly. No agreement on separating banks and industry could be reached, even though the issue was much discussed. The Act stated that savings banks had to be independent institutions, that is, their business efforts should be directed towards safe investments and not ones which were risky but potentially highly profitable.

However, the Act was not clear enough in its implication to fulfil the original goal, that is, to prevent crises among banks caused by industrial fluctuations and the like. A further crisis arose in 1922 when Landmandsbanken, the largest bank in Scandinavia at that time, faced serious problems and had to be restructured (Mørch, 1986). For many years the bank had engaged in increasingly complex, speculative and cross-national activities. At the turn of the century, this business strategy had proved very successful, but after the First World War, the bank ventured into financing enterprises that invested large amounts of capital in weaponry and the transport industry, among others Det Transatlantiske Kompagni, hoping that the Russian market would prove profitable (Bankkomissionen, 1924). This venture failed, the bank lost its capital, and the state and the Nationalbanken were forced to invest the considerable amount of 40 million DKK to rescue the bank. From 1921 to 1927 the bank lost 500 million DKK, or 55 per cent of the total loss in the banking sector (Bengtsson, 1969). Other banks faced similar problems, though not as serious. For example, in 1925 the Andelsbanken (the largest cooperative bank) was closed down, restructured and reopened by the same group of people under its current name, and in 1928 the Privatbanken was forced to suspend payments for two days (Mordhost, 1968). These events made it clear that the bank Act had to be revised. In 1930 a new Act was passed by the government, imposing considerable restrictions on banking activities and clearly defining the functions of a bank compared to those of other financial institutions. Most importantly, overlapping ownership between banks and industrial enterprises now became illegal. Furthermore, a ceiling of 35 per cent (under special circumstances 50 per cent) of the share capital was set as the maximum loan that could be granted to a single customer. Finally, a financial supervision agency (as imposed on the savings banks in 1880) was set up to control the banks and furnished with far-reaching rights to interfere in the banks' loans and business methods.

In 1937, savings banks too were subjected to new restrictions (others had been introduced in 1880 and 1919). The savings banks themselves took the initiative in 1937, wishing to clarify the difference between banks and savings banks in terms of the depositors' risks. Savings banks were restrained from offering bills of exchange, acting as foreign exchange dealers and buying securities (bonds and stocks) on behalf of their customers. Furthermore, the Act emphasized that savings banks primarily were empowered to grant loans and to invest in government bonds and real estate. They were not allowed to invest in stocks, but could grant loans to cooperative societies and similar organizations. Originally, the Act set a limit to the latter, but this proved impossible to respect, as many savings banks were heavily involved in cooperatives, and the paragraph was annulled in 1950. However, the Act stated that a savings bank was only allowed to grant loans to a single customer amounting to 10 per cent of its investment capital. This was significantly less than the banks were allowed.

In spite of these crises, provincial banks continued to increase both in terms of number and size, and also the Copenhagen banks took over many provincial banks. By 1920, Landmandsbanken had 57 branches of which 36 were located in the provinces. Of these 23 were takeovers of existing banks. Deposits in the provincial branches amounted to 296 million DKK, equalling a quarter of the banks' total deposit (Schovelin, 1921). Banks taken over by larger banks did not change their name but merely added their original name to that of the acquiring bank. Furthermore, almost every time a Copenhagen bank acquired a local bank, a new independent bank was established in the area. As a result, both the number of independent banks and bank units expanded. In 1906, the share capital of all provincial banks amounted to 23 million DKK, a little less than the size of each of the three Copenhagen banks. The growth of the provincial banks was mainly caused by rapidly expanding businesses in the cities, and in 1920 the number of new provincial banks reached 180, although it dropped to 160 during the bank crises in the 1920s. In 1905, the provincial banks established their own interest organization, Provinsbankforeningen (the Association of Provincial Banks). The operations of provincial and Copenhagen-based banks were very different, and to avoid being over-ruled by the Copenhagen banks, the provincial banks had to join forces.

From 1945 to 1960 the savings banks increased their loans by around 4000 million DKK to a total of 6417 million DKK. The banks more than doubled their loans, and in 1960 had a total of 10 412 million DKK loans (Olsen and Hoffmeyer, 1968). However, until the end of the 1950s, the structure of the financial sector did not change significantly, apart from the role of Nationalbanken. Gradually, Nationalbanken withdrew deliberately from engaging in private loan activities, and concentrated its efforts on monetary policy and note-issuing.

In 1950 the Savings Bank Act removed the distinction between primary and secondary types of loans, and savings banks were allowed to take higher risks, but still primarily against some kind of security. Deregulation continued in 1959 when savings banks got access to stock-trading, and were permitted to grant small loans without security. The bank Act was revised in 1956, and the demand for balance between stock capital and loans was reduced. The separation between bank and industry was made more explicit in that bank employees were prohibited from being board members of other companies.

In 1949 a group of savings banks took over a bank which they turned into Fællesbanken for Danmarks Sparekasser, thus obtaining access to bank products and operations, such as dealing in foreign currency and stocks. This bank became a kind of 'central bank' for the savings banks. Deposits in this bank came solely from savings banks and were invested in bonds and shares, and only to a very limited extent lent to customers (Winding, 1958).

By the end of the 1950s international trade curbs were being lifted and industry and, to some extent agriculture, expanded. This enabled banks and savings banks to expand their operations, not only in terms of domestic affairs, but also undertaking cross-border payments and other international business transactions related to the export industries. The banks were not allowed to open branches abroad, so instead they established representative offices and consortial banks (with other Nordic banks) in the large financial centres, such as the City of London, and in places that were important trade partners to Danish industry. This made several firms take foreign loans to finance investments, and the Danish banks engaged actively not only in arranging loans on request, but also in encouraging new firms to exploit this possibility. During the 1960s and the 1970s, the large Copenhagen banks became increasingly active in establishing foreign contacts in various financial markets.

The significant change began to occur from the mid-1960s. Until then, the number of provincial banks and savings banks had continued to increase. The expansion of agriculture and industry and the international orientation further supported this development. Had Denmark been dominated by large enterprises, the industrial expansion would probably only have affected the large Copenhagen banks, but since this was not the case all banks and savings banks gained from this development.

From the 1960s, mergers and takeovers by large savings banks, and in particular between local and regional banks and savings banks, commenced. Consequently, the development was characterized by an average growth in size rather than large banks becoming larger. The takeover of smaller banks by the Copenhagen-based banks did not seem to change the life and daily activities of the acquired small banks as products were fairly similar and simple. However, many of the provincial banks managed to resist being taken over by Copenhagen banks. Savings banks did not feel the same pressure of being taken over and losing their independence (only one attempt was made to merge a bank and a savings bank, but it failed, see Mikkelsen (1993) for full details).

Collaboration between the provincial banks was the solution to not losing their independence, but this entailed problems. From the tax authorities' point of view, merging two provincial banks was considered as a closure of the banks concerned and therefore liable to a special income tax. This made it very costly for the banks to start formal collaboration, but Provinsbankforeningen, the interest organization of the provincial banks, put pressure on the government to change this paragraph of the fiscal legislation which happened in 1964, leading to a spate of mergers between regional banks. Some of the most notable subsequent mergers took place in Jutland in the late 1960s (Provinsbanken (1967), Midtbank (1966) and Jyske Bank (1967)). Common to most of these was that they were established from fear of being taken over by Copenhagen banks combined with the need to be able to meet increasingly complex financial demands from customers (especially cooperative businesses). Concentration within the sector did not have the effect that the number of bank branches decreased. On the contrary, during the 1960s the number of branches increased by almost 100 per cent, going from 1544 in 1959 to 2758 in 1969, although the number of independent banks dropped by 200.

The establishment of regional banks was not the ultimate solution to the problems that provincial and small banks were facing, as the need for technology and doing international transactions increased rapidly during the 1960s. Already in 1963, the savings banks had taken the initiative to establish Sparekassernes Data Center, the first collective organization providing access to information technology. In 1970, the banks, primarily on the initiative of the provincial banks, established Bankernes EDB Center with the similar purpose of making the introduction of new technology cheaper and more effective for all parties. Almost every bank and savings bank now had access to very advanced IT systems, even though not all branches were able to utilize this capacity, but it gave them the possibility of offering more and more advanced services to their customers. In 1971, another notable collective organization was established between banks and savings banks, Pengeinstitutternes Betalingsformidlings Center, an organization that coordinated payments between banks and savings banks. It was set up by the trade associations of banks and savings banks in continuation of the agreement on wage accounts in 1963 that made employees independent of having the same bank as their employer. As to training, collaboration was started with the banking and savings bank schools. Finally, an example of collective collaboration between provincial banks was the establishment of the Provinsbankernes Clearingsbank in 1973 that coordinated surplus and deficits of capital between provincial banks, a model very similar to Fællesbanken of the savings banks. A comprehensive network of collective organizations and agreements between the various kinds of banks and between banks and savings banks characterized the sector to the advantage of both the small local and the large national banks and savings banks.

Another area of change concerned the ceiling on interest rates on deposits which had existed since 1930. An agreement was entered into between the trade associations of banks and savings banks, and neither the state nor the Nationalbanken was involved. By the end of the 1960s a group of local and regional banks in mid- and east Jutland claimed the agreement had the effect that the Copenhagen-based banks dictated the interest level. Vejle Bank, since 1965 one of the banks most critical of the agreement, withdrew from the agreement in 1968 by raising its interests on deposits to 1 per cent above the agreed level of 7.5 per cent. It was excluded from the trade associations Provinsbankforeningen and

Bankernes Fællesrepræsentation, as the majority of the provincial banks supported the agreement, although they, to some extent, sympathized with Vejle Bank. The trade association of the banks (that included the Copenhagen-based banks) tried to make Nationalbanken force the small banks to follow the agreement by denying them loans, but Nationalbanken refused, sharing the opinion that the agreement restrained competition. In 1973 the disputed agreement was abandoned, due to new monetary policies from Nationalbanken which imposed a ceiling on interest rates and loans.

The savings banks were particularly active in merging and collaborating. For example, Bikuben Savings Bank (established in 1857 and based in Copenhagen) had grown by taking over or starting collaboration with smaller savings banks. More important was the establishment of Sparekassen SDS in 1973 as a merger between three regional savings banks of equal size, located in different regions of Denmark (Sparekassen Falster-Østlolland, Sparekassen København-Sjælland and Sparekassen Midtjylland). Consequently, the merger resulted in no overlapping network of branches. Headquarters with 70 employees were set up in Copenhagen to coordinate operations. In practice, Sparekassen SDS was a very decentralized organization and the regional savings banks continued to decide on their own investments and transactions, having both the competence and capital to handle very large regional business transactions (Kristensen and Høpner, 1994).

At the same time the bank and savings bank Acts were merged into one and Denmark joined the EEC. It had been suggested that there was a need to revise the Savings Bank Act as these institutions had fully exploited the possibilities of engaging in bank business stipulated by the Act of 1937 and were now finding it increasingly difficult to expand and have loans met with securities. A level playing field between saving banks and banks was the aim of the suggested changes. Naturally, the banks were not very interested in this revision; on the other hand they were not strongly opposed. One of the main problems in creating a single regulatory regime was the different demand for share capital: 10 per cent of the total loans and guarantees for banks and only 4 per cent for the savings banks. Banks were not interested in lowering the level, and it was impossible, even in a period of transition, to have the savings banks meet the rules applying to banks. After some debate, the government proposed a level of 8 per cent, but with a more restrictive statement concerning the banks' share capital, and a more gentle taxation of the savings banks. Simultaneously, public representatives were introduced on to the boards of banks, as had been the case in savings banks since 1937, and both types of institutions were subject to tighter control. The difference between banks and savings banks was, in all significant aspects, removed legally, and only their name and way of organizing made them different (savings banks still had to be independent institutions).

Finally, the new Act introduced a paragraph on cross-border establishment in order to meet demands for harmonization when Denmark joined the EEC. Foreign banks and savings banks were allowed to start up branches or subsidiary banks in Denmark, as was the case with Danish financial institutions in other member states. However, this led to no dramatic changes, as only a handful of foreign banks were established after the deregulation. The same was the case of Danish banks and savings banks abroad. Not until 1976 was the first foreign branch of a Danish bank established (in Luxembourg), followed in 1978 by the establishment of around five Cayman Island branches, which were set up for more 'speculative' reasons, that is, to avoid restrictions on offering loans in foreign currencies. These foreign branches were owned by the large Copenhagen-based banks, as the provincial banks and savings banks did not have the capacity, or the actual need, to be represented abroad. From 1973 Danish banks and savings banks were linked to the international payment system SWIFT, and thus got 'lines' to foreign markets. Smaller provincial banks and savings banks did not get their own 'lines' but made agreements with one or several larger banks. Another aspect of internationalization was financial loans, that is, loans in foreign currency that banks could offer their customers, which increased during the 1970s. These loans enabled the banks to avoid the risk of currency fluctuations, a risk that the customer now had to take, but the actual reason for the banks to venture into this type of operations was that Nationalbanken introduced a lending ceiling. Financial loans were not considered as loans offered by a Danish bank, but as foreign transactions on behalf of a customer.

An effect of the restrictions on interest on loans from 1970 was that the collective agreement on interest rates on deposits was abandoned. The discussion on agreement and regulation of the interest rate was one of the most pivotal topics of the 1970s, especially between the large and the small banks. Some regional banks claimed the agreement on interest rates reduced competition, and hence protected the increasing market share that the large Copenhagen banks had gained by taking over smaller banks. To counter this development, a group of regional banks established an association called Regionalbankerne. In 1979 this association bought up a small bank in Copenhagen (Seisby Bank) with the purpose of increasing their market share in and around Copenhagen, as the number of Copenhagen-owned branches in the provinces increased markedly.

The battle between the large Copenhagen banks and the regional banks intensified after Privatbanken, Handelsbanken, and Den Danske Bank (the successor to the Landmandsbanken) in 1975 made an informal agreement on sharing information on changes in interest levels, fees, and commissions. In 1978 this agreement was supplemented with an agreement between the eight largest banks on a maximum interest level on loans. A few days later, the two trade associations of the banks and savings banks agreed that the interest on deposits should follow the rate set by the Nationalbanken. In addition, between 1975 and 1980 the government introduced restrictions on the interest rate margin, implying that the margin was not allowed to exceed a certain level. In other words, the room for competition had almost disappeared due to cartel agreements and monetary policy.

During the 1960s and the 1970s the structure of banks and savings banks changed towards slightly larger units and more branches, but still with a fairly clear ideological difference between the large Copenhagen-based banks and the majority of other regional and national banks and savings banks. Danish banking institutions were becoming more concentrated with less autonomous locally based organizations. Mergers, networks and collaborations reduced the number of independent banks, though numbers of branches grew.

From 1980, changes became more significant. The first notable change occurred when the Nationalbanken lifted its restriction on interests and loans. This caused a pronounced change in the cartel agreements between the major banks. Some banks, for example Jyske Bank, exploited the new possibilities to raise the rate of interest on deposits. These opportunistic measures were followed by insurance companies that tried to enter into the bank market in the mid-1980s. Furthermore, a series of small aggressive banks were established in the mid-1980s with high expectations of yielding great profits from exploiting the 'free market'. However, customers, both corporate and private, turned out to be less prone to change banks than some had expected. Those who changed banks were often customers with low profitability, or customers unable to renew their credits in one of the old banks or savings banks. Therefore, the risk profile of some of these new banks increased rapidly. Several of them either had to close down or were taken over by established banks with the recession in the late 1980s and the early 1990s. Although some failed, they succeeded in increasing competition and slowly but surely competition became a part of the sector's vocabulary.

The concentration of the 1960s began to follow another track as mergers and takeovers increased in size. In numbers, banks decreased only by eight during the 1980s and savings banks by 45. What occurred was a so-called second generation of mergers. Some of the regional banks that had been established in 1960s were merged into national banks or banks that covered a larger geographical area. Examples of these are Kronebanken (a merger in 1983 between Sjællandske Bank and Fredriksborg Bank), Jyske Bank (merged with Finansbanken in 1981 and Vendelbo Bank in 1983) and Andelsbanken (merged with Hellerup Bank in 1988). During the 1980s the largest banks became increasingly dominant as a result of taking over regional banks that either ventured into the merger voluntarily or were 'forced' to do so by the Danish Supervision of Banks and Savings Banks due to economic crises. In 1982, Den Danske Bank took over the lead from Handelsbanken in terms of size, increasing its balance by around 13 per cent during the first five years of the 1980s, and by 1985 the bank covered 17 per cent of the total balance of the sector. This increase was larger than most other banks, although the three largest banks' balance increased during the same period by 11 per cent, to a total share of 43 per cent (Finansrådet, 1993a). In terms of employees a similar change took place between 1980 and 1987. Around 10 000 employees were hired in that period, and the number of employees in the sector reached 51 766 in 1987, the largest number of employees ever. This increase was not followed by new branches, as in the 1960s and the 1970s when the number more than doubled to 3464 in 1980 (there was 'a branch on every street corner'). Branches were closed down, but at a very slow rate, and reached around 3000 in 1989 (Finansrådet, 1993a; Mikkelsen, 1993).

The nature of the banking business and the sources of profitability also changed in the 1980s. Corporate loans increased, as did private customers' deposits. Two areas showed a drastic change: profits due to exchange rates and value adjustments and interbank transactions. 1983 and 1985 were peak years in terms of profits due to profits on investment portfolio and currency transactions. Profits were huge – the largest ever in the sector (Finanstilsynet, 1993). Foreign loans from Danish banks and savings banks doubled from 1980 to 1990, but interbank transactions increased by eight times thus dominating international transaction by accounting for more than 75 per cent of all foreign business (Danmarks Nationalbank, 1991). Foreign banks establishing themselves in Denmark played no notable role in this. The few branches that were set up in the 1970s did not increase in number. Four foreign branches were operating in 1980, and only two more were established during the following ten years. In terms of balance they accounted for less than 1 per cent, although this is not a totally fair description of their activities, as business handled by foreign (for them domestic) enterprises does not always show in the statistics

(Wendt, 1994). The Danish banks were more aggressive, trebling their number of branches abroad, reaching 30 by the end of the decade (not including Cayman Island branches). In 1988, the rule requiring all foreign transactions to be approved by the Nationalbanken was abolished, opening further opportunities to the large Danish banks. 'Financial supermarket' became a catchword among the large banks. Savings banks and the provincial banks, however, judged the situation more modestly.

Between 1981 and 1983 losses and loans increased from –1 per cent to 4.5 per cent of the total loans and guarantees, but only 1986 ended up with a deficit for the sector due to losses on appreciation. From 1987 the relative losses stabilized at around 1 per cent. Aside from international fluctuations no single event caused particular problems during the 1980s, which were characterized by a mix of large and small enterprises' problems, and at the end of the decade also, to some extent, those of private households. Domestic problems were, however, the major reason for the economic problems. Interest margin was still the main profit area, although the margin dropped during the decade (Finansrådet, 1993a, 1993b).

Some of the aggressive banks were either taken over or closed due to loans that could not be repaid, often involving a very narrow group of customers. This was the case of Kronebanken in 1984 and Juli Banken and C&G Banken in 1987. These takeovers marked a change in how the sector had solved crises 'quietly' since the 1930s. The Nationalbanken, the Danish Supervision of Banks and Savings Banks, and the state had to put much pressure on the large and medium-sized banks to rescue these banks. Previously, rescuing banks had acquired a network of branches in compensation for the liabilities which they had taken on, but this no longer represented an attractive incentive. On the other hand, as a result of this uncertain situation the confidence in the Danish banking system suffered both domestically and internationally. It was no longer considered safe to deposit money in a Danish bank. A contingency reserve fund was established, guaranteeing private customers' deposits to a maximum of 250 000 DKK. The fund was financed by the banks and savings banks.

In spite of these crises, optimism and a growing belief in free competition prevailed when the bank and savings bank legislation was revised in 1988. Restrictions on cross-border transaction were abolished, not only in Europe but globally, and savings banks were allowed to convert themselves into limited companies. These were some of the many minor changes caused by the EEC harmonization programme and the large banks' pressure towards a more liberal bank Act, but the Act was not changed fundamentally.

In 1990 the banking sector was restructured by significant mergers between the six largest banks. Den Danske Bank, Handelsbanken and, a month later, Provinsbanken merged into Den Danske Bank, and Privatbanken, SDS and Andelsbanken merged into Unibank. The two megabanks were established with a market share of about 60 per cent (a fifty–fifty share, Den Danske Bank being the largest). The mergers were justified by referring to greater efficiency and profitability, exploiting large-scale advantages. Another reason was to make the banks more competitive in the domestic market in relation to foreign banks which some feared would invade the market. These mergers made the changing pattern of concentration (that they became larger) crystal clear. Two large national banks, holding half of all branches (around 1500), a small group (12) of medium-sized national and regional banks and savings banks, holding 30 per cent of the total sectoral balance, and a large group of very small and local banks and savings banks (around 100) covering the last 10 per cent of the market, now characterized the structure of the sector.

Organizationally, the two mega-banks approached the post-merger change process differently. In Unibank the process was in some respects very democratic, and positions were, to the widest possible extent, staffed with the same number of employees from each of the merging banks. In all positions origin was considered when building up the Unibank organization. Den Danske Bank pursued the opposite strategy: the 'best man' got the position. In most cases this turned out to be employees of the former Den Danske Bank and secondarily employees from Handelsbanken (Molin and Pedersen, 1994).

The mergers created a further distinction between the mega-banks and the other banks and savings banks. The largest stockholders in the two banks were domestic institutional investors (primarily the pension fund ATP and the Employees' Capital Pension Fund that held around 35 per cent of the stocks). The remaining shares were divided among many very small stockholders, often customers who could obtain higher interest rates if they were stockholders. By law, stockholders that held more than 30 per cent of the shares had to be approved by the Danish Supervision of Banking, Insurance and Securities, and according to the Act of 1930 it had to be stated in the annual report if any single person or institution held more than 10 per cent of the share capital. Bank employees were precluded from accepting membership on boards of enterprises. However, the boards of the two large banks were, and still are, dominated by top managers from the largest enterprises in Denmark that simultaneously are customers of the banks, although these large enterprises also use foreign banks and other institutions in the capital market. This is most pronounced in the Den Danske Bank, as SDS and Andelsbanken (part of the Unibank merger) had a more mixed composition of boards. Their boards much more resembled those of the remaining banks and savings banks, where scope dominated over scale. Ownership of the smaller banks was not characterized by interest groups, which was mainly due to the large banks' intense buying up of shares in small and regional banks during the 1970s and the 1980s. On average, 30 per cent of stocks in small and medium-sized banks were held by large national banks (Finanstilsynet, 1993), which in connection with the mergers in 1989 resulted in the two banks gaining majority control, sometimes reluctantly, in some local banks. Until 1991 a single bank was not allowed to hold more than 30 per cent of the stocks in another bank.

This transformation of the sector continued in the early 1990s. Instead of expanding, banking was to be made more profitable by rationalizing. Banks, particularly the two large ones, started to lay off employees in bulk, closing down branches and tightening demands for credit appraisal. Between 1991 and 1993 a total of 653 branches were closed or merged, and only 18 new ones were set up by the 14 largest banks. Many of the remaining banks, the small and local ones, went in the opposite direction by setting up more branches than were closed, expanding their number of branches by 32 and hiring additional staff that were recruited among those laid off by the large banks. However, the general situation was reductions, and the number of people employed within the sector dropped by 5549 in this period to 45 465, as the number of branches was cut back to 2340 in 1993 (Andersen, 1995; Danmarks Nationalbank, 1995).

Recession in the Danish and the international economy caused further problems to the banks, especially the large ones, and resulted in major losses. In 1992, the Nationalbanken was forced to issue a declaration of confidence concerning the Unibank, as it was rumoured that it would go bankrupt, due to its financial situation (in 1992 it came out with a deficit of 4 billion DKK) – that is, the Nationalbanken guaranteed that the bank would continue. It was claimed that the problems were caused especially by the Privatbanken's involvement in real estate. However, by reducing these activities, the Unibank survived the crisis and achieved a positive result in 1994.

Crises in the banks, in addition to restrictions on credit appraisal, started a debate on the access of small and medium-sized enterprises (SMEs) to business loans. The Danish Federation of Crafts and Smaller Industries (the trade association of SMEs) claimed that it had become more difficult for SMEs to obtain loans and that they often had to pay higher interest rates than large corporate customers. Even the Ministry of Industry supported this opinion in a report (Industriministeriet, 1992). These accusations were repudiated by the banks' trade association, Finansrådet, claiming that the majority of losses were caused by SMEs and banks' involvements in loans of between 0.5 million and 5 million DKK (Finansrådet, 1993b, p. 49).

In 1994, the Nationalbanken offered a slightly different explanation, pointing to losses being the result of the general recession and that no specific sector or size of enterprise was to be blamed, stressing that the international involvement in the first part of the 1990s had caused significant losses, too, due to the uncertain interbank market (Danmarks Nationalbank, 1994).

In 1991, a new bank and savings bank Act was passed which allowed for cross-sectional alliances, for example, between banks and insurance companies. This Act also allowed banks to hold controlling interests in non-financial enterprises (primarily to help with restructuring). They also had access to an increasing holding of and were able to hold stocks in non-financial enterprises (up to 75 per cent of its shared capital). During the 1990s, international transactions continued to increase as a growing number of enterprises obtained foreign loans through their Danish banking partner, but the number of foreign branches dropped. Although both Den Danske Bank and Unibank had announced that as a result of the mergers they would enter into new foreign markets, their predominant activity remained within domestic affairs.

By the 1990s, small provincial banks had been eclipsed by the two large banks. The walls between banks and enterprises, and between other financial institutions and international markets, were crumbling. Finally, the number of branches and employees were being reduced and replaced by technology (ATM, telephone-banking, and so on). From a very decentralized, almost fragmented, sector, concentration and central control seem to be emerging as the general picture of the banking industry. Has the nineteenth century's strong tradition of local banking disappeared or does some of it still exist?

LOCAL BANKING IN THE 1990s

Until the 1970s, the Danish banking industry was characterized by fairly distinct demarcations. Banks and savings banks were separated by law, and Copenhagen banks and provincial banks were separated in terms of different business connections and activities. During the late 1970s and the early 1980s the distinction between banks and savings banks ceased to exist due to the deregulation in 1975 and the declining market for isolated savings banks' activities. However, the distinction between Copenhagen and provincial banks still exists albeit the dominance of regional banks has almost totally disappeared with the mergers in 1990. In general, profitability has been fairly high in most of these small banks, mainly because they have engaged in few corporate business activities, but rather directed their activities towards private customers – transactions that are considerably less risky. Besides, the demand for capital, when engaging in corporate business transactions, has increased considerably since the Second World War. The large regional and smaller national banks still carry the old tradition of fighting against the large Copenhagen-based banks. However with the growing significance of the mega-banks, will local autonomy gradually disappear?

TWO CASES OF LOCAL AUTONOMY

This issue can be clarified by research conducted in case studies we have made concerning work organization, competence-building (Kristensen and Høpner, 1994) and credit appraisal (Høpner, forthcoming) in two Jutlandic branches of Unibank.

The merger of Privatbanken, SDS and Andelsbanken into Unibank in 1990 did not result in significant organizational changes as the merged banks were already universal banks (one of the problems was getting three of everything). Each of them had its headquarters in Copenhagen and had a network of branches hierarchically divided into small and regional branches, although SDS and Andelsbanken were much more decentralized than Privatbanken. Domestic business in the new Unibank became organized around 46 regional branches, responsible for around 400 smaller branches. The branches operated with three types of employees: clerks with two years of fundamental training in banking, performing fairly simple transactions primarily as cashiers; counsellors undertaking more specific services to a group of customers (private or corporate) for which they were responsible (this concept was developed in 1984 by the Privatbanken and implied that each customer only needed to be in contact with one bank employee); and back office staff, educated within banking, undertaking more product-specific services, often on the request of counsellors. The latter group and corporate counsellors only exist in the regional branches.

Regional branches are treated as independent profit centres, that is, they have to forward balance sheets to headquarters regularly, and they are liable to pay for technological equipment, services, training, and so on, rendered by headquarters or external suppliers. Earnings derive from accounts, fees and commissions. In terms of interest, headquarters reimburses the branch interest on deposits and loans, and the branch's drawing facility is not limited to its balance of deposits. On the other hand, this does not imply that the branch can independently increase its lending activities (and risks).

Branches operated in ways which extended their autonomy and flexibility to deal with the needs of their local community rather than acting as 'clones' of their head office. This can be illustrated by reference to two examples.

In 1991, the corporate training division presented a programme advocating internal training at the expense of external courses. This was a significant threat to the link between the bank and the community. Traditionally, education and training were organized in local schools and colleges, enabling the development of local social solidarity (Kristensen, 1995). However the response of the branches was to use the internal and external courses to help reestablish and improve their relations with local customers. Flexibility, higher degrees of competence, and horizontal mobility were the goals. One of the branches which we studied (previously an SDS branch that had dominated the region) in general agreed to most of these issues, but its interpretation of the content of the training turned out to be quite different from that of the headquarters. Headquarters' ideas about flexibility focused on the branch employees' ability to shift from one type of job to another fairly rapidly, that is, being a full-time generalist. However, the regional branch presented a quite different interpretation of the content of internal training. Flexibility was indeed a good idea, but in relation to customers and not products. Flexibility in relation to customers could turn the counsellors into specialists in specific product ranges, for example, transactions within Nordic countries. If the customers in the region asked for such services, the staff should be able to meet the demands.

The new training programme was perceived by the branch as a kind of 'pick and mix', enabling the branch to improve its competitiveness within the region. Turning the work organization of the branch into two teams, one of private and one of corporate counsellors, it became possible to utilize the increased range of internal courses to meet customer needs. Each counsellor had to find himself or herself an area within which he or she wanted to specialize, but it had to be an area relevant to the branch, and not one that was already covered by other members of the staff.

The counsellors also volunteered to join the external course outside office hours. Courses at local business schools and business colleges were directed towards the local business environment, and were taught by representatives of the local business community. Joining these courses provided insight into the development of local business life and, more importantly, offered the opportunity of making informal business contacts. Due to the publicly financed training system the only expenditures were the books and the working hours that employees sometimes had to spend on examinations. The branch did not have to pay them any compensation. In general, internal courses took place during working hours, and the employees had to receive compensation when courses were programmed to run in the evening or the weekend, but this was an expenditure that the branch had to meet anyway (a formal demand). The result was that the combination of internal and external courses improved the local links of the branch.

At a second branch, credit policy was examined. Business customers in the regional branch were small and medium-sized enterprises. Foreign customers and the 400 largest Danish corporate customers were connected to headquarters, and did not use the bank's network of branches. Eighty thousand small and medium-sized enterprises are serviced through Unibank's network of branches. To be connected to the branch, instead of the headquarters, means that all transactions go through that branch, and that credit appraisal and most of the counselling are undertaken by branch employees. SMEs rarely have any contact with the headquarters, or receive any information from them. Therefore, management in the branch perceived the branch as a local bank with a support base in Copenhagen, furnishing it with extensive product knowledge and international contacts. The branch belonged to the region, being dependent on local business. It had no other way of making a living, as it could not itself invest deposits in other regions. In view of the ongoing rationalization of the branch network, the atmosphere was one of 'profit or perish'. To the individual bank employee, including the branch manager, 'perish' was synonymous with having to search for a new job in another part of Denmark, knowing that few new jobs were being established in the banking sector.

Unibank's central credit policy is not directed towards specific industries, firm size or the like. What is expected is profitability and no unnecessary risk-taking. This gives the branch some freedom concerning credit, but there are two restraints. Around 5–10 per cent of the largest loans or guarantees have to be approved by the central credit office (the limits are confidential), although the preliminary appraisal still has to be made by one of the local counsellors or branch managers. Only in rare cases do other types of loans require confirmation by headquarters, but if the customer's standing is rated as uncertain the loan has to be approved by headquarters. The second restraint is the choice of business customers, or more precisely changing the portfolio. Customers are not easy to move, as their reputation among business associates suffers by changing bank. Therefore, getting rid of customers can be expensive, and something that has to be considered (for example, if a customer can not find another bank he or she often goes bankrupt).

The customer portfolio of the branch we studied to a large extent reflected the local industry mainly within agriculture, electronics and food processing. Being a previous Andelsbank branch, involvements in agriculture were predominant, because of its historical links to the cooperative movement. One of the problems that the branch faced was that agriculture nationally was a declining industry and therefore headquarters was very sceptical of such engagements. Although, this specific area harboured the most profitable holdings and estates, the branch had to produce documentation and arguments in each case (credit approval) and in general (internal credit inspection) which was a heavy burden on the branch's resources.

Simultaneously, headquarters' credit guide was so general that, if followed strictly, credit appraisal would be extremely imprecise and conservative, and to some degree even random, as it did not take into account specific economic changes, such as the remarkable profits made in this region during the summer of 1993. During the summer's heatwave when all other farmers received economic help from the state, many of the local farmers experienced a peak year.

An easy solution would be to withdraw from involvements in agriculture and go into more 'fashionable' industries that were easier to assess, but the branch did not follow this strategy. Instead, the demands for documentation were resolved by using the agricultural network consisting of farmers' associations, accountants that had specialized in agriculture, and so on. The community of farmers had a long tradition for sharing information and it was fairly easy to get access to their files, as long as it was for their own benefit. Having this information it was not only easier to fulfil headquarters' demands for documentation, it also reduced the risk connected to involvements with farmers, as was the case of Andelsbanken prior to the merger (at a national level the Andelsbanken's loss percentage on agricultural involvements was significantly lower than that of other banks during the recession in the early 1980s).

Even within hard-core economic issues, the Unibank branch has, as we have seen, been able to demonstrate local autonomy. Headquarters is not punishing the branch economically or increasing control when it acts opportunistically, as long as it demonstrates profitability. This applies to both the branches investigated. Thus, to headquarters the end result seems to be more important than the means. The crucial point is then how the branches achieve profitability. One can only guess about the economic outcome had the two branches followed the logics of the headquarters by the rule and not established this local autonomy. Had they not tried to integrate with the local community, they would have experienced a serious problem of deficient information.

The Unibank branches have demonstrated that the local integration and autonomy of bank units still exist and are reinforced by the profit-centre organization. But does Unibank differ from Den Danske Bank, the other large bank, in this context? At the time of the mergers Den Danske Bank was much more centralized and operated with far more comprehensive control systems than Unibank (Molin and Pedersen, 1994). However, branches in Den Danske Bank are far from being 'McDonaldized' in the sense of operating with unskilled staff and standardized services. In the branch of Den Danske Bank that we investigated the local degree of credit approval seemed high and no one complained about restrictions and control imposed by headquarters. Branches in Den Danske Bank are profit centres and have the same incentives as other branches to do a good job in their area.

In spite of the creation of the mega-banks, Danish banking is still characterized by a split between Copenhagen and provincial banking logic (central versus local). Bank branches still remain closely integrated and tied to their local communities. This is reinforced by the fact that interest rate profits from deposits and loans are by far the most significant part of the banks' operations, in spite of growing involvement in stocks, bonds, currencies and international business.

CONCLUSIONS

Through our historical analysis and the Unibank case studies we have demonstrated how local autonomy has characterized, and still is characterizing, the Danish banking system. Before the Second World War, financing requirements in the provinces had to be solved by the provinces themselves. Neither the Nationalbanken nor the three large Copenhagen based banks directed capital towards provincial and small-scale industry. But the smallholder economy dominating the industrialization process created a market for local financial institutions that in effect reinforced the dynamics of the local economy. When Landmandsbanken established its network of branches by taking over some of the provincial banks in the first part of this century, it was seen as an attempt to drain the local economic system and new local banks were established to resist this. Before the financial crash during the 1920s, the links between banks and industry, both the small and large banks, were very close in terms of overlap in ownership and individuals. With the bank Act of 1930 these links were separated, introducing restrictions on both capital and individuals involved in banking. The establishment of small local financial institutions became more and more rare after this. Local banks, however, did not disappear in the postwar period, but the number of independent banks and savings banks decreased as they were merged. Physically, the spread of banks and savings banks still increased, as branches were set up and local integration maintained, but now in a different way than through ownership and organization.

During the 1960s and the 1970s the banking sector was characterized by two different types of development, the taking over of provincial banks by large Copenhagen banks and mergers between provincial banks that did not want to be owned by a Copenhagen bank. Different kinds of collective agreements and organizations supported the provincial banks in their efforts, for example, in relation to implementing expensive new technology. The concentration of savings banks seemed less conflictual, as they had fewer links to the SMEs that needed the more complex banking services.

During the 1980s local ties became less visible compared to the size of the banks and savings banks, but the number of branches still increased. Although Handelsbanken and Den Danske Bank had been able to maintain their lead in terms of size, many of the other banks, that had developed from provincial banks to national banks, were not that far behind. Local ties were maintained through very decentralized organizational designs and the continuous dominance of SME involvements. However, by 1990 the structural picture changed dramatically. Den Danske Bank and Unibank became dominant, covering 60 per cent of the domestic market, and local integration of the banks was expected to cease. However, studies of Unibank reveal that the branches were by no means turned into 'ice-cream stalls', incapable of making any decisions without consulting headquarters. In fact local branches were able to build up work organization, training programmes, and credit appraisal methods matching the local community. Maintaining local integration is still a struggle, especially as branches and employees are being cut back, but it is strongly embedded in the Danish context.

Local autonomy in Danish banking has proved to be remarkably persistent even though it has changed considerably during the past two hundred years. The large number of branches and the dominance of the domestic market support this argument, and the explanation is to be found in the Danish smallholder economy.

References

T. Andersen, 'Hvor blev filialerne af?', *Finansfokus*, 1 (1995) pp. 2–5.

Bankkommissionen, *Beretning om forholdende i Den Danske Landmandsbank*. (København: Schultz, 1924).

P. Bengtsson, *En demokratisk bank*. (København: Arbejdernes Landsbank, 1969).

N. Clemmensen, *Sparekassebevægelsen i Danmark: 1810–1914*. (København: Jurist og Økonomforbundets Forlag, 1985).

Danmarks Nationalbank, *Beretning og regnskab 1990*. (København: Danmarks Nationalbank, 1991).

Danmarks Nationalbank, *Kvartalsoversigt – maj*. (København: Danmarks Nationalbank, 1994).

Danmarks Nationalbank, *Kvartalsoversigt – februar*. (København: Danmarks Nationalbank, 1995).

Finansrådet, *Danske pengeinstitutter midt i en omstilling – En international sammenligning*. (København: Finansrådet, 1993a).

Finansrådet, *Kreditgivning til erhvervslivet*. (København: Finansrådet: 1993b).

Finanstilsynet, *Beretning fra Finanstilsynet – Pengeinstitutter m.v.* (København: Finanstilsynet, 1993).

S.A. Hansen, *Pengevæsen og kredit – 1813–1860*. (København: Forlaget Arnkrone, 1960).

J. Høpner, *Bankers erhvervsfinansiering og relationer til virksomhederne*, PhD dissertation. (København: Handelshøjskolen i København (forthcoming)).

Industriministeriet, *Fremtidens finansielle sektor*, Betænkning nr. 1232 (København: Schultz Grafisk, 1992).

P.H. Kristensen, 'On the Constitution of Economic Actors in Denmark: Interacting Skill-Containers and Project-Coordinators', in R. Whitley and P.H. Kristensen, *The Changing European Firm: Limits of Convergence*. (London: Routledge, 1995).

P.H. Kristensen and J. Høpner, *Fleksibilitetens Strukturform – Efteruddannelse, virksomhedsorganisation og arbejdskarriere i Danmark*. (København: Nyt fra Samfundsvidenskaberne, 1994).

P.H. Kristensen and C. Sabel, 'The Smallholder Economy in Denmark: The Exception as Variation', in C. Sabel and J. Zeitlin (eds), *World of Possibilities*. (Cambridge University Press, forthcoming).

F. Lauridsen, 'Generalkonsul Henrik Pontoppidan og de jyske banker', in *Erhvervsøkonomisk Årbog*. (Århus: Erhvervsarkivet, 1968).

R. Mikkelsen, *Dansk Pengehistorie – 1960–1990*. (København: Danmarks Nationalbank, 1993).

J. Molin and J.S. Pedersen, *Fusioner i Danmark i et organisatorisk perspektiv*. (København: Institut for Organisation og Arbejdssociologi, 1994).

K. Mordhost, *Dansk Pengehistorie – bilag*. (København: Danmarks Nationalbank, 1968).

S. Mørch, *Det Store Bankkrak*. (Viborg: Gyldendal, 1986).

E. Olsen and E. Hoffmeyer, *Dansk Pengehistorie.* (København: Danmarks Nationalbank, 1968).

J. Schovelin, *Den Danske Landmandsbank, Hypothek- og Vekselbank – 1871–1921.* (København: Hertz Bogtrykkeri, 1921).

K.E. Svendsen and S.A. Hansen, *Dansk Pengehistorie.* (København: Danmarks Nationalbank, 1968).

P. Wendt, *Penge og kapitalmarked.* (København: Handelshøjskolens Forlag, 1994).

P. Winding, *Det Danske Kapitalmarked.* (København: Bikuben, 1958).

3 The French Deposit Bank: Managerial Professions Between Rationalization and Trust

David Courpasson

INTRODUCTION

The face of French deposit banks has greatly changed since the beginning of the 1980s. Changes in their organization, their employment structures and the characteristics of their markets have effectively moved them into a new era (Annandale-Massa and Bertrand, 1990; Grafmeyer, 1992). Banking in France is changing rapidly, as in many countries. The radical changes in the banking industry which affect professional groups are often analysed in two ways: first, in terms of the impact of computer and communication technology and second, in terms of the impact of deregulation (see, for example, Engwall, Chapter 8 in this volume). In France too, banks have experienced these changes, from a dirigist way of 'managing' the sector to a complex compromise between dirigisme (i.e. regulation) and liberalism (i.e. deregulation) (see Salomon, Chapter 6 in this volume).

The banking law in 1984 and the reforms that followed have destroyed most of the barriers which characterized the French financial system, and have created a level playing field on which the different financial institutions can compete. The release from old constraints such as credit limits or exchange controls has facilitated innovation, increased competition and led to a drastic restructuring of the sector. Moreover, the use of computers and telecommunications is completely changing bank relationships with clients, as well as management methods. At the same time, the progressive construction of the single European market in financial services, which implies the complete liberalization of financial movements and the deregulation of the financial services in EU countries, is a challenge, but also an opportunity for French banks.

The changes involve a new set of relationships between the way in which banks are internally organized and the markets in which they participate. In particular, banks have traditionally depended on long-term 'trust relations' with clients. For several years, however, they have been segmenting their markets with the aim of identifying profitable clients and services. Thus, relations with clients are becoming based more and more on an abstract technical logic market segmentation, in which individual clients are allocated to a segment not on the basis of intimate personal knowledge and trust but as a result of their scores on a technical marketing tool. In this chapter,[1] we examine the hypothesis that these changes in the French banking sector are linked to the end of the model of a 'local market economy' which is based on trust between professional and clients. This trust arose from long-standing relationships based on the knowledge both parties had of each other, derived from inhabiting the same local economic space over a long period of time. The techniques of market segmentation, however, derive from abstract knowledge and are not dependent on time–space contiguity. This 'cultural' and professional change towards abstract knowledge means that alongside the 'old-style' branch manager (still existing in some cases), there now exists the 'market manager', responsible for particular market segments. The two models (segments and concrete local markets) continue to coexist and the problem for the banks is to develop a compromise between these two different principles. The transformation of the middle-management profession is at the heart of a new social regulation (Reynaud, 1979)[2] sought by French banks within the new rules of market organization brought about by segmentation. After having described the sector's traditional regulation and the developments affecting the branch manager's job, we put forward the idea that the 'new managers' are creating a compromise between modernism and tradition in their management of banking relationships. This compromise carries with it the seeds of a renewed professionalism on the part of the manager, a vital factor for French banks.

SOME CONCEPTUAL CHOICES

The existence of non-commercial exchanges, of rules and organizations situated in the heart of markets, is now well-established, and this makes it possible to link together a renewed economic sociology and a renewed economics of organization (Polanyi, 1983; White, 1981; Etzioni, 1988). The idea that business relations are embedded in a social context leads us to focus on specific local business settings; these constitute the social, geographical and professional field within which different commercial relations appear, live and die. The study of the transformation of a profession must be carried out considering the interaction of the profession with the socially constructed markets in which it operates. The case of the bank serves as an illustration of this phenomenon, inasmuch as there is a tension between the two principles of professional integrity and market success, a tension which the professional managerial actors are helping to resolve through their transformation strategy.[3]

In the UK and American sociological tradition, the profession is associated with a particular sort of occupation, capable of sustaining and legitimating a claim to self-regulation (in the spheres of certification and disqualification in particular). In the Durkheimian perspective, the term 'profession' is associated with the existence of a set of duties which act as a collective discipline and a form of social cohesion. The profession is thus the means of avoiding individualism and the numerous conflicts which occur in industrial societies (Durkheim, 1967). It is in this latter Durkheimian sense that we refer to managerial professions. One of the most important problems that firms have to solve is the end of solidarities that arise from close and frequent social interaction. Changes in working life such as the increase in geographical and career mobility and the rationalization and standardization of working practices destroy these 'social links'. The concept of 'corporate professions' focuses on new logics of solidarity which emerge gradually. Management based on new concepts of duty and social cohesion is, for us, clearly a corporate profession, which participates in this broad movement of professionalization. Implicitly it becomes a whole array of different jobs which are nevertheless similar in the competences required, in the kinds of performance that seem to be assessed, even in the profiles required in these jobs. Professionalization in this sense acts as a sort of self-regulation of the management labour market, at least in France.

Finally, we speak in this chapter about the 'rationalization' of business relations, in a sense very near to the Weberian approach (Weber, 1967). The present idea in the sector is effectively that a 'competence', a form of specialization associated with technical skills, clearly identified, enables a precise role to be assigned to the salesperson. The sector is moving from a 'mechanical'[4] conception of the business based on social and family interaction (such that management of a bank branch could be passed from generation to generation), in which professional duties, codes and disciplines were learnt from an informal mode of apprenticeship, undertaken in a stable market with durable networks of knowledge. It is evolving towards a more 'organic' conception of business based on a new logic of competence, controlled both by standardized tools (for example, for lending practices), by standardized career and learning paths, and by very similar performance appraisal criteria. The new commercial relation is not assessed in a more or less 'meritocratic' way; but the idea of merit has changed. Before, it was judged in a socially specific market context; with rationalization, it is completely internalized in a specific organizational field. That is why the present modernization of the banking sector is a form of rationalization.

THE TRADITIONAL BANKING SECTOR: DOMESTICITY AND LOCALIZATION

Three principles have historically been behind the running of the French deposit bank sector:

- a market relation principle based on the reciprocal trust between customers and sales staff
- a competence principle based on social knowledge of markets and a qualitative appreciation of risk
- a time relation principle based on both the length of time of relations with a customer and the salesperson's relation with his or her bank

Reciprocal Trust

The business of banking is, in part, speculation. It is based on the management of uncertainty concerning the ability of customers to repay loans, whether they be private individuals or companies. The traditional banker makes use of intuition in lending practices, as well as the almost emotional trust he has in the customer.[5]

> When a customer becomes a friend, we can sometimes think that he [*sic*] wouldn't betray us or take us for a ride. Even if we're not always certain, that's also part of risk management, showing trust to keep [the customer's] trust. (Branch Manager)

Indeed, the trust is long-shared. If the banker at times defends a customer's case in the face of the bank's opposing economic logic, the customer will show undivided loyalty. This loyalty is made all the stronger by the fact that the individuals concerned remain the same over a long period of time and establish reputations as good bankers in their local area. As with lawyers (Karpik, 1989, 1995) and other professions (Freidson, 1970), the banking market is a 'judgement market' where the nature of the business relation emerges from the face-to-face interaction between the customer and the banker, leading to trust (or rejection), which then becomes the salesperson's main resource in the development of the sales activity, and the sometimes decisive argument on behalf of the client when requesting credit. When this face-to-face interaction generates trust between the two parties, the relationship is maintained, even when this appears to be contrary to the bank's overall economic logic.

Social Competence

Trust is established not just through face-to-face interaction but also through the banker's use of information concerning the local market which is as objective and exhaustive as possible. The salesperson must, therefore, be an integral member of the local 'knowledge-sharing' network, where information, prescriptions and recommendations are exchanged. Being in this position allows him to anticipate future changes either by putting forward offers to potential clients, or by identifying risks which need to be integrated into the analysis of any lending. This social competence comes through his length of service on a branch's territory, or thanks to his position as a local notable, especially in rural areas where the branch manager is associated with numerous activities and associations.

> You mustn't miss a thing; celebrations, fetes, inaugurations ... That's when you meet people, and when people talk about each other. (ex-Branch Manager)

The banker's social competence also comes from a thorough knowledge of the workings of the decision-making process of granting credit in his bank. In this way, he knows just how far he can go in his territory. As with any commercial profession, the problem is to find the best compromise between the necessary 'double trust', relation, with the market and with the firm. The rules and procedures of risk management are quite different in the two fields. The banker must know these rules precisely so that he can balance his personal involvement in the customer's projects, and his involvement with the bank.

> We know who's on the Credit Committee, who's in charge of granting credit, who to pass information on to, depending on the stakes of a deal.

All this helps us to assess the limits of reason and the degree of personal involvement. (Office Manager)

The Length of Time of the Commitment

Trust and the model of social competence are reinforced by the length of time over which the commercial relationship exists. First, the trust is reinforced by the amount of time over which there occurs mutual investment and common experiences which can confirm the solidity of a link. Time also reinforces the banker's 'social learning' and competence. The customer's behaviour reinforces this principle, since the customer balks more often than not at the idea of changing bankers. The commercial relation establishes itself through the banker's loyalty to his branch, and the customer's loyalty to his bank, and even to a particular branch. Therefore, the length of time of the banker's relation with his bank influences the quality of the bond to the market at the same time. It is as if the banker cannot invest himself in his commercial activities on a long-term basis unless he has given proof of his solid commitment as regards his organization. He also gains some solidity from his identity, midway between bank and market, from these two areas of action: the organization and the market.

We can analyse the so-called traditional banker's profession, and more specifically that of the branch manager, thus: the latter is in some ways the crystallization of the link between the organization and the market. The kind of commercial action we have analysed is based on the capacity of the manager to organize the relationships both between the branch and the head office, and also between the branch and customers. Thus, the bank manager became one of the main actors in ensuring the efficiency of the French banking sector, since it was based on the local delegation of numerous decisions concerning the granting of credit.[6] In the Durkheimian sense, the profession of bank manager constituted a set of duties and disciplines which created social cohesion between the organization and the market.

THE BRANCH MANAGER AND MODERNIZATION: FROM TERRITORY TO SEGMENT

In recent years, banking has experienced the effects of modernizing practices concerning the rationalization of sales work (especially lending, but also shares and other financial services). Central to this has been the creation of market segmentation models which divide the customer base and shape the 'back organization' to meet the so-called needs of each segment. There are two elements to these changes.

First, there is the segmentation of customers, for example, by age group or socioprofessional class. This can sometimes lead to having up to twenty or thirty segments. The bank then organizes different strategies for approaching each segment (with 'segment men [*sic*]' in the branches and at head office).

Even if appellations differ from one bank to another, with more or less complex stratification, a general 'model' of the structuring of private individual clientele can be given as follows:

- stratum 0 reserved for wealth management
- stratum 1 reserved for estate management
- stratum 2 reserved for high-quality local customers
- stratum 3 reserved for non-priority customers, benefiting from a number of products but of a low value
- stratum 4 reserved for non-priority customers, who are often not assigned to any particular clientele manager

In the market for bank services to professions and small businesses, the rules are often less clear. Banks include in this segment one-man businesses and small firms with less than ten salaried employees or an annual turnover of less than 5 or 10 million French francs.

Finally, the company segment is generally defined to include all companies, small and medium-sized firms, subsidiaries of large groups, or large companies with more than 15 or 20 salaried employees or an annual turnover of roughly more then 10 million French francs.

The second major element of this change is the specialization of the sales staff in relation to the different segments. This also concerns the defining of job descriptions, skills needed, and policy in relation to salaries and career management *vis-à-vis* the sales staff.

If we try to analyse the effects of this rationalization on the managerial professions, we can distinguish three essential elements:

- An increase in the technical nature of market relations which makes the branch manager's position rather vague compared to previously
- The differentiation of markets into three large segments which undermines the status of the traditional branch manager

● Finally, the rationalization process which separates responsibility for sales and markets (undertaken by 'segment managers') from responsibility for control and coordination of branches and for control of local labour markets. What then becomes of the local branch managers who have based their position on this dual control for decades?

Sales Outlet and Segment: A Difficult Reconciliation

The main transformation in the professional universe of bank management is in the setting up of a new organizational structure and hierarchy taking market segments into account. In many banks the branch managers and market managers (for private individuals, one-man firms or companies depending on the case) coexist whether they like it or not. In other words, two not always reconcilable hierarchical legitimacies coexist: one is linked to the sales territory and the stakes of each deal (the sales outlet legitimacy), and the other linked to the type of customer (the segment legitimacy). Within any particular branch or area, branch managers and market managers will each have a number of employees whom they will be managing. The cohabitation of the two is often a difficult experience:

Today, it's obvious we're getting in each other's way. In the same branch there's the branch manager who remains the manager but who has, nonetheless, lost quite a lot of his prerogatives, and the segment managers who are, in fact, the sales teams' managers. The General Public[7] manager here has 10 people working with him. He dictates the rules himself to a certain extent. The branch manager is supposed to be above him to advise and direct, but in reality he is often dispossessed through a lack of precise information. (General Public Salesman)

The coexistence of branch managers and market managers means that, in certain large branches today, many sales people are no longer sure who is the boss. In smaller branches or offices the problem is less frequent. The sales outlet manager (i.e., the branch manager) is still the local boss, although more often than not he is under the General Public Market manager based in the larger, main branch.

But the present situation remains unclear. This change in the hierarchies is difficult, to a greater or lesser extent depending on the area and on the bank. It is, indeed, directly linked to a shift in identity which transforms the dominant legitimacy in the bank; legitimate authority is ruled less by the volume of business and the extent of the boss's zone of action than by the prestige and economic weight of the segment he manages.

Sales Activity and Managerial Activity

The problem posed consists not only of the branch managers' weakened, hierarchical legitimacy, but also of the change in their relation *vis-à-vis* the commercial transaction, and, therefore, their relation to the market. Historically, the branch manager has had the local monopoly over the bank's involvement in the social life of a local market; as we have seen, his autonomy endowed him with a certain prestige, as much in his own branch as in the rest of the organization. The position as sales outlet manager has long been the banker's reference position: a necessary stage, a springboard, or the ultimate post. He is still the 'crowning glory' of the 'frontline actors' (Grafmeyer, 1992).

The differentiation between segments upsets this reference position by changing the nature of the market. From being concrete, physical and contextualized, the market is becoming abstract; it depends more on technical criteria than on knowledge of the individual client; the risk under analysis is dealt with using ratios and sophisticated tools. The legitimacy of the 'super salesman' is evolving; the legitimate boss is no longer necessarily the person who knows the customers and business deals the best, but the one who masters risk-analysis techniques, business finance, or business law the best. Where, now, does the branch manager stand in this universe transformed by the rationalization of decision-making? He remains free to develop a less precise job: that of manager, or administrator of a profit centre. Less directly involved with the market itself, he is responsible for the business's profitability. This is a new function for which many are not only ill-prepared, but which, above all, does not correspond to their professional history, which is made up of 'feats of arms' and unusual career paths.

What we like in this job is the remarkable side to people's pasts, going into detail about things, part of their private life in fact. Having a passion for a job in the domain of finance doesn't mean having a passion for money. I've discovered loads of really strange things, people have told me quite incredible stories – you discover a great company hidden away in some hangar, or an incredible guy at the back of an office somewhere. That's also what banking is all about. (Branch Manager)

The change is therefore experienced as a decisive shift in professional and personal identity, and career. Not only must the branch manager change job, but also his 'spirit'.

Rationalization and Market Control

In addition, market segmentation has three complementary effects which the managerial profession is experiencing. The first is that this way of managing the different markets makes more individual assessment of commercial performance possible. In addition to the performance of the branch as a whole, there is also that of each segment and, especially, of each salesman; the segment objectivizes his activity and brings in criteria for measuring performance (such as, for example, a salesman's success rate within the framework of a sales drive on a given product), that is to say it makes it possible to read each salesman's activity and perhaps even make it negotiable. This objectivization has very direct effects on ranking; a new hierarchy can be created between the sales people. The hierarchy of prestige or importance of business deals is substituted by a hierarchy of individual 'productive' performance, which had previously remained implicit, or at least had no direct effect on the salesman's fate.

A second effect involves the greater transparency of local markets and customers that segmentation affords. Thanks to the division of sales areas and especially the salesmen's duty to report back, each branch's real market becomes clearer and more accessible to the central sales management. The computerization of a branch's activities which accompanies the segmentation, also, of course, increases the ability of the central coordination staff to master the sales areas.

Third, the responsibility for the job market also returns to the bank's central authorities. Since the 1980s, the recruitment of sales people has been based on relatively standardized criteria regarding level of education, and careers are managed in a much more global way. Policies concerning the flexibility of the sales population have led to the banks opening up the frontiers of the internal job market. If before mobility was often viewed in relation to a rather limited sales area, generally around a main branch or group of smaller branches, in the 1990s the salesman's scope of mobility is clearly the whole company. With segmentation, it may even become sector-based since the salesman's abilities are tending to become interchangeable from one bank to another.

In this context of greater standardization and flexibility, it is obvious that branch managers are losing a great number of their prerogatives which were based on the bank's acceptance of the specific character of local product and job markets.

The middle-management profession in the bank is, therefore, going through a difficult stage. Not long ago, some banks considered eliminating the 'mythical'[8] function of branch manager and replacing it with three 'market managers' overseen by an 'area manager' responsible for directing several branches. Few precise choices have yet been made; such a decision would have a major impact on what the organization of banks' networks could or should be like very shortly, and how the autonomy/centralization dialectic may be managed in this sector. That is why the bank's senior executives hesitate to make any crucial decision in this domain, preferring to see how the profession evolves on its own.

THE NETWORK MANAGER: TOWARDS A NEW PROFESSION?

We will now try to specify what type of branch network management 'model' French deposit banks are moving towards. Two functions are at the heart of this redefinition: market manager and area manager.

The Market Manager: A New Managerial Model

First and foremost, the market manager (market segment manager) demonstrates in the present structure of his job a combination of three types of ability:

- Technical ability linked both to the knowledge of financial and risk-analysis techniques relevant to his particular segment, and to the knowledge of products on offer to that segment
- Managerial ability of a new style, linked to the ability to directly lead a sales team, based on the 'industrial sales-manager model'; we mean that he has in mind very precise objectives of 'production', of 'prospecting' activity, and that he is himself evaluated on the collective economic performance of his sales team
- Social ability; this remains, but it is not at the heart of the market manager model. Whilst a good knowledge of the clientele is required, the banker's social integration in an area is not considered a deciding factor

In other words, the appearance of this model seems to mark the banker's current shift of allegiance and direct involvement from the market (or at least from an intermediate position between market and organization) towards the organization. It could be said that the behaviour of the market manager is shaped by the organization's structure and systems rather than the specific characteristics of the local market-place.

More precisely, the rationalization process makes the organization's rules unavoidable for its employees who have to adapt their practices to the new model. People try to preserve their job by accepting the new working conditions because if they do not, they risk being marginalized and even excluded. They have to construct a new form of professional 'corporate identity' as described by Dubar (1991): that is to say, an identity based on their involvement in the whole organization as a structure rather than an identity based on place and function. In doing so, they become less bankers and more managers. Their identity is more 'flexible', capable of being adapted to a standardized managerial model (for example, a market manager can be a market manager in very different sectors: banks, insurance, department stores, even some parts of industry).

The second aspect is in some respects a consequence of this shift, and concerns the great 'interchangeability' of the new bosses. Previously, the importance of specific territorial characteristics, recognized as central to business success, made the branch manager's position stable; staying in the same area promoted efficiency. In the 1990s, the desire to standardize the technical aspects of lending through models of market segmentation and credit scoring means that social knowledge and competence has decreased in importance. There is now a tendency to neglect the need for the banker to involve himself in local affairs. The homogenization of a technical model of the market relation goes together with the possibility of increased mobility of personnel. Even if the rate of mobility is tending to decrease a little in the face of the excesses of the 1980s, it is clear that a professional labour market of market managers who have little allegiance to particular geographical areas is forming. Indeed such managers may have little allegiance to their present employers and will be willing to move to another bank, even into another sector. Rationalization, therefore, tends to be accompanied by a noticeable shift in the operation of companies' internal and external labour markets.

The Managerial Coordination Functions: The Area Manager

The area manager (a more or less constant terminology depending on the company) is in fact the manager of a group of branches, organized according to a geographical area logic. He is in some ways a 'super branch manager' whose main function is to manage a territorial area in conjunction with the market managers, and the main branch managers where they still exist. This position represents the search for a compromise between a territorial and market segment logic in banking. It is the interface role between the old and the new ways of conducting banking business. He is not only the hierarchical superior of branch managers and market managers, but, in addition, he must simultaneously combine in his activity the 'vertical' protection and performance of his sales territory (the group of branches) and the 'horizontal' defence of the interests of the coexisting segments within it. In other words, the area manager function crystallizes to an even greater extent a form of compromise between the organizational logic linked to the market segment, and the social logic linked to the territory. We can see such professional groups emerging in the banking sector, whose main characteristic is precisely to build such compromises through the daily search for consent between the two conflicting logics:

> My job is, in some ways, to get people who don't always agree to live side by side. The segment manager may want to do some thing or another to increase overall results. But one action may go against a branch manager's one, for example if the latter manager is in contact with a company manager who also has personal accounts in a branch. Coordination then becomes indispensable. There are power clashes, but also clashes concerning ways of working. (Area Manager)

Furthermore, the area manager is tending to become the reference point according to the American sociology of professions (see Hughes, 1958) both for branch managers and market managers. The latter often see themselves occupying this position in the future. It is thus little by little replacing the branch manager function in the bank's hierarchy of social status. Above all, however, the compromise developed by the area manager seems progressively to resemble a search for balance between banking conservatism and the necessary degree of commitment to the client's projects. There is, indeed, in the segment/territory antagonism, opposition between technical rationality in the bank's decision-making,[9] and a form of rationality inherited from traditional practices based on affectivity and 'mutual acquaintance' which constitute the means for the qualitative analysis of the market (Wissler, 1989).

The area manager is, at the same time, in close enough contact with the field to understand a certain social logic, and close enough to the organization to accept, in part, the principles of orthodoxy. He keeps a customer portfolio to continue to be involved in the commercial work undertaken in the field; in particular, he has more often than not responsibility for clients in the high stratum of wealth management. To a certain extent, we can say he occasionally defends the field logic. Indeed, when times are difficult for the economy, many salespersons tend to shelter behind the technical tools. They reduce risk by following the rules rigidly. In doing so they also reduce profit potential. Consequently, other actors must consider certain files with a different pair of eyes 'to give them the chance' that current edginess would normally disallow. Here, social competence and discretion takes the upper hand; area managers in this way combine the technical and social logics. Social competence becomes most useful at a time when uncertainty (about employment in particular) brings about hidden professional strategies behind arguments of technical rationality.

CONCLUSION: THE PARADOXES OF MODERNIZATION IN FRENCH BANKS

The most noticeable evolution in French deposit banks since the early 1980s has been the rapid specialization of business relations. The managers and sales people in banks are becoming specialized in particular types of clientele and the branch is also becoming an area devoted to a particular market segment. The characteristics of each segment are constructed and known through formal technical models which are the basis upon which organizations, work roles and systems of rules are based.

In this atmosphere of increasing technical rationality as regards relations with the customer, a need is felt for a balance between technical, managerial and social specializations. In other words, there is a need to go back towards the roots of the banking professions with a personalized approach. Indeed, many salespersons do not feel very comfortable with the technical approach to customer relationships, partly because it is not always coherent with their learning process (mainly based on field-work), but mainly because they experience the negative reaction of numerous clients facing a diminution of quality in the personal relations they have with their 'own' banker. A sense of depersonalization is felt by many clients, and there is a real convergence between their opinion about the essential personal component of a 'good' service and the salesperson's opinions.

At the outset of the process of rationalization of market management, the banks seemed to forget that there was an irreducible social dimension to any commercial activity. Paradoxically, the professional actors are themselves reintroducing it, partly through the crystallization of a tacit compromise between the legitimate practices and competences of the market segment logic and the legitimate practices and competences of the local market logic. This evolution demonstrates that the professional commercial actor needs a dual cultural and economic legitimacy in order to operate, as described in the sociology of professions (Heilbron, 1986). It is on this necessity for both an identity and a practical way of working that a new managerial profession is being built in French banking.

The issue at stake for the French banking sector lies more in the search for a compromise between the social logics of concrete markets and the organization's technical logics in the granting of credit than in the search for a compromise between local autonomy and central control. In our opinion, the bank's dilemma is not a question of the centralization or decentralization of powers, but of the link between a social model and a technico-economic model of business practices. The modernization of the sector lies in bringing these together rather than in purely fostering a process of rationalization of roles and procedures. This is because rationalization comes up against an irreducible paradox. The need to standardize tools of analysis must be tempered by the need to be discretionary in their application according to one's detailed social knowledge of the client.

Furthermore, in French banks, the very idea of modernization goes hand in hand not only with rationalization, but also with a decentralization of decision-making. Through market segmentation, the banks have introduced policies to increase the levels of delegation to each salesman so that the banking institution may say 'yes' on the spot as often as possible. This increase in the local delegation of responsibilities to the sales outlet is accompanied by an increase in the ways of assessing individual sales performance and greater centralization of information on product markets thanks to branches being computerized. Therefore, decentralization in banks (and in numerous companies organized in networks) is at the heart of a yet unresolved paradox which is even increasing with segmentation. On the one hand, salespersons' responsibility is made more concrete through a greater degree of delegation; on the other hand, the salespersons are made more apprehensive by the pressure of assessment and daily reporting. There undeniably lies an economic logic (the greater the freedom of action, the greater the need to check results) but also a social paradox (the salesman is endowed with a professional image founded on his autonomy in the field of action). There is therefore a paradox between the highly controlled decentralization of risk management and a personalization of performance management and of its effects on the salesman's destiny.

The professional actors are themselves caught up in these multiple paradoxes while their own work roles are still evolving. The interaction between decentralization and the forming of new competences brings about not only often difficult shifts of identity, from 'generalization' to specialization, from reporting locally to reporting to the organization, but also withdrawal strategies (according to Sainsaulieu, 1985), linked to the fact that the actors do not know the market and human resources mode that the bank will adopt in the near future.

These changes can be seen as located within the framework of four models shaping the activity of bank managers and employees:

- the social competence model
- the technical competence model
- the centralized risk management model
- the decentralized risk management model

The following figure attempts to illustrate these alternatives.

Within this field of alternatives, we have come across branches and regions which seem to be taking the direction of one or another of these 'ideal' positions in a more or less definite way. The problem for bank management is to find some meeting points between these models: if the markets are effectively mainly run by social logics, the salespersons must prioritize social kinds of behaviour and of competence and not just technical ones. To understand this requires that the paradoxes of rationalization are unravelled. This is a reasonably optimistic point of view, which takes into account the real capacity of the 'corporate professions' to adapt themselves to a new system of organizational rules.[10]

If we try to generalize, we see clearly that the evolution of the structures of firms (including the industrial firms) towards the decentralization of profit centres encourages the managers (in particular, middle managers) to continue to occupy an intermediary position between acting as purveyors of technical rationality and control and acting in ways which promote trust and informality. The new 'social pacts' that modern organizations are searching for lie in the balance they will be able to construct between these logics. In organizations with less hierarchical levels, the role of managerial professions is precisely to find out the compromises between standardization and the irreducible contingency of the local management and professional context. In this gap, not only is the emergence of a model of managerial competence at stake, but also a large part of the paradoxes of modernity in the productive organization. We see that an important paradox in so-called 'modern' organizations lies in the tendency towards

82

Figure 3.1   Alternative models for the activity of bank managers

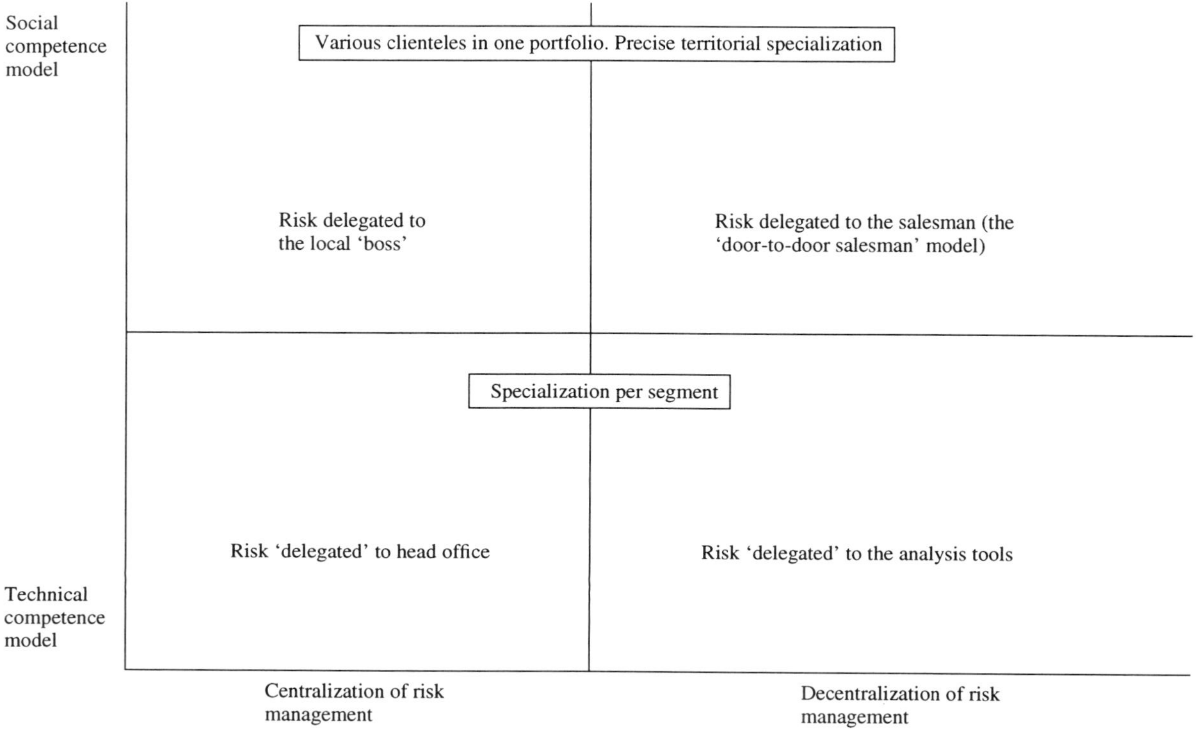

Social
competence
model

Various clienteles in one portfolio. Precise territorial specialization

Risk delegated to the salesman (the
'door-to-door salesman' model)

Risk delegated to
the local 'boss'

Specialization per segment

Risk 'delegated' to the analysis tools

Risk 'delegated' to head office

Technical
competence
model

Centralization of risk
management

Decentralization of risk
management

the standardization of skills on the one hand, and on the other hand, forms of human resource management that tend to favour the individual and singularity – 'each man is able and required to build his own job' (Courpasson, 1994a). Numerous tools of innovation tend to create tensions between elements aimed at mobilizing the actors in a common objective (the common concern of 'quality', for example), and at the same time elements promoting or creating a predetermined order or behaviour (for example, the formal procedures of quality certification) (Eymard-Duvernay and Marchal, 1994). This general tension exists and is clear in the French banking sector.

Notes

1. This chapter is based on the results of approximately ten case studies carried out between 1989 and 1993 by the author with five high street banks of varying size and location. The aim of these studies was to analyse the transformation of the sales professions and business relationships in French banks. On this subject, see Courpasson (1994a, 1995).
2. The concept of regulation as used here is derived from Reynaud who refers to the social activity of creation of rules; for him, a social group (like a firm, or like an economic sector, for example) is mainly based on a 'joint regulation' between different kinds of actors. In our case, this theoretical model would demonstrate that market segmentation practices have destabilized the historic joint regulation of the banking sector, based on a certain model of relationship with the markets. (See Courpasson, 1995.)
3. In a different framework Granovetter (1985), taking up the Ben-Porath (1980) study of diamond merchants, maintains that the solidarity of a profession may be a condition for existing trust in a market not turning into wrongdoing. The profession provides an ethical type of coherence (p. 492) which ensures that each business relation is conducted in accordance with general principles but related to the specific instance.
4. We also utilize the Durkheimian distinction between mechanical and organic solidarity to bring out the nature of this transformation (Durkheim, 1967).
5. We use the male pronoun as an indicator of the social reality of French banking. The management groups have been predominantly male until quite recently.
6. The strength of the traditional model led to the fact that the real decision was made more often than not by the actors in the field, despite the apparent centralization of the credit-granting system. This reality of decision-making was due to the fact that the strategic information was held almost exclusively by the branches, thanks to their privileged position in the heart of local markets and to the control they operated on their customer networks. That is why many bank managers or regional managers continue their commercial activity so as not to lose contact with all the decision-making parameters when they 'move' to head office.

7. The General Public Market includes the private customers and the Professional Market which is not yet autonomous.

8. Mythical in the sense that banking employees identify the nature of the bank manager by reference to legendary individuals whose style and behaviour give a concrete representation to the idea of good management.

9. Which is characterized by precise debt ratios, or by the classification of customers under three colours depending on an application file's 'quality': red (the 'impossibles'), orange (the 'possibles'), and green (the 'accepteds').

10. This view is quite different from that explained in the Quack and Hildebrandt chapter concerning the comparative evolution of the relationships between banks and SMEs in France and Germany; their vision is more pessimistic. This difference comes first from the comparative methodologies they use which lead them to postulate the existence of very distinct national models that they have, to some extent, to oppose. In that approach, there is 'always' a better model than the other. But the second reason is more crucial; we consider in our approach that the evolutions we are analysing are not finished, that is to say, French banks are in a transition where there is no real model for the end point. We can analyse this transition as a series of negotiations and compromises that are presently emerging in the sector. Therefore, there is not a pessimistic and an optimistic vision of the change which could be opposed. What is important is to analyse banking's way of bringing together opposite logics of business action as well as can be expected.

References

D. Annandale-Massa and H. Bertrand, *La gestion des ressources humaines dans les banques européennes: quelles stratégies?* (Paris: Economica, 1990).

Y. Ben-Porath, 'The F. Connection: Families, Friends and Firms in the Organization of Exchange', *Population and Development Review*, 6, 1 (1980) pp. 1–30.

D. Courpasson, 'Marché concret et identité professionnelle locale. La construction de l'identité par le rapport au marché', *Revue Française de Sociologie*, 35, 2 (1994) pp. 197–229.

D. Courpasson, 'Modernity and Professions. The 'Corporate Professions' at the Heart of Organizational Paradoxes', paper presented for the workshop on knowledge workers, Human Capital Mobility Programme, Lyon, November (1994).

D. Courpasson, *La modernisation bancaire. Sociologie des rapports professions/marchés*. (Paris: L'Harmattan, 1995).

C. Dubar, *La socialisation. Construction des identités sociales et professionnelles*. (Paris: Armand Colin, 1991).

E. Durkheim, *De la division du travail social*. (Paris: PUF, 1967).

L. Engwall, 'The Invisible Hand Shaking the Visible Hand', ch. 8, this volume (1996).

A. Etzioni, *The Moral Dimension. Toward a New Economics*. (New York: The Free Press, 1988).

F. Eymard-Duvernay and E. Marchal, 'Les règles en action. Entre une organisation et ses usagers', *Revue Française de Sociologie*, 36, 1 (1994) pp. 5–36.

E. Freidson, *Profession of Medicine*. (New York: Harper & Row, 1970).

Y. Grafmeyer, *Les gens de la banque*. (Paris: PUF, 1992).

M. Granovetter, 'Economic Action and Social Structure: The Problem of Embeddedness', *American Journal of Sociology*, 91 (1985) pp. 481–510.

J. Heilbron, *La professionnalisation comme concept sociologique et comme stratégie des sociologues*, in *Historiens et Sociologues aujourd'hui*. (Université Lille 1: Presses du CNRS, 1986).

E.C. Hughes, *Men and Their Work*. (Glencoe: The Free Press, 1958).

L. Karpik, 'L'économie de la qualité', *Revue Française de Sociologie*, 30, 2 (1989) pp. 187–210.

L. Karpik, *Les avocats entre l'Etat, le public et le marché*. (Paris: Gallimard, 1995).

K. Polanyi, *La grande transformation*. (Paris: Gallimard, 1983).

S. Quack and S. Hildebrandt, 'Bank Finance for Small and Medium-Sized Entreprises in Germany and France', ch. 5, this volume (1996).

J.D. Reynaud, 'Conflit et régulation sociale. Esquisse d'une théorie de la régulation conjointe', *Revue Française de Sociologie*, 20 (1979) pp. 367–76.

R. Sainsaulieu, *L'identité au travail*. (Paris: Presses de la FNSP, 1985).

D. Salomon, 'The Problematic Transformation of the Banking Sector in France: The Case for Consumer Credit'.

M. Weber, *L'éthique protestante et l'esprit du capitalisme*. (Paris: Plon, 1967).

H. White, 'Where Do Markets Come From?', *American Journal of Sociology*, 87, November (1981) pp. 517–47.

A. Wissler, 'Les jugements dans l'octroi de crédit', in *Innovations et Ressources Locales, Cahiers du Centre d'Etudes de l'Emploi*, 33 (1989) pp. 67–121.

4 The End of the German Model? Developmental Tendencies in the German Banking Industry

Herbert Oberbeck and Nestor D'Alessio

INTRODUCTION

Since the early 1980s changes have taken place in the German banking industry which are transforming its business environment. Market saturation in the segment of basic bank products and services, falling profitability in the lending business, increasing operating costs, changes in the saving and investment behaviour of the private clients and growing uncertainty on the corporate side of the business are indicators of the forces at work which have transformed the business parameters of the firms and are forcing the banks to revise their marketing strategies, rationalization concepts, and personnel policies.[1]

Our purpose is to clarify to what extent the changes are mere adjustments within the business system or whether they imply a break with established practices which traditionally have been associated with the 'German model'. The German model refers to a 'bank-based' finance system administered by 'universal banks' using their internal techniques of resource allocation in response to demand. The banking institutions are oriented to the corporate side of business, possessing closed and comprehensive relationships with the rather financially conservative German private clients. The universal banking system also requires staff with high training standards capable of selling and administering a wide range of products (Krummel, 1980; Gardener, 1992).[2]

The starting point of this chapter is a comprehensive presentation of the developments and shifts which occurred in the 1980s. In a second step we will outline new facts which indicate how the firms are acting to cope with the changing business environment. Later on, we will try to identify areas of uncertainty and causes of friction with which the firms will be confronted in the process of managing the changes at the firm level. Finally, we will discuss the character and significance of the observed changes.

THE CHANGES OF THE 1980s

Market Saturation in the Segment of Basic Bank Products and Services as a Result of a Successful Business Strategy of the Banks

The 1960s and the 1970s were decades of growing expansion in the retail banking segment. Traditionally the business field of the Sparkassen and cooperative banks, the commercial banks discovered in the 1960s the increasing importance of retail banking in the framework of a society whose members were leaving behind the austerity and privations of the immediate postwar years and were avid consumers. As bait to attract the future clients the Deutsche Bank offered in 1959 a consumer credit with a maximum of 2000 DM without security.[3] This was the starting point of a race to win private clients: commercial banks, cooperative banks and Sparkassen directed all their energy towards integrating private households into a dense net of bank products and services. Current accounts were sold to private households as the pivot for other financial products and services. The term '*Allfinanz*' primarily meant, at the beginning, not the cooperation between banks and insurance providers but the practice of offering a technologically supported 'product package' to households which consisted of a current account as support for a comprehensive organization of payment transfers including all the regular payments by standing order or direct debit, automatic overdraft credit (two or three times the monthly personal income), a savings account and consumer credit. Originally called 'wage or salary accounts', they enabled the German banks to transform their traditional payment system into an electronic one and to win private clients. Fees for traditional forms of money transfer for wage and salary payment were higher than fees for direct transfer into the account. Thus the German firms were gradually forced to adopt the new method of payment, whereas their employees had to open a non-interest-bearing account with a bank of their choice, thereby increasing the funds available to the banks.

Simultaneously with the move to electronic payment systems and as part of the new market-oriented business strategy a restructuring of the work organization took place. The back office work functions were separated from those of the front office. As market-oriented functions were separately defined and freed from a great part of the administrative work, the front office activities assumed predominantly a service and advisory character with sales goals. At the same time, the banks gave the advisers and credit officials a greater prerogative to issue credit to the private clients as well as to the commercial ones. This process was supported by the development of integrated customer and account data bases, which made it possible to scan all the existing business connections and consequently the risks as well. These data bases were also connected to automatic control programs (Baethge and Oberbeck, 1986).

Additionally, during the 1960s and the 1970s an expansion of the banking branch networks took place. Whereas there were 32 227 branches in the year 1962, their number grew to 44 344 in 1979. The expansion of the branches occurred simultaneously with a territorial restructuring of the offices in accordance with the requirements of the local markets. Accordingly, the technologically supported one-man branch of the Sparkasse was no longer a rarity in the countryside at the end of the 1970s. This made it possible for the inhabitants of small villages and suburbs to handle their bank affairs in the local office. This frequently included not only withdrawals and deposits but also advice on credit and securities.

During most of the 1980s the German banks tried to improve the basic model outlined above for the private sector. By the end of the decade 90 per cent of private households were covered with basic products and services: current account with automatic overdraft credit, savings book and a comprehensive organization of payment transfers which included all regular payments by standing order or direct debit, so that automatic transfers and direct debiting represented 90.8 per cent of the number of the cashless payments and 81.1 per cent of the volume of the cashless payments at the end of 1987 (BIZ, 1989). This shows not only the success of the business strategy in the past but also the emergence of a new constellation, which can be interpreted as market saturation in the segment of basic banking products and services.

Increasing Competition among the Banks for the Savings of Private Clients and Changes in the Saving Behaviour of German Households

In an atmosphere of increasing competition the German banks did not remain inactive while trying to retain the savings of private clients. Alongside the traditional savings accounts, they developed innumerable savings products with various maturities, interest rates, special bonuses and termination dates. The statistics presented in Figure 4.1 show, however, that the banks were not completely successful in retaining the savings of private clients. Their share in the annual increase of personal assets dropped from 42.8 per cent in 1980 to 26.0 per cent in 1989. In comparison, the share of the life insurance market grew from 15.2 per cent to 20.1 per cent in the same period. Above all, bonds placed partially through investment funds have been the beneficiaries of the changes in the saving behaviour of private clients. With their fixed interest rates, bonds offer German private clients the security associated with traditional savings accounts. The banks currently control the growing investment fund industry with a market share of 72 per cent, by comparison with only a 10 per cent share for insurance companies and 13 per cent for independent financial advisers. However, they have tried to compensate for the loss of 'cheap money' due to the decline of savings deposits by charging relatively high fees for transactions in their investment funds.

On the other hand, apart from the uncertain profitability of some of the products offered, their proliferation obstructed the banks' attempts to achieve a more complete standardization and computerization of the work process. The bank advisers were gradually confronted with a greater range of products, whereby even small variations to basic products required separate forms and processing programs. A consequence of this development was that the integration and standardization gains of the first rationalization round were in part negated and processing costs actually increased (Krönung, 1994).

Increasing Operating Costs Along with Falling Profitability in the Lending Business

It would be an exaggeration to claim that German banks are facing a 'cost crisis'. All the same, it cannot be denied that previously successful business strategies have been attracting increasing costs, not compensated for by profits from traditional credit business. The figures in Table 4.2 present the income statements of the three bank groups in the 1980s, showing that operating costs grew in absolute terms in the three bank groups during the 1980s but not as a percentage of total assets. Relative costs have indeed decreased which means that the banks have become more productive in terms of the relation of total assets to operating costs. At the same time

90

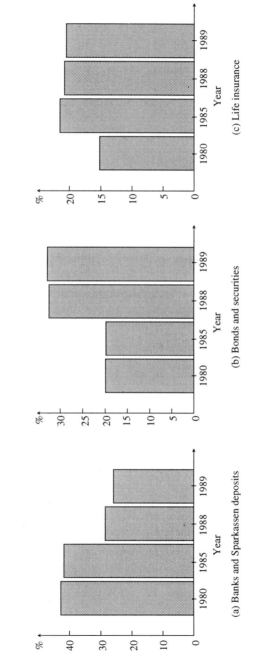

Figure 4.1   Annual increase of personal assets in Germany (%)

(a) Banks and Sparkassen deposits

(b) Bonds and securities

(c) Life insurance

Source: Graf von der Schulenburg, 1991.

and in spite of its growth, the margin of intermediation as a percentage of total assets fell and this means that traditional lending business became less profitable in the 1980s. In contrast, one observes an increase of income from commission-based products (services that the banks offer their clients at fixed commissions) in absolute terms. As a percentage of total assets, however, they remained almost constant in the Sparkassen and increased in the big banks and cooperative banks only at the end of the decade. Operating costs represented an increasing share of the income from the lending business and even surpassed it in the case of the big banks in 1987. On the other hand, income from commissions and fees increased but only partially compensated for the falling profitability in the lending business so that operating costs as a share of gross income were higher at the end of the decade than at the beginning. This increase in operating costs as a percentage of the net interest incomes (in spite of growing total assets) was a consequence of the falling profitability of business lending and was not fully compensated for by the growing revenues from commissions and fees.

However, as the statistics presented in Table 4.1 show, the changes affected the various bank groups in different ways. The margin of intermediation for the big banks is smaller than that enjoyed by the Sparkassen and cooperative banks, since the latter serve above all the medium-sized and small firms which is a more profitable segment than the larger corporations served predominantly by the commercial banks. On the other hand, the larger banks attract rather wealthy private clients, who are more likely than the clients of the Sparkassen and cooperative banks to search for commercial investment opportunities negotiated on the basis of commissions. This is reflected by the statistics on commissions and fees: as a share of total assets they are notably higher in the larger commercial banks than at the Sparkassen and cooperative banks. Furthermore, the statistics suggest that the commercial banks try to compensate for the loss of relatively cheap money by earning commissions and fees and/or by using the money markets. By constrast, the Sparkassen and cooperative banks can still rely on a relatively high and stable deposit base which provides resources for a profitable lending business with medium-sized and small firms as well as with private clients.[4] However, regardless of the structural differences between the three bank groups, which open up different alternatives for the individual banks, all the banks must deal with the same basic problems. These result from the necessity to retain savings as a basis for supporting a profitable lending business, satisfying the demands of relative wealthy clients searching for new investment opportunities, and preventing the increase of operating costs.

Table 4.1 Big banks, Sparkassen and cooperative banks: income statements (in million DM and as % of total assets) and relations between operating costs and incomes

Year	Net interest income (1)			Income from commission and fees based products (net) (2)			Operating costs (3)			Operating costs as ratio of net interest income (3)/(1)	Operating costs as ratio of net interest income plus net income from non-financial products (3)/(1)+(2)
	Total	Index	As % total assets	Total	Index	As % total assets	Total	Index	As % total assets		
Big banks											
1983	9,010	100	3.12	2,583	100	0.89	7,858	100	2.72	0.87	0.67
1985	9,416	104	2.80	3,343	129	1.00	9,063	115	2.70	0.86	0.71
1987	9,999	110	2.50	3,671	142	0.92	10,442	132	2.61	1.04	0.76
1989	11,398	126	2.31	4,812	186	0.97	11,571	147	2.34	0.99	0.71
Sparkassen											
1983	21,993	100	3.63	2,114	100	0.35	13,392	100	2.21	0.60	0.55
1985	22,856	104	3.32	2,232	105	0.32	14,946	111	2.17	0.65	0.59
1987	23,586	107	3.01	2,470	116	0.32	16,876	120	2.16	0.71	0.60
1989	24,314	110	2.78	3,141	148	0.36	18,409	137	2.11	0.75	0.67

Table 4.1 Continued

Year	Net interest income (1)			Income from commission and fees based products (net) (2)			Operating costs (3)			Operating costs as ratio of net interest income (3)/(1)	Operating costs as ratio of net interest income plus net income from non-financial products (3)/(1)+(2)
	Total	Index	As % total assets	Total	Index	As % total assets	Total	Index	As % total assets		
Cooperative banks											
1983	11,505	100	3.66	1,184	100	0.37	8,643	100	2.74	0.75	0.68
1985	13,041	113	3.24	1,424	120	0.35	11,400	131	2.83	0.87	0.78
1987	13,693	119	3.04	1,675	141	0.37	12,352	143	2.74	0.90	0.80
1989	14,749	128	2.97	2,255	190	0.45	12,976	150	2.61	0.87	0.77

Source: Deutsche Bundesbank, Monatsbericht (1990). Own calculations.

Growing Uncertainty on the Corporate Side of the Business

In terms of corporate governance the 'German model' has been characterized as a 'bank-based system'. Major stakes in corporations are held by the big banks, the commercial private banks and to a lesser extent by the Landesbanken (main banks of the Sparkassen system) directly or as proxies for individual shareholders. With substantial equity as well as credit exposures, the banks exert a significant monitoring role in the management of corporations, including active boardroom participation and guidance on the basis of available inside information. This monitoring role is reinforced by the existence of intercorporate relations and interlocking directorates between the banks and non-bank enterprises.

However, since the 1970s changes have taken place which seem to have affected the relationship between the banks and corporations. As one indicator of a more distant relation between the corporations and the big banks, the increasing sales by the banks of corporate ownership shares in the recent past has been mentioned (Sabel *et al.*, 1993). At the same time, the corporations have become less dependent on bank credits, so that the share of bank loans for the capital investments of non-financial firms has tended to decrease. Also, many large corporations began to act in the finance markets on their own, not only to manage their specific financial risks but to make a profit as well.[5]

It is difficult to ascertain to what extent these changes have affected the system of corporate governance in Germany but there is considerable evidence of tension and uncertainty between the commercial banks and the corporate businesses. On one side, representatives of the banks are calling for the corporations to abandon the use of complex and proliferating financial instruments. On the other side, representatives of larger corporations accuse the banks of not being prepared to support their expansion in the framework of a global economy.

However, it is not only the large banks that are confronted with a new constellation on the credit side of the business. Despite the competitive advantages of the Sparkassen and cooperative banks in the market segment of small to medium-sized firms, their lending activities also became less secure due to the increasing volatility of the business environment. At a time of changing product and service markets, technological rationalization, organizational restructuring, outsourcing and internationalization, the traditional loan business on the basis of collaterals is insufficient. The banks need not only more but also new types of information to evaluate commercial risks, to give advice and to organize preventive intervention if necessary. This is causing banks to rethink the organization of their credit activities. They are trying to develop not only new techniques of collecting information about the firms to whom they lend money but also to enlarge and enhance their advising activities (Ecker, 1995). Even though the efforts of the banks show that they are reacting quickly to the new business requirements, the fact that they are following paths with which they are not familiar cannot be ignored.

THE ANSWERS OF THE BANKS TO THE NEW BUSINESS ENVIRONMENT: AREAS OF UNCERTAINTY AND CAUSES OF FRICTION

We do not think that there is 'one best way' to cope with the new business constellation considering the different starting points of the individual banks in terms of market position, size and organization. However, it is possible to assume that all the banks will be establishing priorities, which address

- product and marketing strategy
- the structure of the delivery channels
- client segmentation
- the supporting role of the technology

and aim to reduce staff and operating costs. These factors do not represent a definite plan but they indicate the direction in which the German banking system is changing (D'Alessio and Oberbeck, 1994).

Redefining the Product Range and Delivery Channels

We indicated above that German banks developed innumerable savings products in the 1980s. In the 1990s, the banks are checking the profitability of the products and the functionality of the product range in terms of the rationalization of the work process. Simultaneously, in order to reduce the product range, they are trying to develop a new concept of banking products. In the past, products were predominantly developed in isolated form and sold with the help of cross-selling techniques. The products became 'packages' from the point of view of marketing but not in terms of standardization and technological support. In the 1990s, banks have been reducing the number of products offered and creating 'product packages' based on standardized work procedures and integrated technological support. In contrast to the past, this rationalization process focuses upon packages rather than isolated products. A reduction of administrative work and a more efficient use of technology are the objectives of this strategy.

On the other hand, cautious but resolute testing of new self-service techniques such as multifunctional ATMs or telephone banking in addition to direct marketing by the commercial banks and some of the larger Sparkassen indicate a rethink not only of their product ranges but also of the channels of delivering them. Apart from the use of automated machines for delivering money and bank statements, comprehensive self-service was neither a technological option nor a business strategy of the German banks in the 1970s and the 1980s. Instead, the banks emphasized personal contact with clients. However, this might change in the medium term if the results of the tests being carried out in the 1990s are positive and a new round of restructuring in the branch networks, stressing self-service and the role of advisers working outside of the branches, takes place. In this respect, the banks are discussing an adjustment of the branch networks to client structures at the local level, to be achieved by means of a more accurate differentiation of the branches and the ranges of services offered. Three types of branches are distinguished within the system of the future: first, automated branches, where only self-service of standard bank transactions is available; second, branches in which self-service is combined with a minimum of personal service and advice; and third, branches in which the full range of products and services of the banks is offered (Terrahe, 1992).

New Criteria for Market Segmentation and Client Selection

The redefinition of the product range and the channels of delivery is accompanied by new ideas about market segmentation and client selection. These ideas are not only based on the observed changes in the behaviour of clients but also on expectations concerning future developments relating to private consumption. It is expected that many consumer savings will stagnate partly as a consequence of relatively high unemployment. This will create a further polarization of incomes in German society leading the banks to stress the business importance of the relatively wealthy client segment, which in the search for better investment opportunities will offer the banks the possibility to engage in profitable business.[6]

Corresponding to these expectations the banks are trying to define more accurately their client segments and developing investment alternatives with higher levels of advice and service. In addition to the contents of these alternatives, which are matched to similar client segments at the level of the firm, the emerging strategies display different trade-off options relating to the cost/output balance in the area of securities business. Whereas the 'discount broker solution', which is offered by a small number of banks as a telephone banking service, combines low prices with little or even no advice the 'adviser solution' combines high prices in exchange for 'expert' advice. These solutions are two of a gradation of options and should not be seen as determined solely by the income level of clients. The 'discount broker solution' is often appropriate for wealthy clients who have a high degree of financial information, and who are therefore capable of executing their investment orders over the telephone without any form of advice.

New client segmentation means not only more investment alternatives for clients with potential investment surpluses but also the reduction of services and advice for clients with low incomes. As expressed by the representatives of a large Sparkasse, one-quarter of the clients accounted for three-quarters of the proceeds, leading to the conclusion that the objective of the bank should be to concentrate their activities on this client segment and to reduce the service and advice offered to the rest. At the same time, through a review in the magazine *Der Spiegel*, it has become public that some big banks and Sparkassen are rejecting less wealthy clients, unemployed persons and social welfare recipients (*Der Spiegel*, August 1994). In this regard, the rethinking of the delivery channels appears as an instrument to adjust the range of services and advice to the new criteria of client segmentation.

Tightening the range of standard products, redefining the delivery channels, providing a more accurate segmentation and selection of clients and importing new technological developments in support of these changes will probably shape future strategies in German retail banking. However, this restructuring process will not be smooth and will give rise to areas of uncertainty and frictions, which we shall now outline.

Uncertainties Relating to the Differentiation and Selection of Clients

The purpose of the new schemes of segmentation and selection of customers is to attract or retain clients, who, searching for better investment opportunities than the traditional savings products, offer the banks the chance to realize a profitable transaction. Each firm (or network of firms in the case of the cooperative banks and Sparkassen) considering the income structure and the potential saving/investment capacity of its own clients, must develop differentiated client strategies. These involve offering investment options which, while covering the technological, advising and delivery costs at the same time, prevent the flight of clients to other banks. This flight can be caused not only by high commissions and fees but also by the minimum amounts demanded by the bank for the maintenance of accounts. This can be high for clients with small surpluses but even a small surplus might lead a client to reject standard savings products and seek another bank with smaller minimum amounts. On the other hand, since the minimum amounts (if correctly calculated) are a result of the technological, advising and delivery costs, the right combination of the three factors in accordance with client structures becomes crucial for the success of the business strategy. This means that in relation to segmentation and selection of clients, the firms are moving in an area of great uncertainty, where an incorrect decision could easily lead to customer flight. A growing client fluctuation with consequent increasing costs would contradict the original aim of the strategy, that is, to perform more efficiently and generate growing profits (Schlesinger and Heskett, 1991). This possibility is made more likely by the development of investment funds which make private clients less dependent on their *Hausbank*. They can remain in their bank without having to tackle the exhausting procedures which accompany a bank switch within the comprehensive electronic payment system and at the same time can invest in the fund of another bank.

Uncertainties Relating to the Restructuring of the Branch Networks

Another area of uncertainty concerns the restructuring of the branch networks. In view of the changes and shifts described above, the firms will have to redefine the role of the branches in accordance with their marketing and business strategies. As in the case of the client segmentation, which will be decisive for the restructuring of branches, the wrong combination of segmentation, localization, service and advice could lead to an exodus of clients to other banks.

We do not think that the German banks will follow the path of the American and to some extent of the British banks, which have withdrawn from non-profitable localities without further ado. The long tradition of local integration of the Sparkassen and cooperative banks represents a business resource which they will not throw away overnight, and in the case of the large commercial banks, the branch network is not old enough to suppose that a drastic reduction will take place in the near future.[7] However, it cannot be overlooked that as a consequence of mergers, marketing or cost considerations, the German banks in the three groups are relocating or shutting down branches. The number fell from 44 334 in 1979 to 39 807 in 1990, and a new round of rationalization is highly probable, particularly in the urban areas.

Causes of Internal Friction

It is impossible to foresee how the changes and shifts will affect in detail individual banks in terms of employment, work organization, training programmes and compensation schemes. We are, however, observing developments which will cause friction regardless of the particular firm's situation. By supposing that the firms will pursue a systematic tightening of the product range based on new technological and organizational solutions, which include the restructuring of the delivery channels, the rationalization of the work process will predominantly affect the service functions and in part the advising functions in the front office areas. The changes will probably lead to a redefinition of the front office's activities, stressing the selling profile of the employees. Warnings from the managers addressed to the unions point out that the changes do not necessarily have to lead to dismissals but that employees should be ready to accept necessary adaptations in the near future as a condition of retaining their jobs. However, the adaptation process, even if supported by training programmes, will not be easy to manage since it requires not only the acquisition of new knowledge but also a new employee attitude in relation to his or her personal appraisal of the job.

In view of the selling orientation of front office activities as part of the marketing strategy of the 1970s, which stressed the personal contact with clients in the branches, the present insistence on selling and the warning voices of the managers suggest that those strategies were only successful under different business conditions and that the strategies now have to be adjusted. In this respect, the recruitment of selling personnel for the branches without previous work experience in the banking sector represents a novelty in the German banking industry. Even though we are speaking of isolated cases, the decision to break with traditional forms of recruitment indicates a degree of nervousness within the management ranks. They are uncertain whether their traditional practices of recruitment involving a two- or three-year period of comprehensive apprenticeship with further training in the banks can fulfil the requirements of adaptation to the new business conditions.[8]

By means of training programmes, however, the big banks as well as the cooperative banks and Sparkassen are strengthening their financial advisers for the more up-market segment of clients who have potential investment surpluses. This indicates that the banks are trying to adapt their personnel structure to new forms of work organization and marketing strategy. The probable consequence will be the emergence of new lines of occupational differentiation, which no longer can be described merely in terms of the contrast between back office and front office activities. This differentiation process could cause considerable friction concerning, for example, who is selected to do what under which conditions. It may also be difficult to manage staff cooperation in the context of such occupational differentiation. Furthermore, the stress on sales performance in a staff with a relatively clear differentiation in terms of functions and career introduces a disruptive element in the long-standing cooperation amongst branch personnel. This could disrupt the best-conceived restructuring plan unless the transition is managed with caution.

Moreover, the introduction of new compensation schemes which combine salaries and bonuses will probably reinforce the disruptive effects of stressing selling as a central criterion of performance. In this respect, even if the price/cost/risks calculations are correct, an effective management of change demands much more. Bank management has to not only shape the internal processes of differentiation but also maintain a certain balance between the pursuit of volume rates and the quality of advice as well as between sales-oriented activities and risk-evaluating ones. However, these prerequisites for a successful management of change may be given less priority in an atmosphere of increasing competition for market share among the banks – yet another cause of uncertainty for the future.

OUTLOOK

Market saturation in the segment of basic bank products and services, increasing operating costs, falling profitability in the lending business, the growing importance of revenues from commissions and fees as compensation for decreasing net interest incomes, changes in the behaviour of private customers and a growing uncertainty on the corporate side of the business are the factors which we have identified as the driving forces behind the process of change in the German banking industry in the 1980s. They are not only the result of new business and marketing strategies, training and personnel policies executed in the 1960s and 1970s, but also a reflection of the rationalization and reorganization that occurred as a result of broader changes in the economy and society.

More independence for large corporations in financial matters, restructuring of the goods and service markets and also increasing private wealth along with a growing income differentiation have created a new business environment for the German banks and Sparkassen. The period of extensive growth and relatively cheap money is over and new forms of attaining and placing money have developed. Against this background, the question arises as to whether we are discussing mere adjustments within the traditional business system or rather a fundamental transition which is affecting the conception of the 'German model' mentioned at the beginning of this chapter.

At first sight, there are a number of indicators, such as the increase of sales of corporate shares the growing share of institutional investors as the source of funds at the big banks, the new advising activities on the corporate side of the business, and the increasing importance of the investment funds as a new form of collecting money, which might suggest a more dealing-oriented relationship between clients and banks than in the past. The evidence is, however, ambiguous: the big banks retain their decisive presence in the corporations as proxies of individual shareholders. According to Bundesbank statistics, 53.5 per cent of the total nominal value of German shares (excluding shares in insurance enterprises) was on deposit with banks, and the big commercial banks controlled 44.6 per cent of this total (Deutsche Bundesbank, 1989).

On the other hand, the German banks and Sparkassen have to date controlled the investment fund industry, which includes not only investment funds for private customers but also special funds, through which the deposits of the insurance companies are managed. This means that the banks have been able to steer and regulate the process of change, remaining the dominant actor of the finance system. It is not only the traditional techniques of the universal bank system (particularly the internal allocation of resources) which have contributed to the bank's ability to cope with the new constellation without great shocks and without notable disadvantages for their customers. It is also that the German banks have also succeeded – with the support of the Bundesbank and the government – in preventing the proliferation of short-term investment funds with their disruptive effects on the structure of funding. In this sense, the German banks have been a factor of stability in the reproduction of economic and social life.

However, the situation might be changing. The recent authorization of money funds and their short-term investment strategies represent a break with the financial practices of the past, where long-term orientation was one of the most important elements of the 'German model'. Alongside are the new forms of customer segmentation which, adjusting to the increasing income and social inequalities, might in turn tend to reproduce and magnify them. These changes are creating another basis for business, which will probably affect issues such as profitability, liquidity and calculation.[9] This in turn is leading to new organizational forms of universal bank activities, above all by the commercial banks. Not only has the internal divisionalization of bank activities been introduced but also the reorganization of the holdings structures has been discussed. In this sense, the creeping abandonment of the traditional training systems at the firm level appears not only as an instrument to cut costs but also as a prospective solution to a more differentiated universal bank organization structure adjusting to segmented and differentiated markets.

It is too soon to predict the future evolution of the German banking industry given the areas of uncertainty the banks are now facing. However, in view of the cautious behaviour the firms have shown in the past, it is not unreasonable to suppose that they will try and adjust to the new business environments while retaining the advantages derived from institution-oriented banking activities. In times of growing uncertainty, not only close relationships to clients but also a cautious approach to the staff might be the most appropriate strategy. In any case, under these circumstances the *bon mot* of the German economist Adolf Weber is not likely to remain valid. Summing up the findings of his comparative research on the British and German banking industries at the beginning of the twentieth century, Weber used to say that the British banks were developed for people who had money, whereas the German banks were developed for people who had none.

Notes

1. In view of the particular situation of the banks in East Germany, the new *Bundesländer*, the chapter is confined to the development in West Germany. As recent statistics of the Bundesbank show, they have not been affected by the political and economical reunification of the country.
2. The bank industry in Germany is dominated by relatively small firms with no more than local or regional importance, above all the public Sparkassen, controlled by the municipalities, and the cooperative banks. In 1990 in West Germany, 574 Sparkassen with 12 212 branches controlled 30.1 per cent of the total deposits and 37 per cent of the total credits, whereas 3042 cooperative banks with 15 767 branches controlled 18.3 per cent of the total deposits and 15.1 per cent of the total credits. Both bank groups organize their universal bank activities through an integrated network of specialized

firms which back their business in the area of *Allfinanz* and from which they get marketing and technological support. This means that the local firms are indeed part of a highly developed business system. On the other hand, the private universal banks, branches 332 firms with 6289, controlled 28.8 per cent of the total deposits and 25 per cent of the credit volume. Respective figures for the three big banks (Deutsche Bank, Dresdner Bank and Commerzbank) with their 3105 branches were 12.6 per cent of the total deposits and 10.1 per cent of the total credits. The statistics suggest that the degree of concentration in the industry is not high.

3. Even though the situation in the labour market then, with its low rate of unemployment and turnover in German firms, indeed represented a form of 'security' for the bank, one cannot overlook the innovative character of this kind of consumer credit. It helped to create a more 'familiar' relationship between banks and clients.

4. In 1989 whereas 27 per cent of the deposit basis of the big banks flowed from other credit institutes the respective share at the Sparkassen was 13 per cent and the cooperative banks on 11 per cent.

5. The downfall of the Metallgesellschaft, one of Germany's largest trading companies, which lost over $1 billion in the oil futures market and almost went bankrupt, shows the growing risks banks are facing on the corporate side of the business. The financial dealings of the corporations have become much more complicated.

6. One factor of growing income differentiation is the accumulated wealth passed on in the form of inheritance, which will be reinvested in the 1990s (Dudler, 1991).

7. The closure of branches in Great Britain justified only in terms of profitability has raised a controversial discussion about the significance of the branches not only as business resources for the banks but also for the development in the local markets (*The Economist*, 14 November 1992 and 9 January 1993). In the USA the closure of branches in the 1980s has predominantly affected areas of low and moderate income (Obermiller, 1988). This fact suggests that the banks are eroding the developmental objectives of the legislators: under the law the banks' offices are required to place a part of the accumulated money in the areas where they are located particularly in the 'low and moderate income areas' (Hamars, 1994).

8. At the end of the 1980s almost 90 per cent of the banks' employees had passed an examination as *Bank* or *Sparkassenkaufmann*. The largest part of this personnel passed later through a further training programme to reach the qualification level of *Fachwirt*. Not only the high qualification level as a result of the generous training policies of the banks but also the job security and the satisfactory compensation schemes contributed to the high social status of the bank's employees, which even now still persists. (The firm could select the training candidates from a great number of applicants.) In contrast to this practice the banks are also recruiting personnel without previous work experience in the banking sector. The training courses last six weeks.

9. The authorization of the money funds associated with a growing trading of commercial papers issued by firms could lead to more 'liquidity' and 'short termism' in the future.

References

M. Baethge and H. Oberbeck, *Zukunft der Angestellten*. (Frankfurt: New York, 1986).

BIZ (Bank für Internationalen Zahlungsausgleich), *Zahlungsverkehrssysteme in elf entwickelten Ländern*. (Frankfurt: Fritz Knapp Verlag, 1989).

N. D'Alessio and H. Oberbeck, '"Lean Banking": Klassische Rationalisierung mit anderen Vorzeichen oder Metapher für eine neue Marktorientierung der Finanzdienstleister', in *SOFI-Mitteilungen*, 21 (1994) pp. 53–64.

Deutsche Bundesbank, *Bankstatistiken*. Series 1, July (1989).

Deutsche Bundesbank, *Monatsbericht*, August (1990) pp. 28–31.

H. Dudler, 'Strukturwandel der Vermögensbildung im Reifeprozeß von Volkswirtschaften', in *Beihefte zu Kredit zu Kapital*, Heft 11. (Berlin: Duncker & Humblot, 1991) pp. 53–74.

F. Ecker, *Banken und Unternehmer im Feuer*. (Passau: Neve Presse, 1995).

E.P.M. Gardener, 'Banking Strategies and 1992', in A. Mullineux (ed.), *European Banking*. (Oxford: Blackwell, 1992) pp. 107–29.

J.-M. Graf von der Schulenburg, 'Organisations – und Steuerungsfragen aus der Sicht eines Versicherungsunternehmens', in *Beihefte zu Kredit und Kapital*, Heft 11. (Berlin: Duncker & Humblot, 1991) pp. 221–36.

M. Hamars, 'Les banques au secours du banlieus', *Alternatives économiques*, 116 (1994) pp. 46–7.

H.-D. Krönung, 'Chancen und Risiken von Lean Banking', *Die Bank*, June (1994) pp. 324–9.

H.T. Krummel, 'German Universal Banking Scrutinized', *Journal of Banking and Finance*, 4 (1980) pp. 33–55.

P. Obermiller, 'Banks and the Brink: The Effects of Banking Deregulation of Low-Income Neighborhoods', *Business and Society*, 27, 1 (1988) pp. 7–13.

C. Sabel, J. Griffin and R. Deeg, 'Making Money Talk. Towards a New Debitor-Creditor Relation in German Banking', *Working Paper presented at the Conference on Relational Investing, Center for Law and Economics Studies, Columbia University (1993)*.

L.A. Schlesinger and J.L. Heskett, 'The Service-Driven Service Company', *Harvard Business Review*, September–October (1991) pp. 71–81.

J. Terrahe, 'Das Rationalisierungsmotiv der Banken ist längst dem Kundenwunsch gewichen', in *Banken International*, Handelsblattbeilage, 91, May (1992).

5 Bank Finance for Small and Medium-sized Enterprises in Germany and France*

Sigrid Quack and Swen Hildebrandt

INTRODUCTION

During the 1980s and 1990s, the relationship between banks and non-financial companies in most European countries has been affected by the expansion of international financial markets. Their emergence allowed non-financial companies to directly access money and capital markets and thereby undermined the intermediation role which banks traditionally held in many countries. Furthermore, many national governments have taken policy actions to remove regulations which formerly protected financial markets from international competition (Canals, 1993).

The impact of internationalization and deregulation, however, is not the same in all segments of corporate finance. Whereas disintermediation has increased among large and multinational companies, small and medium-sized enterprises (SME) are often excluded from direct access to international and capital markets and still rely on the national banking system (Gardener and Molyneux, 1990). In order to understand the effects of global pressures on bank finance for SMEs, we therefore suggest that it is

* We would like to thank the bank managers whom we interviewed for their cooperation and the CNRS for financial support for our research in France. The interviews in Germany were carried out together with Brent Keltner, RAND. A first version of this chapter was presented at the EMOT workshop on Financial Services held in Paris, September 1994, and was published in the discussion paper series of the Wissenschaftszentrum, Berlin (see Quack and Hildebrandt, 1995a). The current article has been considerably revised and also includes new empirical material. The authors have benefited from careful comments on earlier drafts by Bernard Ganne, Michel Goyer, John Griffin, Christel Lane, Glenn Morgan and Jacqueline O'Reilly. We are also grateful to Sabine Hark and Ricos Thanopoulos for discussions which helped to clarify the argument.

necessary to analyse more carefully how these pressures have been mediated by specific institutional contexts (see also Salomon, chapter 6 in this volume).

Our analysis is informed by theoretical approaches which consider economic behaviour and institutions not as opposed to but as interpenetrated with each other (Granovetter, 1985; Sorge, 1995; Whitley, 1992). In the following, we refer to institutions as socially constructed, routine-reproduced rule systems which provide stability and meaning to social behaviour. Such arrangements can emerge from three arenas: the state, sectors and organizations. Campbell *et al.* (1991) and Jepperson and Meyer (1991) have outlined how the state as actor and structure shapes preferences of economic actors, market structures and forms of competition. Authors such as Hollingsworth *et al.* (1994) have studied varying governance mechanisms operating in different societal sectors or industries. Other authors have shown how the organization of companies is shaped by the institutional context (Maurice *et al.*, 1986; Sorge and Warner, 1986; Lane, 1989, 1995; Sorge, 1991). Evidence suggests that these mechanisms are also at work in the banking sector (Deeg, 1992; O'Reilly, 1994; Quack *et al.*, 1994; see also contributions in this volume). However, little is known so far on how economic and institutional changes are interrelated in this specifically state-regulated sector.

In this chapter, we examine developments in bank finance for SMEs in Germany and France during the 1980s and early 1990s.[1] Germany and France are interesting cases to study because, historically, the involvement of the state in the economic and financial system differed considerably and industrial policy favoured different types of companies. Institutional differences have also influenced the relation between banks and their corporate customers. In the traditional German *Hausbank* relation, companies give priority to one bank which runs most of their banking business, the relation is long-term and regarded as a partnership. Such lead banks have not played the same role in France, and particularly SMEs did not enjoy the same frequency and continuity in the contact with banks which acted much more like *fournisseurs* delivering financial services on the spot. As a consequence, French SMEs in the past have often suffered from a shortage of long-term loans, whereas these were available to a greater extent to their German counterparts.

We are interested to see how recent institutional and economic changes have affected bank finance for SMEs under such distinct systems of economic coordination. The analysis is based on case study data[2] from the banking sector and secondary material for the SME sector. The results show that in a period which was characterized by increasing competition in both countries, deregulation and despecialization in France, and institutional stability in Germany, banks in Germany and France followed different strategies. Furthermore, there are persistent if not increasing differences in the bank–company relationship between both countries. Global pressures have been translated in different ways and with distinct consequences. We argue that this divergence is the result of distinct organizational forms and practices which became institutionalized in the SME and banking sector of each country during the postwar period and generated different constraints and opportunities for banks when the institutional and economic context changed in the 1980s.

The first section analyses how changes in the institutional and economic context during the 1980s have affected banks in both countries. The second section describes how industrial policies have shaped the SME sector and, thereby, have laid different foundations for what banks consider as their SME customer base in Germany and France. The third section investigates prevailing differences in structures and competencies of banks originating from their position in distinct financial systems. In the last section we then examine the impact of these institutional arrangements on activities in the 1990s and strategies of German and French banks towards SMEs.

CHANGES IN THE INSTITUTIONAL AND ECONOMIC CONTEXT

In earlier studies, Zysman (1983) and Cox (1986) classified both the German and French financial systems in the postwar period as credit-based and bank-oriented. They also pointed out that each system is governed by a distinct type of coordination between the state, banks and non-financial companies. Whereas the German corporatist system is governed by bargaining between strong collective actors (Streeck, 1992), the French statist system is organized around the central state which delegates tasks to functionally specific actors (Jepperson and Meyer, 1991). German banking regulation has been orientated towards universal banking and the federal state and *Länder* governments have historically promoted competition between commercial, savings and cooperative banking sectors of equal size and with a similar range of activities (Deeg, 1992). In contrast, the French financial system has been centralized around the state as main actor, favoured a high degree of specialization between commercial and medium–to long-term credit banks and restricted the activities of savings and cooperative banks (Boissieu, 1990). Direct state control allocated finance primarily to large, often state-owned companies. Since the 1980s, however, the context of financing SMEs has undergone changes in both countries which we will describe in more detail in the following paragraphs.

During the 1980s, the French government undertook various legal and institutional reforms which concerned the allocation of finance for investment, activities of different banking groups, the privatization of banks, and the openness of the French financial system towards international markets (Chanel-Reynaud, 1994). With rising budgetary deficits, the state was no longer able to maintain the former state-administered system which had been based on three elements: (1) the setting of money market rates by the Banque de France, (2) the control of the quantity of credit through upper ceilings for bank lending, and (3) a system whereby state-owned and parapublic banks specializing in corporate lending were guaranteed preferential conditions for loans to certain industries (Zysman, 1983). The credit ceiling system was abolished in the mid-1980s and since then an increasing proportion of loans have been indexed on market-based interest rates (Taillepied and de Bressieux, 1994). Banks no longer have access to quasi-unlimited refinancing from the central bank. Specialized banks lost their privileges and now have to compete with commercial banks and other banking groups. Competition was also fostered by the 1984 Banking Act which eliminated the former specialization of banks and grouped all banks together under the same legal framework. This allowed cooperative banks to extend lending beyond their traditional customer groups in agriculture and small crafts businesses. Savings banks which before had been confined to collecting savings were allowed to diversify their activities into lending to personal and since 1987 also to SME customers (Duet, 1991).

Other government initiatives such as the creation of a secondary market in 1982 and the introduction of investment certificates in 1983 aimed to develop capital markets (Boissieu, 1990). The rise of capital markets was supported by fiscal reforms which increased the demand for shares and investment funds. Furthermore, the privatization of state-owned enterprises made shares available to a wider public. Between 1985 and 1992, the volume of share issues tripled even though growth rates slowed down after the stock market collapsed in 1987 (Taillepied and de Bressieux, 1994). The availability of a broader range of financial products with different maturities has led to a shift away from traditional savings accounts which served the financing of housing, state and industry. At the same time, investment into Organismes de placement collectif en valeurs mobilières (OPCVM) and life insurance expanded rapidly (Artus, 1991; Zerah, 1993). The rise of capital markets and financial innovations, accompanied by an increasing openness of the French financial system, also had considerable effects on the financing of the French economy which until the 1980s was highly indebted and dependent on bank finance. The financial reforms in the 1980s gave large companies direct access to capital and money markets which they used to reduce their gearing ratio from 65 per cent in 1985 to 33 per cent in 1992 (Cieply, 1995). The extent of disintermediation on both the saving and lending side is reflected by the data presented in Figure 5.1. The proportion of household assets in savings deposits decreased from 42 per cent in 1980 to only 26 per cent in 1989 whilst the proportion of assets in shares expanded rapidly from 14 per cent to 41 per cent during the same period.

As a result of the financial reforms, French banks were confronted with a dilemma (Cieply, 1995; Chanel-Reynaud, 1994). On one hand, the refinancing of banks has become more costly and sensitive to fluctuations in market interest rates because banks have less access to tax-privileged savings funds and depend more on the interbank market. A study of the Conseil National du Crédit (CNC, 1993b) estimated that the shift from savings to OPCVM created additional costs for the banks of 6–30 per cent of their income. On the other hand, banks now have to carry more risks in lending since the state no longer guarantees fixed interest rates and unlimited refinancing. Large companies exert increasing pressure on banks' prices and conditions. The privatization of commercial banks has also contributed to these pressures as shareholders now have higher expectations concerning the profitability of banks. Compared to the former state-administered system, there are fewer legal and economic incentives for banks to engage in lending to the corporate sector.

The negative effects of the reforms on lending are most significant for SMEs because most of them are still excluded from capital markets and dependent on bank loans. In order to compensate for these disadvantages, the French government introduced special incentives for bank lending to SMEs. First, in the early 1980s a tax-privileged savings deposit named Comptes pour le développement industriel (CODEVI) was introduced. Banks have to transfer 86 per cent of their CODEVI deposits into subsidized loans to SMEs. The capacity of banks to forward such loans, however, is limited because deposits are restricted by an upper limit per person (FF 15 000, extended to FF 30 000 in October 1994) and each bank can only lend from its own deposits.[3] Second, a credit guarantee institution named Société Française de garantie de financements des Petites et Moyennes Entreprises (SOFARIS), whose main shareholders are the state and commercial banks, was founded in 1982. Guarantees are directed at companies

Figure 5.1   Financial assets of the personal sector in Germany and France, 1975–90 (%)

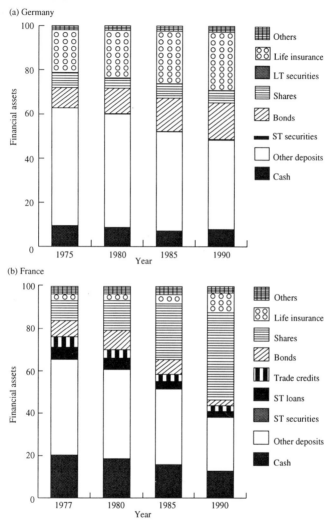

(a) Germany

(b) France

Notes: ST = short-time; LT = long-time; cash includes other transferable deposits; life insurance represents net equity of households on life insurance reserves and pension funds.
Source: OECD, 1992, p. 49.

which do not have sufficient collateral or capital of their own, for example, business start-ups and companies in transition. The guaranteed loan volume is limited to 5 million FF per company and the risk divided between the bank and SOFARIS. Third, a specialized bank for SMEs was set up from a merger of three smaller institutions which were already in charge of financing SMEs before. The Crédit d'Equipement des Petites et Moyennes Entreprises (CEPME) offers medium- and long-term loans (3–20 years) for investments to SMEs and also gives credit guarantees. Evidence which we present in this chapter suggests that the scope of these measures was too narrow to counteract the negative effects of the financial reforms on bank lending to SMEs.

In contrast to France, the German financial system has experienced more continuity during the 1980s and early 1990s. Changes resulted primarily from the market environment and increasing competition between banks. In order to understand the different mode of change it is helpful to review the policy of German governments during the postwar period which favoured a competitive open economy and an early liberalization of the banking sector. Restrictions on capital movements, for example, were lifted in 1957 and interest rates became liberalized in 1967. The government aimed at increasing competition in the banking sector by removing restrictions on the opening of new branches in 1958, abolishing an anti-competition accord in 1968 and bringing the legal status of savings and cooperative banks closer to commercial banks in the 1970s (Oellerking and Holzgrabe, 1990). The liberalization of the German banking system thus took place much earlier than in France.

The reconstruction period after the Second World War was also decisive for the establishment of public institutions which encouraged the provision of bank finance to SMEs (Harms, 1992; Lane, 1995; Vitols, 1995b). This includes public banks such as Kreditanstalt für Wiederaufbau (KfW) and Deutsche Ausgleichsbank (DAB) which distribute subsidized loans and start-up capital. In addition, public credit guarantee institutions (Bürgschaftsbanken) were established by the trade corporations, banks and Länder governments in the 1950s to help business people who wanted to set up or expand a business but did not have the necessary collateral for a bank loan. All these institutions have in common that their programmes are handled through the banking system. Due to their continuity and consistency, German support programmes have contributed to the institutionalization of standards for credit assessments in banks and strengthened business relations between banks and SMEs.

As a result of the liberalization in the 1950s and 1960s, German banks were confronted with the impacts of international financial markets at an earlier stage than French banks. This happened primarily through increasing competition between banks and changes in the demand of large corporate customers. Since the mid-1970s, savings and cooperative banks entered into direct competition with large commercial banks which had traditionally served this customer group (Oellerking and Holzgrabe, 1990; Deeg, 1992). At the same time, however, large German companies began progressively to finance their long-term investment from internal sources. Between 1978 and 1989, their provisions for possible losses and liabilities of company pension schemes increased from 21 per cent to 33 per cent of the total balance sheet (Deutsche Bundesbank, 1992a). Large companies also built up their own financial departments which participated directly in international financial markets. As in France, the increasing independence of large companies from bank finance allowed them to exert pressure on banks. For reasons which we will consider below, however, disintermediation on the lending side did not affect German banks to the same extent as French banks (see also Canals, 1993).

Throughout the 1980s, German banks were also able to maintain a comparatively stable position in the savings market. As Table 5.1 shows, German households in 1991 still held 41 per cent of their assets in savings deposits compared to only 26 per cent in France. These deposits provide banks with relatively cheap funds for their lending. The shift to investment products has been less pronounced in Germany than in France even though money-market funds have rapidly attracted funds from households since their introduction in 1994. This is related to the more conservative attitudes of German investors which have been reinforced by fiscal policy and market strategies of German banks which until recently charged high fees on investment products and issued only shares and investment certificates with a high standard of value. According to Oberbeck and D' Alessio (chapter 4 in this volume), German banks were able – with the support of the Bundesbank and the government – to limit the proliferation of short-term investment funds. In the absence of attractive investment products for a wider public, German households invested an increasing proportion of their assets in bonds and life insurances. Again, negative effects on banks' refinancing costs were limited by the fact that German banks control the bond market (Canals, 1993) and maintain close cross-shareholdings with insurance companies which invest a considerable part of their funds in banks (OECD, 1992).

Changes in the market environment together with the creation of the single European Market have also induced modifications in German banking law. Changes in legislation, however, have been more gradual than in France and German banks were able to influence legislation through their trade associations. This is illustrated by the following examples. For smaller savings and cooperative banks, the requirements of the European capital and solvency standards were difficult to accomplish because their legal status does not allow them to augment their own capital by other means than retained profits. Therefore, the savings and cooperative banks' associations engaged in negotiations with the state. On the other hand, the commercial banks through their association tried to prevent any privileged treatment of their competitors. A compromise was finally found which allows savings and cooperative banks to issue special participation certificates and cooperative banks to include part of their liability surcharge in the calculation of their own capital. The second example is related to the rise of financial innovations during the 1980s which created the need for savings banks to negotiate new rules and rights in their relationship to commercial banks and *Länder* governments. In the late 1980s, several savings bank laws were reformed in order to enable savings banks to trade securities on their own account and to participate in the market for derivatives (Oellerking and Holzgrabe, 1990). In both cases, legislation mediated between the different interest groups and guaranteed savings and cooperative banks particular rights which enabled them to fulfil their special mission.

The results suggest that in each country global pressures have been transmitted by different actors and with different outcomes. In France, state-imposed financial reforms led to a break with established legal and competitive rules in the banking sector. In Germany, changes were more gradual, resulted from the economic sphere and were more easily absorbed by the strategies of banks and their associations. German banks appeared to have a larger capacity to counteract disintermediation than French banks. One of the reasons is that German banks compensated diminishing margins with large companies by expanding their business with SME customers. In order to understand why this was the case for German but not to the same extent for French banks it is necessary to examine more closely how structures, practices and perceptions of SMEs and banks are institutionally anchored in the broader societal context of each country.

DIFFERENCES IN CUSTOMER GROUPS: INDUSTRIAL POLICY AND SMEs

The German and French system of economic coordination assigned different roles to companies of different size and thereby influenced the industrial structure of each country. These policies have also shaped the characteristics of what banks consider as their corporate customer base.

This is particularly true for banks' definition and perception of SME customers. As we will show, structures and strategies of banks reflect differences in both the characteristics and dynamics of the SME sector *and* the perceptions which banks have of the profitability and riskiness of these companies in each country.

In short, SMEs in Germany are on average larger, better-established and more growth-orientated than in France. German SMEs cluster more homogeneously around the ideal type of a so-called *Mittelstand* firm whereas French SMEs split into a few larger, stable companies on the one side and many small and unstable companies on the other side. French SMEs are more vulnerable in their financial structure, have less capital of their own and are more in debt (Quack and Hildebrandt, 1995a). The segment of larger SMEs with a continuous demand for a varied range of financial products is, as a study of the Conseil National du Crédit suggests, considerably smaller in France than in Germany (de Saint-Louvent, 1992).[4]

According to Lane (1991), these differences go back historically to the period of industrialization. After the Second World War, German and French governments followed distinct industrial policies which reinforced existing differences. German governments considered SMEs as an important pillar of economic reconstruction and pursued a policy which offered SMEs a dense network of support for economic, technological and financial development. Banking legislation enabled strong local savings and cooperative banks which provided decentralized finance to SMEs. Together with German labour market institutions such as vocational training and cooperative industrial relations, these measures created a stable business environment and a supportive public climate in which smaller and medium-sized companies flourished. In the 1990s, the typical German SME is in a more mature period of the life cycle but still predominantly family-owned.[5] As German SMEs often provide specialized products and are more involved in exports, they have avoided exclusive ties with large buyers and are less dependent on subcontracting than their French counterparts (see also Lane and Bachmann, 1995).

French SMEs never became embedded in an institutional network and decentralized system of finance similar to that of their German counterparts. Instead, French SMEs for a long time relied on networks of family and local neighbourhood ties which made them more inward-looking and economically retarded than SMEs in other countries. Since the Second World War, the French SME sector has undergone considerable changes as an indirect result of the French state support for the development of the large industrial company sector. This policy often disrupted local networks between large and small companies, favoured large companies at the expense of independent networks of small enterprises and economic centres at the expense of peripheral regions (Dubois and Linhart, 1994). The destabilizing effect of these measures can be seen from the fact that the average life duration of a new company in France decreased from 25 years in 1960 to only 15 years in 1990 (Bizaguet, 1991).

Many of the larger SMEs in France (companies with more than 150 million FF turnover) have been transformed into subsidiaries of large enterprises which control their financing (Matray, 1992). Since the 1980s, large companies have also established intercompany cooperations in which they provide finance for their suppliers (Cieply, 1995). SMEs which are part of these networks have gained more independence from banks. On the other hand, there is a cluster of small and predominantly young SMEs which are in the majority family-owned, but often in financial difficulties (Bizaguet, 1991; Matray, 1992) because they are undercapitalized and having to cope with late payments from their clients.[6] It is the problems of this group which explain the high turnover of French SMEs compared to the greater stability of their German counterparts. In France, about 20 per cent of new business set-ups expire during the first year and 50 per cent by the fourth year of their existence (Bizaguet, 1991). The rate of bankruptcies has been increasing in both countries, but it is much higher in France (1.6 per cent) than in Germany (0.4 per cent) (CNC, 1993a).[7]

It is only since the 1980s (Ganne *et al.*, 1993) that there have been attempts by the French government to improve the institutional support for SMEs by regional decentralization of the political administration and the foundation of parapublic financing institutions like the CEPME and SOFARIS. So far, however, no significant change has occurred either in the allocation of resources to SMEs or in the connotation attached to them in public opinion. The definition which French banks use for SME customers (DM 17–70 million turnover) also ignores many of the smaller companies compared to the broader definition of German banks (DM 1–100 million turnover) (Kirchhoff and Bauer, 1994; Quack and Hildebrandt, 1995b).

To summarize so far, industrial policy and also the readiness of banks in the past to provide finance for SMEs have laid the foundations of banks' current customer base. The empirical evidence revealed differences in the characteristics and public perception of SMEs. There are definitively fewer large and high-yielding customers among French than German SMEs. There is a higher proportion of younger companies which are more difficult to assess and the greater polarization of French SMEs raises more problems for banks in trying to spread risks. However, one should be careful not to oversimplify the impact of such indicators in the strategic decision-making of banks. As Friedland and Alford (1991) argue, profit and risk are culturally constructed categories whose definitions vary widely across nation states. The more narrow definition of SMEs that the French banks have compared to their German counterparts suggests that national models of industrial development have also become ingrained in bank managers' perceptions of what a profitable or risky customer is.

PREVAILING STRUCTURES AND PRACTICES IN THE BANKING SECTOR

As outlined above, state intervention and regulation in Germany and France ascribed different functions to the banking sector, favoured distinct patterns of competition and cooperation between banks, and channelled funds in specific ways to various types of companies. In this section we will analyse how these institutions have become ingrained in the structures and practices of the banking sector. First, we refer to distinct capacities which similar banking groups in both countries developed at the sectoral level. Second, we analyse different organizational forms, practices and types of work organization in the corporate lending departments of German and French commercial banks.

One of the main differences at the sectoral level is the extent to which savings and cooperative banks are involved in lending to SMEs. In Germany, savings banks are the most important banks to provide loans to SMEs. In 1980, they accounted for 37 per cent of bank loans to companies whereas commercial banks held a market share of 26 per cent and cooperative banks of 15 per cent (see Table 5.1). Although statistics are not comprehensive, the available evidence indicates that the dominance of savings banks is even stronger in financing SMEs (see below). Savings and cooperative banks are strongly engaged in the development of the local economy and maintain close contacts with local business and political institutions. Local banks do not operate as isolated entities but form part of a network with other member banks and centralized refinancing institutions (Landesbanken and genossenschaftliche Zentralbanken) which allows them to share refinancing, information and strategic planning at the same time as it delimits local areas of business. According to Vitols (1995a), the pooling of deposits through centralized refinancing institutions enables savings and cooperative banks to overcome problems of risk transformation and to refinance at a more advantageous rate than large commercial banks. Furthermore, within each group, member banks share a considerable amount of information on customers. For example, the savings banks' group operates a data base with financial information on approximately 100 000 predominantly small and medium-sized companies. This data base enables member banks to process an analysis of credit-worthiness based on detailed breakdowns by industry, company size and form of business organization (DSGV, 1993). Savings and cooperative banks are also engaged in a continuous exchange on strategic planning

Table 5.1   Market shares of German and French banks in lending to firms, 1980–93 (%)

(a) Germany[1]

	1980	*1985*	*1990*	*1993*
Commercial banks	25.9	24.7	38.4	29.4
Savings banks[2]	36.9	36.5	29.6	34.2
Cooperative banks[2]	15.4	16.8	14.6	14.0
Specialized banks	2.2	3.7	3.7	10.7
Other credit institutions[3]	19.6	18.3	13.7	11.7
Total (billion DM)	724	968	1429	1835

(b) France

	1980	*1985*	*1992*	*1993*
Commercial AFB banks	46.7	41.1	45.3	44.0
CDC and savings banks	20.1	17.5	14.2	15.0
thereof:				
Savings banks	0.0	0.0	0.7	0.9
Cooperative banks	7.5	8.7	11.8	12.1
Specialized credit institutions	16.5	20.6	12.8	12.6
thereof:				
CEPME	0.0	2.9	1.7	2.0
Discount houses[4]	9.1	11.0	15.0	15.5
Other credit institutions	0.1	1.1	0.9	0.8
Total (billion FF)	n.d.	1712	3184	2978

[1] Shares include mortgage loans on commercial property. Since 1990 including East Germany.
[2] Including regional and central institutions of savings banks and cooperative banks.
[3] Includes mortgage banks, hire purchase banks and postal banks. 1993 without postal bank.
[4] Sociétés Financières et Maisons de titres.
Sources: AFB, 1990; Banque de France, 1993, 1995; Deutsche Bundesbank, 1981, 1986, 1993, 1994. Own calculations.

and human resource management which reduces the expenses of each bank and gives small banks access to more sophisticated business practices than each could afford on their own.

In France, in contrast, the banking sector has been dominated by large commercial banks whereas local and regional banks remained weak. In 1980, most of the lending to companies was undertaken either by commercial AFB banks[8] (47 per cent) which concentrated on short-term loans or by specialized long-term credit institutions (17 per cent) and the state-owned Caisse des Dépôts et des Consignations (CDC) (20 per cent).[9] Cooperative banks had a market share of only 8 per cent and savings banks played no role at all in corporate lending (see Table 5.1).[10] French savings and cooperative banks lacked most of the network synergies of their German counterparts. They were on average smaller than in Germany and pursued their market and personnel policies in greater isolation from each other. The situation was slightly different with regard to French cooperative banks. For example, Crédit Agricole, which ranked among the largest French banks, had a centralized refinancing institution. Nevertheless, the cooperative banking sector in France remained more fragmented than in Germany. Five groups were operating in different regions and different customer groups (Crédit Agricole, Banques Populaires, Crédit Mutuel, Crédit Cooperatif and Crédit Mutuel Agricole et Rurale-Group). As a result of this particularism, French cooperative banks could not benefit to the same extent as their German counterparts from the pooling of refinancing and information. Only two of them, Crédit Agricole and Banques Populaires, have a sufficient business volume and customer base and a multi-level structure at the national and regional level to exploit group advantages (CNCA, 1993).

The institutional and social context also shaped organizational forms and competencies of commercial banks. Differences exist with regard to (1) the degree of decentralization and (2) business practices and work organization. Commercial banks in Germany decentralized their lending decisions at an earlier stage and to a larger extent than in France. According to Deeg (1992), since the mid-1970s German commercial banks tried to expand their business with SME customers. In order to compete with savings and cooperative banks, commercial banks delegated more discretion to the regional and local level. Regional credit departments and larger branches were staffed with specialized relationship managers in charge of a certain portfolio of business customers. In other cases, the branch manager would deal with SME customers. In France, however, most lending to companies was centralized in the Paris headquarters. There was no specialized staff for business customers at the branch level and no specialized organizational units at the regional level. Small loans to SMEs would be processed by the branch manager and larger ones referred to the central headquarters.

Furthermore, commercial banks in Germany used a broader range of information to assess loan applications combined with a dual decision-making structure whereas in France they based loan decisions primarily on financial analysis undertaken by individual managers along hierarchical reporting lines (Quack and Hildebrandt, 1995b).[11] In German banks, balance sheet analysis was accompanied by an evaluation of the investment project as far as product markets, technology and competitors were concerned. German *Hausbanks* could also draw to a greater extent on information from the current accounts of the company (Dietsch, 1993; Homé, 1991). The loan had to be approved by the relationship manager and the group leader of the credit department or – in the case of a larger loan – by their superiors. In contrast, French banks based their loan decision mainly on information about the balance sheet, the current financial situation and collateral (see also Cieply, 1993). The back office had only a support function and the approval of the loan was up to the relationship manager or the next highest manager.

These business practices reflect a different degree of social homogeneity between banks and their corporate customers. The relationship between French bank managers in the central headquarters and large companies has been embedded in the friendship networks of French elites (Birnbaum, 1977; Bourdieu, 1989; Suleiman, 1978). The heads of banks and large firms share a common educational background from one of the Grandes Ecoles and follow a similar career pattern (Swartz, 1985; de Quillacq, 1992; Kadushin, 1995). As a result, bankers and managers tend to know each other and to share a large amount of background information and assumptions about their respective interests and behaviour. As other studies have shown (Tolbert, 1988; Scott, 1991), homogeneity in the social context can reduce the necessity for organizations to elaborate internal structures such as different assessment methods. Furthermore, the role of the French commercial banks under the system of credit ceilings was more that of an administration than that of a risk-taking institution.

In Germany, close relationships between large banks and large companies have been based on shareholding, delegated voting rights and interlocked directorates (Elston, 1993). However, most bank managers, including top managers, have made their way up through internal career ladders and hence do not share the same amount of educational and social background with their counterparts in large non-financial companies. In addition, the liberalization of interest rates in 1967 forced German commercial banks at an earlier stage to develop more differentiated techniques to control their risk portfolio. Formalized practices which German commercial banks developed for large companies could also be applied to SME customers whereas the French 'elite model' was not transferable to business relations with owners and managers of SMEs who come from a different social background.

To sum up, the analysis of the banking sector showed institutionalized patterns which correspond to those found earlier in the SME sector. In the German corporatist system, savings and cooperative banks developed strong group institutions which enabled them to compete successfully with commercial banks in the lending market whereas their counterparts in the French statist system remained weak and fragmented. Although commercial banks in France developed similarly close ties to large companies as in Germany, they could not easily extend their expertize to SMEs because it was based on personal ties.

DIFFERENT BANK STRATEGIES AND OUTCOMES FOR SMES

During the 1980s, banks in both countries experienced increasing competition and disintermediation, but they did so to a different degree. As changes were more gradual in Germany the main banking groups could more easily adapt by developing new customer groups and restructuring existing activities. Financial reforms in France, in contrast, implied a profound break in the distribution of market shares and business practices and exposed banks to previously unknown pressures on their profitability. French banks thus had to reconsider more profoundly their global strategy and activities. In each country, strategic decision-making and organizational restructuring was embedded in a distinct set of institutionalized forms and practices which we have described above. In the following, we will analyse what implications this had for banks' activities towards SME customers.

As mentioned earlier, German banks were able to compensate their diminishing returns from large companies by expanding their business with SMEs. Whereas in large companies finance by bank loans decreased from 14 per cent in 1978 to 8 per cent in 1989, in small companies it rose from 25 per cent to 32 per cent and in medium-sized companies from 22 per cent to 24 per cent (Deutsche Bundesbank, 1992a).[12] Commercial banks, in particular, marketed actively amongst medium-sized companies which are considered as the most lucrative customers and thereby entered more directly into competition with savings and cooperative banks. Many customers of savings and cooperative banks started to use commercial banks for foreign business, security and leasing (Kirchhoff and Bauer, 1994). By expanding into the SME market, commercial banks could stabilize their market share in lending to all companies until the end of the 1980s (see Table 5.1).

Based on the group infrastructure which they had developed in the past, German savings and cooperative banks could maintain their dominant position as lead banks of SMEs. According to a company survey, in 1989 nearly one out of two German companies (44 per cent) considered a savings and one out of three a cooperative bank as its *Hausbank*. Only 13 per cent of companies reported a primary relationship with one of the three large German commercial banks and very few with foreign banks. In 1991, savings banks provided 57 per cent of the credit volume to craft businesses, followed by cooperative banks with 24 per cent and commercial banks with only 11 per cent (Ellgering, 1993). After the German reunification, the network structure of both groups proved efficient in supporting East German member banks in establishing their lending business. Within three years, the market share of the total savings banks group again approached preunification level after it had dropped to 30 per cent in 1990.[13]

Financial reforms in France favoured investment products and capital markets at the same time as they opened up the lending market for new competitors. At first, French banks expanded in investment and capital market products as well as in traditional lending. SMEs were one of the target groups in the lending boom during the second half of the 1980s. At the end of the 1980s, however, when it became clear that banks had many bad risks in their loan portfolios from the downturn in the real estate market, and that the recession made lending even more risky, bank managers began to perceive the SME market increasingly as a problem market. Most banks changed their strategy from a sales orientation to credit rationing[14] which according to Cieply (1995) affected predominantly SMEs. Ten years after the financial reforms, French banks have shifted their activities increasingly from interest- to fee-generating business and larger commercial banks have moved from national to international activities.[15]

The strategies and activities of French banks reflect their position at the time of deregulation and therefore vary more than in Germany. During the 1980s, commercial banks were able to increase their share of company loans from 41 per cent in 1985 to 44 per cent in 1993 (see Table 5.1). As part of the specialization and segmentation strategy (see Courpasson, Chapter 3 in this volume) banks established regional business centres in which specialized managers would deal with SME customers. The work organization and decision-making procedures, however, remained unchanged (see above). Commercial banks expanded their market share mainly through increased short-term lending. This was at the expense of specialized credit institutions whose market share decreased from 21 per cent in 1985 to 13 per cent in 1993.

After deregulation, cooperative banks were able to achieve the highest growth rates in lending. Based on prior experiences in lending and existing links to specific groups of SMEs, cooperative banks expanded considerably their medium- and long-term lending. Overall, they increased their market share from 9 per cent in 1985 to 12 per cent in 1993. Savings banks, however, could only gradually expand into lending to companies because they had to consolidate their group[16] and to build up technical structures and skilled personnel. With a market share of less than 1 per cent, they are still a tiny dwarf compared to their German counterpart (Duet, 1991).

Overall, SMEs remained of secondary importance for French banks and gains from this market segment did not offset the decline in profits which banks experienced from the 1980s in wholesale lending. This is reflected by the diminishing proportion of bank lending in the overall financing of French SMEs from 60 per cent in 1985 to 43 per cent in 1992 (CEPME, 1993). Disintermediation and declining profitability in lending are also indicated by the rapidly decreasing proportion of net interest income which French banks have experienced since 1988 compared to German banks (see Figure 5.2).

In the mid-1990s, German and French banks' strategies towards SMEs are far from converging. German banks' assessment of the profitability of SME customers is positive and they continue to compete for SME customers[17] whereas their French counterparts perceive SMEs as a risky customer group and have reduced their lending (Cieply, 1995). The outcomes for SMEs also vary considerably. First, the volume of bank loans has shown much stronger cyclical variations in France than in Germany. Second, French SMEs continue to rely more on overdrafts and less on long-term lending than their German counterparts (see Figure 5.3). Third, the bank–company relationship still differs in qualitative aspects. Although German companies during the 1980s have multiplied their business relations with banks they still maintain a stable and close relationship to one or two lead banks (Kirchhoff, 1990). In France, on the other hand, financial reforms have increased the number of ruptures between banks and SMEs and reinforced the habit of companies of 'shopping around'.

Figure 5.2   Net interest income of German and French banks, 1988–93 (% of average balance sheet total)

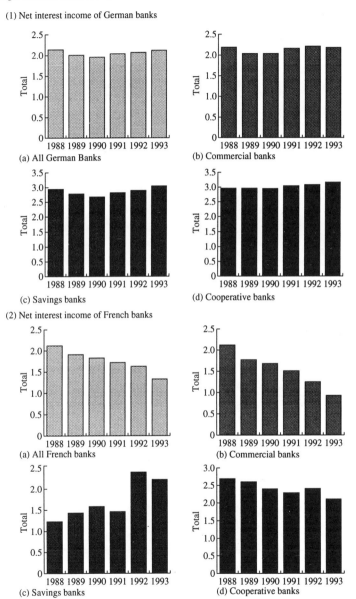

(1) Net interest income of German banks

(a) All German Banks

(b) Commercial banks

(c) Savings banks

(d) Cooperative banks

(2) Net interest income of French banks

(a) All French banks

(b) Commercial banks

(c) Savings banks

(d) Cooperative banks

Source: OECD, 1995.

124

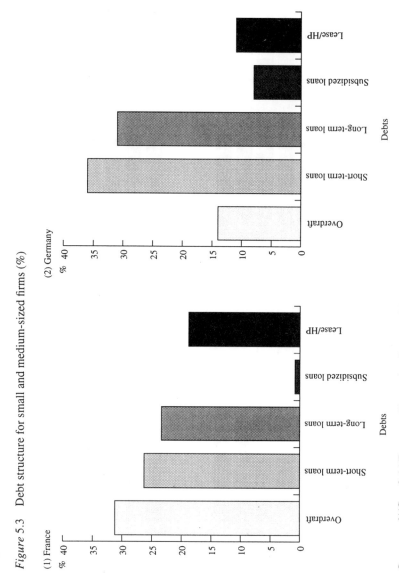

Figure 5.3 Debt structure for small and medium-sized firms (%)

(1) France

(2) Germany

Source: 3i/Cranfield European Enterprise Centre (1992), cited in Davis, 1993.

The persistent differences in the closeness of the bank–company relationship point once more to the influence of institutionalized practices in the banking sector. Human resource policies in French commercial banks were not as suitable for establishing continuous business relationships with SMEs as in German banks. As Courpasson (Chapter 3 in this volume) points out, the specialization of business relations in French banks was accompanied by new recruitment procedures based on standardized criteria favouring university education and a more global management of internal careers. In the large commercial banks, the majority of managers dealing with SMEs are university graduates. As a side effect of the growing number of graduates, however, promotion has also become faster and a relationship manager on average will stay no longer than three or four years with the same customer group. Human resource management in German banks strives for job stability which is the basis for long-term personal links between bank managers and directors/managers of SMEs. Although German banks tend to recruit slightly more graduates than in the past, in most cases a relationship manager will still come up the internal career paths and stay at least five to seven years with a customer group. This relationship is not only an important source of stability in the bank–company relationship but also provides the basis for information-sharing between banks and companies (for more details see Quack and Hildebrandt, 1995b).

CONCLUSIONS

In this chapter, we set out to examine the effects of internationalization and deregulation on bank finance for a specific customer group, that is, SMEs, in two distinct systems of economic coordination. The analysis revealed that different types of coordination generated specific modes of adaptation with different socioeconomic outcomes. In Germany, the internationalization of financial markets affected banks primarily through changes in their market environment. Different banking groups renegotiated – with the support of the state – changes in the legislative framework which facilitated their adjustment to new market demands. German banks were able to soften the negative impacts of investment products on their refinancing costs whereas on the lending side, they intensified their business activities towards SMEs to compensate for shrinking margins with larger companies. Even though the *Hausbank* relationship is gradually losing some of its exclusiveness, the majority of German banks and SMEs still maintain a stable long-term relationship. In France, where the financial system was more isolated from international markets, the main impact of external pressures was on the state as the central actor who then initiated various changes in macroeconomic policy and regulation. The growth of capital and money markets made refinancing more costly for banks and privatization increased pressures on profitability. At the same time, banks faced more insecurities and risks due to the abolition of state subsidies and guarantees. As a consequence, French banks after a short boom period reduced their lending activities in favour of fee-based business in other market segments. The relationship between banks and SMEs has retained its loose character and, in fact, even worsened if we look at the increasing number of breaks in links between banks and their clients. Deregulation and despecialization were to the disadvantage of SMEs, and particularly those which have to mobilize their finance outside larger industrial groups.

The analysis revealed three possible, and as we think, complementary explanations for this divergence. First, institutions and incentive structures remain different. Whereas in Germany legislation and public institutions continuously favour credit-based finance, French legislation throughout the 1980s aimed at developing capital markets. Little was done to ensure the access of SMEs to capital markets and indirect support for bank lending to SMEs was introduced only in the early 1990s. Second, a closer look at the nature of SMEs in both countries showed that German SMEs offer a much larger and more homogeneous customer base including many larger SMEs which are regarded as high-potential customers whereas in France there is only a small number of independent SMEs which reach the size and economic stability that make them attractive customers for banks. Third, the results show that the strategies of German and French banks towards SMEs during the 1980s varied depending on organizational and human resource capacities which they had built up in the past.

The results contradict the argument that deregulation will lead to a general convergence of market structures and strategies of banks in different European countries. The example of SME finance, rather, suggests that customer groups, forms of competition and business practices are deeply rooted in the institutionalized social arrangements of each country which constrain and empower different options for future developments.

Notes

1.	As the subject of this article is a French–German comparison, we focus on developments in West Germany. For an analysis of the role of banks in the transformation process in East Germany see Griffin (1993) and Deeg (1994) and for more details on ownership in East German enterprises see Carlin and Mayer (1995).

2. Our sample consists of ten French and nine German banks. In each country, there are commercial, savings and cooperative banks included. During the period from October 1993 to December 1994, semi-structured interviews were conducted in each bank with representatives from different management functions (for details see Quack and Hildebrandt, 1995a).

3. With the exception of the specialised Crédit d'Equipement des Petites et Moyennes Entreprises (CEPME) which does not collect CODEVI but distributes subsidized loans to SMEs based on funds allocated by the public Caisse des Dépôts et des Consignations (CDC).

4. Whereas in France, the survey counted 17 000 companies with a turnover of between 50 and 500 million FF, the number in Germany was nearly twice as high (31 000 companies).

5. Three out of four German companies with a turnover of 50–300 million FF and one out of two German companies with a turnover of 300–500 million FF are family-controlled (de Saint-Louvent, 1992).

6. On average, the realization of payments from the buyers takes about 66 days in France compared to only 29 days in Germany (CNCA, 1993).

7. The proportion of bankruptcies for Germany might be underestimated, because German courts reject them often in the case of small companies without estate.

8. Most of the commercial banks in France belong to the Association Française des Banques (AFB).

9. The latter financed primarily companies involved in social housing programmes.

10. In France, no separate statistics for lending to SMEs are available.

11. These differences also appeared when only medium- and long-term lending was considered.

12. In per cent of the total balance sheet.

13. Commercial banks could temporarily increase their lending because some of them merged with parts of the former East German state bank which had undertaken most of the lending in the former GDR. Before the reunification, East German savings banks were not allowed to lend to companies.

14. From 1991 to 1993, French banks reduced the volume of short-term loans to companies by one-third from 1.021 to 723 billion FF (Banque de France, 1995).

15. The three largest AFB banks generate about half of their business volume and income abroad, whereas it is only one-third for the German Commerzbank and one-fifth for the Deutsche Bank (Conner, 1994).

16. Within ten years, the number of saving banks decreased from 467 in 1983 to only 35 in 1993.

17. Since the end of the 1980s, however, activities of German banks *vis-à-vis* SMEs – in parallel with developments in the personal customer market – have become more strongly focused on core customer groups (Kirchhoff and Bauer, 1994).

128   *Bank Finance in Germany and France*

References

AFB (Association Française des Banques), *10 années qui ont marqué le monde bancaire 1980–1990. Rapport annuel 1989.* (Paris: AFB, 1990) p. 45.

J.-F. Allegret and J.-F. Goux (eds), *Système financier et système productif, Cahiers Monnaie et Financement, 23.* (Lyon: Centre de recherche Monnaie–Finance–Banque, 1994).

P. Artus, 'Les banques, les assurances et le financement de l' économie', *Les cahiers français, Banques et assurances,* 252 (1991) pp. 34–9.

Banque de France, *Statistiques monétaires et financières annuelles, 1992.* (Paris: Banque de France, 1993) p. 513.

Banque de France, *Statistiques monétaires et financières annuelles, 1993.* (Paris: Banque de France, 1995) p. 437.

P. Birnbaum, *Les sommets de l'Etat. Essai sur l'élite du pouvoir en France.* (Paris: Editions du Seuil, 1977) p. 186.

A. Bizaguet, *Les petites et moyennes entreprises, Que sais-je? 2642.* (Paris: PUF, 1991) p. 127.

C. de Boissieu (ed.), *Banking in France.* (London: Routledge, 1990) p. 190.

P. Bourdieu, *La Noblesse d Etat.* (Paris: Edition de Minuit, 1989) p. 568.

J.L. Campbell, J.R. Hollingsworth and L.N. Lindberg, *Governance of the American Economy.* (Cambridge: Cambridge University Press, 1991) p. 441.

J. Canals, *Competitive Strategies in European Banking.* (Oxford: Clarendon Press, 1993) p. 284.

W. Carlin and C. Mayer, 'Structure and Ownership in East German Enterprises', Discussion Paper FS I 95–305. Wissenschaftszentrum Berlin für Sozialforschung, Berlin (1995) p. 27.

CEPME (Crédit d'Equipement des Petites et Moyennes Entreprises), 'Dossier P.M.E.', *CEPME Service des études,* Paris (1993) p. 32.

G. Chanel-Reynaud, 'Les conditions réelles de la réussite de la réforme financière', in J.-F. Allegret and J.-F. Goux (eds), (1994) pp. 19–49.

G. Chanel-Reynaud, S. Cieply, A. Clerc, C. Mercier and D. Saby (eds), *Réforme financière et transformations des entreprises, Collection Les chemins de la recherche, 30.* (Lyon: Centre Jacques Cartier, 1995).

S. Cieply, 'Nouveaux modes de financement et transmission des entreprises', mimeo, Mémoire du D.E.A. Lyon, Centre de recherche Monnaie–Finance–Banque (1993) p. 265.

S. Cieply, 'Impact de la réforme financière sur la structuration de l' industrie française: l' histoire de l' émergence et de la propagation d' une contrainte financière', in G. Chanel-Reynaud *et al.* (eds), (1995) pp. 53–86.

CNC (Conseil National du Crédit), *Les garanties et le crédit aux entreprises.* (Paris: CNC, 1993a) p. 271.

CNC (Conseil National du Crédit), *Indices du développement des OPCVM sur l'activité des établissements de crédit.* (Paris: CNC, 1993b) p. 135.

CNCA (Caisse Nationale de Crédit Agricole), *Observatoire Entreprises.* (Paris: CNCA, 1993) p. 113.

D. Conner, 'Top Twenty Take to Travel', *The Banker,* 49 (1994) pp. 49–52.

A. Cox, 'State, Finance and Industry in Comparative Perspective', in A. Cox (ed.), (1986) pp. 1–59.

A. Cox (ed.), *State, Finance and Industry. A Comparative Analysis of Post-War Trends in Six Advanced Industrial Economies*. (Brighton: Wheatsheaf, 1986).

E.P. Davis, 'Wither Corporate-Banking Relations?', in K. Hughes (1993) pp. 85–107.

R. Deeg, 'Banks and the State in Germany: The Critical Role of Subnational Institutions in Economic Governance', mimeo, Cambridge, Mass., MIT (1992) p. 525.

R. Deeg, 'Banking in the East: The Political Economy of Investment in Eastern Germany', Discussion Paper FS I 94-303, Wissenschaftszentrum Berlin für Sozialforschung, Berlin (1994) p. 47.

Deutsche Bundesbank, *Statistische Beihefte zu den Monatsberichten der Deutschen Bundesbank*, Reihe 1, *Bankenstatistik nach Bankengruppen* (Frankfurt a.M., 1981, 1986, 1993, 1994).

Deutsche Bundesbank, 'Längerfristige Entwicklung der Finanzierungsstrukturen westdeutscher Unternehmen', *Monatsberichte der Deutschen Bundesbank*, October (1992a) pp. 25–39.

M. Dietsch, 'Des relations banques entreprises exemplaires', *La Revue Banque*, 538 (1993) pp. 42–4.

DSGV (Deutscher Sparkassen- und Giroverband), *Jahresbericht*. (Bonn: DSGV, 1993) p. 137.

P. Dubois and D. Linhart, 'Industrial Networks and Corporate Cultures. The French Case', in S. Mako and P. Novoszath (eds) (1994) pp. 63–89.

D. Duet, *Les caisses d'épargne, Que sais-je? 2582*. (Paris: PUF, 1991) p. 126.

I. Ellgering, 'Aspekte zu künftigen Anforderungen an das Firmenkundengeschäft der Sparkassen und Landesbanken', in K. Juncker and E. Priewasser (eds) (1993) pp. 775–91.

J. Elston, 'Firm Ownership Structure and Investment: Theory and Evidence from German Panel Data', Discussion Paper FS IV 93-28, Wissenschaftszentrum Berlin für Sozialforschung, Berlin (1993) p. 43.

R. Friedland and R.R. Alford, 'The Public Order and the Construction of Formal Organizations', in W.W. Powell and P.J. DiMaggio (eds) (1991) pp. 232–65.

B. Ganne, A. Michelson, D. Navell and P. Totterdill, *PME et systèmes industriels locaux entre l' internalisation de l' économie et les politiques d'aides au développement en France, en Italie et en Grande-Bretagne, Rapport final du Contrat PPSH 60 C*. (Lyon: Groupe Lyonnais de Sociologie Industrielle, 1993) p. 163.

E.P. Gardener and P. Molyneux, *Changes in Western European Banking. An International Banker's Guide*. (London: Routledge, 1990) p. 300.

M. Granovetter, 'Economic Action and Social Structure: The Problem of Embeddedness', *The American Journal of Sociology*, 91, 3 (1985) pp. 481–510.

J.R. Griffin, 'Investment and Ownership in a Volatile Economy: German Banks and the Case of East German Privatization', mimeo, Department of Political Science, MIT, Cambridge, Mass. (1993) p. 40.

C. Harms, 'The Financing of Small Firms in Germany', Working Paper, The World Bank, Washington (1992) p. 35.

J.R. Hollingsworth, P.C. Schmitter and W. Streeck, *Governing Capitalist Economies. Performance and Control of Economic Sectors*. (New York: Oxford University Press, 1994) p. 316.

F. Homé, 'Les relations banques entreprises en République Fédérale D'Allemagne', *La Revue Banque*, 513 (1991) pp. 170–5.

K. Hughes, *The Future of UK Competitiveness and the Role of Industrial Policy*. (London: Policy Studies Institute, 1993).

R. Jepperson and J.W. Meyer, 'The Public Order and the Construction of Formal Organizations', in W.W. Powell and P.J. DiMaggio (eds) (1991) pp. 204–31.

K. Juncker and E. Priewasser (eds), *Handbuch Firmenkundengeschäft*. (Frankfurt a.M.: Fritz Knapp, 1993).

C. Kadushin, 'Friendship among the French Financial Elite', *American Sociological Review*, 60, April (1995) pp. 202–21.

U. Kirchhoff, 'Wachsender Wettbewerb der Kreditwirtschaft um mittelständische Unternehmen', *Die Sparkasse*, 8 (1990) pp. 353–60.

U. Kirchhoff and C. Bauer, 'Neuorientierung des Firmenkundengeschäfts in den Sparkassen', *Die Sparkasse*, 4 (1994) pp. 174–80.

C. Lane, *Management and Labour in Europe. The Industrial Enterprise in Germany, Britain and France*. (Aldershot: Elgar, 1989) p. 328.

C. Lane, 'Industrial Reorganization in Europe: Patterns of Convergence and Divergence in Germany, France and Germany', *Work, Employment and Society*, 5, 4 (1991) pp. 515–39.

C. Lane, *Industry and Society in Europe. Stability and Change in Germany, Britain and France*. (Aldershot: Elgar, 1995) p. 236.

C. Lane and R. Bachmann, 'Risk, Trust and Power: The Social Constitution of Supplier Relations in Britain and Germany', Working Paper Series, WP 5, ESCR Centre for Business Research, Cambridge (1995) p. 53.

S. Mako and P. Novoszath (eds), *Convergence versus Divergence*. (Budapest: Hungarian Academy of Sciences and Communication and Consultation, 1994).

L. Matray, 'L' impérieuse nécessité, des fonds propres', *Revue d'Economie Financière*, (1992) pp. 3–27.

M. Maurice, F. Sellier and J.-J. Silvestre, *The Social Foundation of Industrial Power. A Comparison of France and Germany*. (Cambridge, Mass./London: MIT Press, 1986) p. 292.

OECD (Organization for Economic Cooperation and Development), *Insurance and other Financial Services. Structural Trends*. (Paris: OECD, 1992) p. 156.

OECD (Organization for Economic Cooperation and Development), *Bank Profitability. Financial Statements of Banks 1984–1993*. (Paris: OECD, 1995) p. 196.

C. Oellerking and M. Holzgrabe, *Sparkassen und Genossenschaftsbanken im Spannungsverhältnis zwischen Moral und Ökonomie: Strukturelemente, Organisationsgrundsätze und Geschäftspolitik*. (Frankfurt a.M./Bern/New York: Peter Lange, 1990) p. 252.

J. O'Reilly, *Banking on Flexibility. A Comparison of Flexible Employment in Retail Banking in Britain and France*. (Aldershot: Avebury, 1994) p. 297.

W.W. Powell, 'Expanding the Scope of Institutional Analysis', in W.W. Powell and P.J. DiMaggio (eds), (1991) pp. 183–203.

W.W. Powell and P.J. DiMaggio (eds), *The New Institutionalism in Organizational Analysis*. (Chicago: University of Chicago Press, 1991).

S. Quack and S. Hildebrandt, 'Hausbank or Fournisseur? Bank Services for Small and Medium Sized Enterprises in Germany and France', Discussion Paper FS I 95–102, Wissenschaftszentrum Berlin für Sozialforschung, Berlin (1995a) p. 23.

S. Quack and S. Hildebrandt, 'Das Geheimnis der Banken. Zum Einfluß von Organisationsstrukturen und Personalpolitiken deutscher und französischer Kreditinstitute im mittelständischen Unternehmensgeschäft', Discussion Paper FS I 95–103, Wissenschaftszentrum Berlin für Sozialforschung, Berlin (1995b) p. 36.

S. Quack, J. O, Reilly and S. Hildebrandt, 'Structuring Change: Training and Recruitment in Retail Banking in Germany, Britain and France', *International Journal of Human Resource Management*, 6, 4 (1994) pp. 779–814.

L.M. de Quillacq, *The Power Brokers: An Insider's Guide to the French Financial Elite*. (Dublin: Lafferty Publications, 1992) p. 506.

P. de Saint-Louvent, *Analyse de la perception de l'offre bancaire par les Petites et Moyennes Entreprises en Grande-Bretagne, Allemagne et France*. (Paris: Bossard Consultant, 1991) p. 267.

P. de Saint-Louvent, 'La perception de l'offre bancaire par les PME. Synthèse du rapport au Conseil National du Crédit', *Banque Strategie*, 80 (1992) pp. 11–14.

W.R. Scott, 'Unpacking Institutional Arguments', in W.W. Powell and P.J. DiMaggio (eds) (1991) pp. 164–82.

A. Sorge, 'Strategic Fit and the Societal Effect: Interpreting Cross-national Comparisons of Technology, Organization and Human Resources', *Organization Studies*, 12, 2 (1991) pp. 161–90.

A. Sorge, 'Cross-national Differences in Personnel and Organization', in A.-W. Harzing and J. van Ruysseveldt (eds), *International Human Resource Management. An Integrated Approach*. (London: Sage, 1995) pp. 99–123.

A. Sorge and M. Warner, *Comparative Factory Organisation: An Anglo-German Comparison of Manufacturing, Management and Manpower*. (Aldershot: Gower, 1986) p. 229.

F. Stokman, R. Ziegler and J. Scott (eds), *Networks of Corporate Power: A Comparative Analysis of Ten Countries*. (Cambridge: Polity Press, 1985).

W. Streeck, *Social Institutions and Economic Performance. Studies of Industrial Relations in Advanced Capitalist Economies*. (London: Sage, 1992) p. 248.

E. Suleiman, *Elites in French Society: The Politics of Survival*. (Princeton, NJ: Princeton University Press, 1978) p. 299.

D. Swartz, 'French Interlocking Directorships: Financial and Industrial Groups', in F. Stokman, R. Ziegler and J. Scott (eds), (1985) pp. 184–9.

P. Taillepied and C. de Bressieux, 'Le financement de l' économie entre 1980 et 1992', *Les notes bleues de Bercy*, 30, Paris (1994) p. 30.

P. Tolbert, 'Institutional Sources of Organizational Culture in Large Law Firms', in L.G. Zucker (ed.) (1988) pp. 101–13.

S. Vitols, 'German Banks and the Modernization of the Small Firm Sector: Long-term Finance in Comparative Perspective', Discussion Paper FS I 95–309, Wissenschaftszentrum Berlin für Sozialforschung, Berlin (1995a) p. 25.

S. Vitols, 'Financial Systems and Industrial Policy in Germany and Great Britain: The Limits of Convergence', Discussion Paper FS I 95–311, Wissenschaftszentrum Berlin für Sozialforschung, Berlin (1995b) p. 36.

R. Whitley (ed.), *European Business Systems*. (London: Sage, 1992).

R. Whitley, 'Societies, Firms, and Markets: The Social Structuring of Business Systems', in R. Whitley (ed.), (1992) pp. 5–45.

D. Zerah, *Le système financier français. Dix ans de mutations.* (Paris: La Documentation Française, 1993) p. 294.

L.G. Zucker (ed.), *Institutional Patterns and Organizations.* (Cambridge, Mass.: Ballinger, 1988).

J. Zysman, *Governments, Markets and Growth. Financial Systems and the Politics of Industrial Change.* (Oxford: Martin Robertson, 1983) p. 358.

6 The Problematic Transformation of the Banking Sector in France: The Case of Consumer Credit

Danielle Salomon

INTRODUCTION

The transformation of the banking sector in France is part of a worldwide movement which began in the USA and the UK during the 1980s and has progressively extended to all the developed countries. This process consists of a generalized move towards deregulation, which modifies the rules of competition in the banking sector and introduces new forms of regulation. A tension appears between, on the one hand, a search for better profitability and, on the other hand, a potential increase in risks and losses. Given that financial crises can have a politically destabilizing impact, policy-makers face a complex environment. Financial systems vary significantly between countries (see, for example, the typologies and differentiations elaborated in Zysman, 1983; Huveneers and Steinherr, 1993) and thus deregulation takes on a special character in each country. In the case of France for instance, a similar sequence has tended to be repeated from one segment of banking activity to another.

As deregulation takes away from the banks part of their captive clients and a substantial portion of their margins, they are led to look for new markets. In so doing, they meet new players whose appearance has been enabled by deregulation, such as insurance companies, large department stores, financial houses and direct marketing organizations. All these new players are intent on winning market shares and therefore they enter an overbidding game, offering their products either more cheaply than previously had been the case or with less regard to the risks which they are taking on. Yet the companies may not have the appropriate analytical tools to adapt their business actions to the new environment. Neither

133

supervisory authorities, nor markets or players have the means to immediately regulate this process of overbidding and the result is often a crisis which impacts both on the profits of the companies and the financial position of their clients. As the crisis of deregulation emerges in any particular case, public authorities become involved to try to correct the problems. This is what happened in the consumer credit activity.

This whole process can be conceptualized as a change from a stable game to a new one searching for its own form of regulations. The new game is influenced by new regulations that create a new situation in which strategic moves can be made at different levels and by various actors or institutions. Each move, in turn, influences the ongoing position of the game that will evolve from it. Although the game is still mainly controlled by public institutions which keep the key resources, it is altered by the impact of increased competition. In this sense, deregulation can be seen metaphorically as a continuous feedback game taking the shape of a spiral progressively oriented in one direction.

This chapter examines a particular example of this process through case studies of two financial institutions (a large deposit bank and a specialized consumer credit institution). The two institutions had very different structures but in the period of deregulation they came to share a common segment of activity, although the way in which they related to their customers was shaped by their internal structures and practices. As the competitive game developed in the sector, a crisis of over-indebtedness emerged which became an issue of public concern, requiring actions on the part of public authorities. (See Thoenig and Dupuy, 1986; also Wright, 1990; and Best, 1990, for examples of how to link organizations, sector dynamics and public action.) The analysis of this process underlines some of the specificities of the French banking sector as well as the actual limits of action both of public authorities and of the major banking institutions themselves. In particular, the banking sector in France consists of a large number of players of various statuses and prerogatives. Among these players, the large deposit institutions hold a leading position, through their financial weight and collective market shares. This situation is a result, among other things, of the specific history of the banking sector in France and of a regulatory system that locked organizations into particular markets. The deposit-backing institutions developed into universal banks which adopted highly conservative positions in the process generating specific mechanisms, rules and practices which reproduced the existing system (see, for example, Pastré, 1985; Achard, 1987). But as the leading and universal actors in this stratified market, they in fact protected all other players. The public authorities have had to take into account these structures and therefore seek to meet international requirements for open competition whilst protecting French banks. As a result, domestic practice has slowed down the rhythms of transformation derived from the international context. Policy-makers in the banking sector have understood the mechanisms of their sector, its limits and the contradictions that can occur.

In this chapter, we analyse the commercial behaviours of the two banking institutions. These behaviours derive from the rules and practices of the different institutions and they have specific consequences in terms of outcomes. Essentially, the deposit bank lacked practices or rules which enabled it to analyse the risk it was taking on when it lent to individuals under the rules of the new deregulated system. The specialist financial institution on the other hand had a very detailed system of risk assessment. The deposit bank overlent to bad risks because of the incapacities of its internal structure. This experience has shown that its structure was not adapted to mass credit-selling. However, rather than taking this opportunity to create a better organization structure, it focused on its commercial aims of retaining or winning new clients and reserved its credit-offering for the groups identified in that strategy. The interaction of the two organizations, the market and the regulatory authorities, led to new games but not those expected by the advocates of deregulation.

THE COMMERCIAL BEHAVIOUR OF THE TWO INSTITUTIONS

In both the companies studied, given the retail aspect of this activity, senior management have delegated to their sales people in the branches the specific duty of achieving certain quantitative and qualitative targets for business. Thus it is a game that involves four different actors: the organization, the hierarchy, the sales agents and the clients. In both companies, the internal structure has a key role in influencing how the sales agents reach their decisions to grant clients loans. Hence, it is necessary to analyse, first, the conditions of implementation of policies elaborated at the head office, second, the way in which the actions of the various internal actors are managed and controlled and third, the way in which information is exchanged and modified between the centre and the periphery, both upward and downward. Information in particular is a major cornerstone of these processes, in so far as it determines the day-to-day acts, the general policies, and the reactions to the environment in a context marked by three features: first, the organization is decentralized; second, accurate data is difficult to obtain; and third, policies have to be translated into internal criteria.

The large deposit bank that has been studied shows a formal structure that generates many dysfunctions. It has had therefore to establish a parallel structure to enable it to work. The contrast is so strong between the formal rules and its actual mechanisms that it can be characterized as a 'mock bureaucracy' (Gouldner, 1964). The parallel structure is based on influential individuals and their personal relationships. These influential people possess a high degree of power, a phenomenon which reinforces the arbitrariness that reigns in the organization.

The internal structure of the deposit bank is highly compartmentalized. Each division has its own norms, values and aims. It collects information according to its own criteria and this information is frequently unavailable, unreliable and not comparable across departments. Along the same lines, the rules of operation are confused and numerous. The instructions come from various centres and are not coordinated or prioritized. The training programmes are poorly adapted, the instructions imprecise, and the objectives numerous. The result is that there is confusion as to the real intentions of the organization and its managers. It has a great number of rules and regulations but they are so complex and contradictory they cannot guide behaviour.

As a consequence, actors within the organization have to find ways of adapting, substitutes for the deficient formal organization. This is provided by systems of personal relationships which develop between powerful managers and their employees. Managers control their own fiefdoms and negotiate with each other about resources, dispensing and calling in favours as required to achieve their objectives. Employees further down the organization need these personal relationships with a 'patron' in order to survive but this makes them subject to the arbitrary whim of the manager, rather than the bureaucratic code which supposedly shapes the organization. Each manager in turn needs his or her 'patron' and thus the whole organization becomes a series of clans in which individuals are located and through which they protect each other and advance their careers.

Clans derive from systems of relationships between the centre and the local areas. The deficiency of the information system and of the formal structure requires the local hierarchy to take over and organize the situation. However the managers of the 21 regions are also directors of the bank and this makes it difficult for the functional services of the head office to work officially with the branches in each area network, if the hierarchical line is to be respected. The result is that local managers have a high degree of autonomy and power to implement the detail of the policies decided in the centre. The only way the centre can counterbalance this is by controlling resources and offering help to local managers when problems emerge which cannot be solved at local level. At these moments, local managers look for protection and help through their personal networks. In such networks, formal rules and norms are put aside and replaced by personal links and trust-based relationships embodied in clans. Clans enable the organization to work by offering a parallel structure to the formal bureaucracy. Membership of a clan and the possession of a 'patron' becomes necessary for fulfilling one's role. Subordinates have to follow the lead given by their superiors in order to get their approval and cooperation which is necessary for their own protection and well-being, in terms of monetary rewards and promotion. This situation favours a conservative approach to the task of banking rather than innovation with the emphasis on reproduction and loyalty to the patron and the clan.

The information that circulates within the bank is embedded in the operations of the clans as internal phenomena. Downward information is either too general, or led by specific ends. For instance, the business targets that are given yearly are based on deficient figures; they are calculated long before they are going to be applied (around 18 to 24 months before) without real adaptation in the meantime. Along the same lines, for instance, when a local manager realizes that losses from loans and credits are increasing, the information system will only provide him with general figures but will not provide him with detail of where the losses are emerging from. As the manager is obsessed with protection of himself and the other members of the clan, he stops offering credit at all rather than analysing more precisely the operation or reviewing the credit-granting criteria.

Similarly the information which is passed up the management hierarchy and provides the basis for top decisions and strategies conveys to the centre messages that prioritize protection of the local managers rather than the facts themselves. As there is very little reliable data and each person is shaping the information to suit his or her own purposes, an internal reality is constructed which does not conform at all to what is actually happening. It thereby becomes impossible to fine-tune the operation of the system. Yet, paradoxically the relationship between banks and their clients is a long-term established interaction that implies follow-up, adaptation and so on, especially when credit operations are involved. The bank however is not capable of doing this in a systematic way. Thus concepts such as creditworthiness cannot be systematically constructed by the bank. They cannot develop a profile of their clients that allows for any accurate understanding of which persons will or will not repay loans and under what conditions. The sales people at the branch level have to rely on their own instincts and intuitions supported by the other members of their clan if things start to go wrong or to refer to conservative criteria of guaranteeing any credit by an equivalent amount of savings or capital.

In this situation, any data that appear clear and reliable take on a special importance. This is the case, for instance, with clients' overdrafts that are followed and discussed between superiors and subordinates on a daily basis. This gets the attention of the employees better than anything else and they often prefer to grant overdrafts rather than formal loans to some clients because of this, even though the two forms of credit have different consequences for the bank's balance sheet and for the clients as far as formal conditions and costs are concerned.

The main problem for the bank is that it prefers to learn and adapt from experience and failures in a way that does not involve changing its structure. There is no space for fine-tune analysis. Each entity within the bank is set targets for numbers of accounts and amounts of deposits. It is compared to the average of other similar entities and the game is to reach these averages rather than to prospect and innovate. Poor information and collective construction of reality prevent the organization from perceiving its environment and then adapting quickly and resiliently to it (see Wildavsky, 1988; Douglas, 1986; Wildavsky and Douglas, 1982). In other words, the organization does not favour risk-taking because the means to analyse and correct it are absent. A business risk tends to become an individual risk taken by the person who grants the credit because of two combined effects. First, all transactions occur within a personalized interaction and therefore any failure can be felt as a personal betrayal especially since the means to follow up, prevent and correct are absent. Second, any failure can be used against someone instead of used to teach him how to analyse and behave differently. Thus a commercial risk becomes a personal risk and individuals therefore avoid risk-taking.

The bank is thus a kind of organization which strictly separates risky business from non-risky business in a binary approach, the first one becoming unacceptable and the second one acceptable. It is not able to classify or create a hierarchy of risks according to their level of acceptability. This does not mean that the bank does not take real risks. Risks are taken in spite of the inherent conservatism because the lack of information means that people do not realize that what is internally classified as non-risky, therefore acceptable, in fact entails considerable risk of default (Landau and Stout, 1979).

This is what happened with consumer credit in 1986. The bank sought to increase its market share of this business and bring it up to its general level of market share. This decision was based on rational factors such as apparently comfortable margins in this area of business, enhancing the marginal utility of the branch network of agencies, diversifying into related areas and so on. The decision was helped by the introduction of a scoring tool supposedly resolving the risk involved in granting credit. This scoring tool, however, delegated to the local branches the authority to accept any business up to 50 000 French francs provided the score was above a certain value. This was considered as a green light to the agent to grant the credit. These facts combined to make this activity seem non-risky since both the centre and the local managers supported it and also the tools and its associated rules were a means of protecting the individual from any personal responsibility since in the event of the loan going bad the agent could blame the scoring tool.

However in 1989–90, losses began to mount. Although the losses themselves eventually became visible, there were no systems for identifying precisely which accounts were at risk nor any special mechanisms put in place to help those people who were going into debt. Managers' response only served to increase confusion by insisting that the rules be respected. The agents themselves denigrated the efficiency of the scoring system and went back to their usual criteria for classifying customers.

THE SPECIALIZED FINANCIAL INSTITUTION

The case of the specialized financial institution contrasts dramatically with that of the deposit bank. Since its creation in 1953, the specialized institution has sold consumer credit to a middle-class clientele. Since 1959 it has been part of a single holding company made up of specialized institutions. Its origins in this sector had meant that it had built systems allowing it to work with a mass of credit transactions and to minimize any losses from bad loans, including restructuring personal debts so that individuals had a better chance of paying off their loans after getting into difficulties. When consumer credit controls were lifted after 1986 it was therefore able to capitalize on its years of experience in managing and innovating within the consumer credit field.

The various dimensions of the organization are on the one hand extremely clear and worked out and on the other hand combined together in a coherent whole. There is tight integration of all its elements as well as strong differentiation. Specialization occurs in such a way that every member of the company is in a position to innovate. The division of work is precise and gives to each member of the organization a specific mission to fulfil. It is accompanied with precise rules, tools and procedures that allow every participant to realize with efficiency the tasks which are set.

The management and information system is made up of numerous instruments and statistics that permit precise analysis. All these instruments fit together and give adequate information necessary for particular levels of the organization. Data is processed in real time or at the latest with a one-day delay. The information is then available to everyone and becomes the basis for cooperation between individuals. Information is analysed according to objectives that are given and negotiated every month, checked regularly (generally weekly or twice a month) and followed every day in each of the business units.

This cooperation is obtained for a number of reasons. First, the division of work makes everyone necessary and therefore prompts them to cooperate with one another. Second, the relationship between superior and subordinate is contractual and laid out in a detailed manner. Every individual has quantitative and qualitative objectives to fulfil and needs his or her superior to help achieve these objectives. On the other hand, every superior needs his or her subordinates to accomplish their objectives which are, in turn, aggregated and become the manager's own objectives. Third, the objectives defined are ambitious and need real effort to be accomplished. Fourth, the efforts made by the structure, the collectivity and each individual are all turned towards these objectives and the procedures or work organization that allow them to be achieved. Fifth, individuals are not appointed forever to one position, but on the contrary, geographical and professional mobility is systematically encouraged. Thus everyone learns the constraints of other jobs and is in a position both to understand them and to negotiate with them. Sixth, the performance of the individuals is analysed on the basis of the variation of its results and not punished. Therefore the rewards of the organization are strictly linked with the skills that are needed inside the firm: these include not just commercial objectives but also capacities to integrate various teams, to train and lead teams, to contribute to technological innovations and so on. As a result employees are led to cooperate and invest themselves into what is a demanding game that the firm sets for them even though chances for promotion are slim. The cooperation obtained here is dynamic, in so far as each individual is an equal member of the group and receives as a counterpart of his personal commitment the collective and symbolic rewards of the success of the organization as a whole.

The organization is able to implement its centralized policies at local level. The service offered to the clients is standardized from one place to another. This does not mean that no problem ever occurs, but the general capacity for self-analysis and the respect given to people inside the organization means that these can be resolved to the benefit of all parties.

Sooner or later problems show up and appear in the commercial and analytical statistics which enables managers to deal with them. Similarly the objectives which are set derive from a firm understanding of how business is produced. Deviance from the targets is soon spotted and rather than adopting a punitive stance towards the actors involved, the organization utilizes data to correct the problem. This self-analysis and the tight integration of the various elements allow the rules, the procedures and tools to be permanently adjusted. The organization can then capitalize on its errors and past experiences and redefine explicitly its general or specific goals. These objectives work as concrete ends that guide the efficiency of people and actions in a pragmatic way. The data and information system are indispensable in defining and reaching these goals.

Each person is responsible for playing his or her part in the preservation of the organization as a whole. The hierarchical level one holds shows the capacity of the person both to belong to the group and to contribute to its internal values and objectives. A manager can become a recognized specialist in his or her functional area, because he or she has time to learn, to interact with external specialists and to apply a standardized approach, learned in other positions in the firm: analysis, definition of goals and of analytical tools, objectives, steps and procedures to reach them, and so on. The degree of personal investment allied with internal standardized norms of action and understanding means that each high-level executive is in a sense a guarantee of the reproduction of the organization's internal order.

This reproduction is not static but continually changing, ensuring that new rules or innovations are compatible with the original structure. In that perspective, this company is an auto-poïetical organization, a whole, which finds its unity not through the identical reproduction of its parts over time but through the underlying principles of learning whereby it adapts to the environment (Varela, 1989; see also Hahn's discussion of Luhmann, 1994).

The organization relies on tight integration, internal differentiation to correspond to its environment, and good internal responsiveness. It is able to control risks not simply by being conservative but by being innovative with products, but utilizing rapid feedback mechanisms to assess the success or failure of innovations. The organization's skill and renown in this respect led to it being a sought-after partner in joint ventures with insurance companies, department stores and other institutions seeking to expand into consumer credit.

These two organizations, the deposit bank and the specialized institution, almost appear as two opposed ideal-types. The question which arises is why the deposit bank did not learn from the example of the specialized institution since the latter organization was both more profitable than the bank (see Tainio *et al.*, 1991, for a discussion of the evaluation of the performance of banks) and also met the requirements of the supervisory authorities more clearly. The answer to this lies in the structure of French banking itself and not just at the level of management strategies (see, for example, the accounts in Wright, 1990; Boyer and Durand, 1993; Aglietta, 1993). In the history of the banking sector in France and the way it is organized and managed the large universal banks have an important position from which they are given the opportunity to define key norms and consequently to protect themselves, even allowing for their own deficiencies.

THE FRENCH BANKING SECTOR AND THE DOMINANCE OF LARGE DEPOSIT BANKS

In spite of deregulation since the 1980s the banking sector remains stratified. History, regulation, social class and inertia are the main explanations for the stratification. The existing financial institutions have been created throughout the past two centuries. According to historians, each time a new need appeared, a new kind of organization was created, generally with the help of the state. In the nineteenth century the savings banks, the issuing bank (Banque de France) and the major banks were founded. These institutions coexisted with specialized institutions created for specific aims; Crédit Agricole for financing agriculture, Crédit Central du Crédit Hôtelier for hotels, Crédit d'Equipement des PME for small and medium firms and so on (see Bouvier, 1993). Each of these channels collected the deposits of their corresponding clientele and either directly or indirectly through a centralized organization (for instance Caisse Nationale de Crédit Agricole for the local Caisses de Crédit Agricole, Caisse des Dépôts et Consignations for the savings banks and the Crédit Local de France) re-lent the money to the sector's clients. Generally each of these activities benefited from specific conditions or privileges. For instance the Crédit Agricole group did not pay any tax until the Caisse Nationale was sold in 1988 to the Caisses Régionales (established at departmental levels). The Caisse des Dépôts received the right to collect the notaries' transactions and savings banks were able to collect deposits and pay interest free of tax at fixed rates (which the banks were not allowed to do) (see Fournas, 1993, for an exhaustive list of the privileges of each type of financial institution).

This structure was not significantly changed until the German occupation and the Liberation (Andrieu, 1992). In 1945, in line with the general approach that prevailed in the Liberation measures (Andrieu *et al*., 1987), the four major deposit banks which constituted 72 per cent of the total balance sheets of the top twelve French banks at the time were nationalized. The law confirmed tight frontiers around banking activity. One main idea guided this process which led to a separation of 'Business Banks' (known as banques d'affaires in France) from deposit banks: the banks had to serve the reconstruction of France. The state managed and controlled these major institutions as well as taking a close interest in the establishment of any new organizations in the sector. This does not mean that all the financial sector was nationalized and that no new firm would appear. Several specialized institutions were created in the 1950s, because they would undertake activities (for example, financing consumption or housing) that large banks were avoiding, though they might participate in the financing of these ventures so long as they were kept at arm's length.

In the period from the 1950s onwards, the state introduced various measures to shape the activities of the banks within the interventionist logic of the system. The price of banking transactions was fixed, the provision of credit was directed and controlled, foreign exchange operations were limited and so on. Simultaneously, the reconstruction had led to economic growth that benefitted everyone and particularly the middle class. The majority of people were employed and paid salaries, which necessitated that they had bank accounts.

In 1966 and 1967 new measures were taken to introduce some competition between the financial institutions. The state sought to increase the level of savings and investments in the country. The separation between commercial and investment banking was abolished; any bank could freely open a new branch without special authorization and the Banque Nationale de Paris, BNP, was created by the merger of BNCI and CNEP, surpassing in size Crédit Lyonnais and Société Générale. Between those three leading banks and the second rank of banks there then started a competitive struggle for new customers, based primarily on opening new branches. From 1967 to 1975 the numbers of bank branches doubled from 7776 to 15 133. In 1966 18 per cent of households had a bank account; by 1972, the figure was 62 per cent and in 1984 92 per cent (Bonin, 1989). The deposit banks collected only a quarter of the savings in 1965 but in the period 1975–85, more than half of all deposits went to the banks, with households having more than three-quarters of bank deposits in the 1970s. This period has been characterized as one in which competition was organized by the state (Bouvier, 1993; Pastré, 1985; Achard 1987). Conditions for credit were still controlled by the state but economic growth meant an increasing market for the banks which maintained high margins. Competition occurred mainly through the extension of branch networks which drew in new groups of the population, rather than on the basis of new products with better margins attracting new customers. Furthermore, there were few foreign competitors challenging the national institutions in this period.

The 1984 Banking Act was the first symbolic step towards changing the system though it had to be followed up by a series of concrete measures to deregulate the French banking sector, such as the abolition of credit limits and the creation of new capital markets. All the banking institutions were affected by the Banking Law of 1984, except the Post Office, Banque de France, Caisse des Dépôts et Consignations and Trésor Public. The different sectors of the banking industry are represented by their professional syndicates or their central institution, which are all members by law of the AFEC, the Association Française des Etablissements de Crédit. The AFEC negotiates directly with the supervisory authorities on behalf of the banking sector as a whole. Each particular type of bank belongs to its own industry organization which in turn belongs to the AFEC. Nine of these 'sub-sectoral' organizations are recognised under the law.[1] Among three of them a concentration movement has started (savings banks, Crédit Agricole, Banques Populaires), although in others such as the banks (member of Association Française des Banques, AFB) and the financial institutions (member of Association Française des Sociétés Financières, ASF), there can still be new entrants. The goal of the supervisors (as revealed in a number of articles by key people such as the Secretary of the Commission Bancaire, the Governor and Deputy Governor of the Banque de France, the Secretary of the Conseil National du Crédit (see Raymond, 1991; Cassou, 1991, 1992; Butsch, 1991) has been to gradually dismantle the privileges and restrictions under which the various groupings have operated and equalize competitive conditions.

Despite deregulation, the opening of frontiers and the real competition that has started between the institutions, there remain strong factors ensuring stability. First of all, the commercial banks benefit from a dominant position and they remain conservative, thus influencing and protecting the whole sector. Second, commercial as well as social reasons make the relationships between bank institutions and their clienteles rather stable. Third, the various factors – stakes, internal capacities, clients, and so on – combine together in ways which reinforce the structure of the sector and its compartmentalization. For example, the breaking down of regulatory barriers between the deposit banks and the mutual banks has not undermined the method of operating amongst the deposit institutions since the two groups share the same kinds of preoccupations, resources and constraints. Altogether the big three banks plus Crédit Agricole represent more than 50 per cent of deposits and of debts. Furthermore, even if their constraints are not the same, the banks' capacity to innovate is if anything reduced even further. For example, Crédit Agricole is not a heavily centralized organization. It might therefore be expected that it could be more innovatory. However because each regional unit (known as Caisse) is an autonomous operator in deposits, capitals, internal criteria, information systems and so on, the diversity of the 69 Caisses makes it difficult for the group to coordinate at a national level any campaign apart from their common name and image (see the article in *Les Echos* 12 April 1995). Their strength comes from their global deposit and capital base, and their intricate relationship with local customers but as a group, Crédit Agricole will reinforce the way in which the large deposit banks work.

It is the smallest of the more specialized firms that are devoted to innovation and creativity. This is their functional role in the sector but what usually happens, with a slight delay, is that the large banks absorb these innovations, either by producing similar products, or by purchasing the company that produced them in the first instance. The large banks absorb the innovation, forcing the small firms to find a new innovation, thus creating a spiral of innovation and absorption.

The stability of the system is also reinforced by customer inertia. Habit, expectations of a standardized service (with few significant differences between firms), a conservative attitude towards finance and the organizational resistance to allowing customers to change banks all contribute to this inertia. Statistics confirm this phenomenon, although they also show a worsening of relations between a class of clientele and banks. According to a study conducted on behalf of the AFB in 1993, sixteen per cent of interviewed persons declare having changed their bank after a dispute, although only 5 per cent declare having directly responded to a more competitive offer from another bank.[1] Our own analysis of low- and middle-class clientele shows that they criticize increasingly the way banks treat people with low revenues or end-of-month cash handling problems, although at the same time the majority of people have a good opinion of banks and of their bank. As to the 5 per cent who have changed, they are mostly composed of urban, executive people. Altogether, this group shows that there does exist an alternative to remaining with the same institution but in order to attract these new clients a bank has to achieve significantly higher standards than the ordinary. However the numbers of customers who do move remain small in spite of aggressive campaigns based on new strategies run by Barclays and Paribas (with its Direct Bank).

If change has begun it remains slow due to the continued predominance of the large deposit banks which are particularly conservative. As has been shown, their internal structure is incapable of responding adequately to the new challenges. Where they do respond they simply create new forms of destabilization. As a result the supervisory authorities are faced with a major problem. Their attempts to deregulate the sector founder on the conservatism of the large deposit banks. This can be illustrated by reference to the case of consumer credit.

THE CASE OF CONSUMER CREDIT

Consumer credit showed a sudden increase in the late 1980s for a number of reasons. First of all, deregulation enabled the players to operate on new segments and led them to find new sources of margins. Second, the banks adopted quantitative criteria that pushed them to offer credits aggressively, given the security they found in scoring. Third, this offer met an equally strong demand. Credit had been legitimated both by housing policies which encouraged purchase through long-term loans and by the inflation that turned indebtness into an economically rational decision. According to a study by the Commission Bancaire (1991) in just two years between 1986 and 1988, consumer credit increased from 181.6 billion to 316 billion French francs. However, this expansion occurred with little change in the internal systems of control. So long as the macroeconomic situation was good, customers were able to pay back their loans. When the economic situation deteriorated, the banks were incapable of adapting and instead continued to lend. The result was that loans became non-performing as individuals and companies defaulted.

The crisis that resulted prompted a demand for public action. In the face of opposition from the banks, the Secretary for Consumer Affairs pressed forward a plan to help debtors to reschedule their loan repayments. The plan depended on the cooperation of many groups – the banking institutions, their representatives, consumer associations, the Department of Justice, the Treasury, the Banque de France – all working together under the coordination of the Secretary for Consumer Affairs. The plan was based on a two-stage model. In the first phase, debtors would come before local commissions presided over by a Préfet or, in his absence by the Trésorier-Payeur-Général (TPG, local chief of all finance administrations). The secretary of the commission is appointed by the Director of the Banque de France, and the other members are a representative of the consumer associations, a representative of the banking institutions, and a member of the local administration, for example from the Department for Consumer Affairs. The commission tries to establish a plan for the settlement of debts with the agreement of the main creditors. Usually the plan aims to decrease the monthly instalments in order that the family can meet them given their monthly revenues. In the case of failure, the debtor can take the case to the second stage, the local court of justice, that will judge the case with legal but limited rights. The law was voted on 31 December 1989 and the plan came into action from 1 March 1990. In French terms this is a very speedy implementation of legislation, showing the degree of seriousness with which the indebtedness crisis was seen by the politicians. By the mid-1990s the 116 local commissions had considered more than 335 000 cases of over-indebtedness.

The seriousness of the situation had arisen from a number of factors. Local authorities, for example, found that the amount of unpaid rents which they were owed were increasing as indebted consumers juggled their responsibilities between paying off the banks and paying their rents. This became a political problem for local officials as the debtors came to local social services departments requesting help with the payments which the municipalities were unable to provide because of the diminishing resources of the welfare state generally. In this respect the Secretary for Consumer Affairs, who was herself elected for a low-class municipality close to Paris, was particularly sensitive to these problems. The Banque de France also undertook a decisive role as it felt itself helpless in getting the banks to moderate their credit offers, a fact that had, in its opinion, two consequences: first, it meant that it was difficult to get inflation under control and second, it meant that the banks would soon face heavy losses which would become its responsibility.

The success of the law has however been mixed. In social terms, it appears that the poorest amongst the debtors have not been helped by the conciliation procedure of the local commissions. In economic terms, it appears that the law did not lead the banks themselves to look for better ways to manage their risks.

With regard to the latter, the banks have not learned to cope with their risks, but they have learned to position themselves and their marketing efforts in ways which reduce their risk. The result is a new segmentation of the market for consumer credit. The banks now reserve their credit offers for their good clients. The specialized institutions on the other hand organize for the other players (insurance companies, department stores, new financial institutions entering the credit segment, and so on) the sale and collection of loans. The latter have proved, thanks to the crisis, that managing risks was the key element in this business. Thus these institutions such as the one studied have recovered and enlarged their market share as well as generally improving their reputation for good risk management. The banks, on the other hand, reverted in the credit area to their basic strengths. For example, one bank offered consumer credit at 9 per cent, when the market was offering between 12 and 17 per cent, depending on the amounts, product, and so on. Ten days later all the commercial banks had aligned their offer with the first one. They used the cheap resources derived from their non-remunerated deposit accounts to fund their credit activity. The specialized institutions on the other hand still had to borrow the money they lent, and therefore had to pay the market price for these funds. As this stood between 12 and 17 per cent, they were unable to offer credit of 9 per cent. On the other hand, the banks' lending was accompanied by restrictive conditions, in contrast with the specialized institutions. Banks set minimum amounts, minimum delays in repayments, minimum savings in the bank, and an obligation to pay salaries direct into the bank as conditions on their loans. In other words the actual offer of banks became centred around holding the client's financial activities in total within their grasp. In this way, they sought to reinforce their grip on the client based on their traditional power and mode of activity. They did not create any new ways of learning about risk management for this would imply an internal organizational revolution which they were unable to achieve.

LIMITS TO PUBLIC ACTION

Through a detailed analysis of the two banking institutions and the distinctive games they play to face their common segment of activity, we have shown that the structure of the banking sector raised specific problems that the public authorities could not completely cope with. Instead they have to find complementary and versatile ways of dealing with the situation, using whatever comes within their reach and acting according to the circumstances. The banks on the other hand respond in three ways: first, by protecting themselves from the supervisory authorities; second, by acting on short-term imperatives without a long-term policy; and third by partially externalizing the costs on to their weaker clients.

Although the supervisory authorities have strong and extended powers, their capacities to act effectively are limited. Supervision of the banking sector is divided up between the Ministry of Finance, the Treasury and the Banque de France. However, the main authority is the Banque de

France as far as control is concerned, through the Commission Bancaire (CB) which is in charge of checking that legislation is being applied. The Governor of the Banque de France can control the number of firms in the negative sense that he can allow firms to go bankrupt or alternatively he insist that the share holders or the rest of the sector supports any bank in difficulty. In addition the Banking Act of 1984 has given the power to the Comité de la Réglementation Bancaire (CRB) to issue any regulations deemed necessary under its prerogatives. The Commission Bancaire has the power to control and sanction the players, elaborate rules and regulations and even decide upon the dissolution of institutions. In addition, the Commission Bancaire can promote any new accounting rules either to harmonize them with the European Community, or to improve disclosure, thus, in principle, making certain types of balance sheet risk more visible. Partly these measures have been taken to bring France into line with the decisions of the Basel Committee and the European Union but others derive from national imperatives. Even so these enlarged powers, frequently criticized by the financial institutions, are not sufficient to regulate the evolving banking sector, and more specifically to press the banks to both modify their internal structures and collectively regulate their behaviours in new ways.

Banks are necessary to any modern economy and government. In France, they are strategic actors. They support the franc and implement the investment policies of the state. They are helping the state to overcome the fiscal crisis arising from the increased demand for pensions by developing the new tax-free products issued by the government (see Sturdy *et al.*, Chapter 7 in this volume). They help to finance public deficits. They give information to the fiscal administration. They receive the deposits of the population and secure their savings. The banks' reputation, individually and collectively, contributes to the reputation of the financial centre of Paris and of the supervisory authorities. Thus the losses revealed at Crédit Lyonnais made foreign institutions suspicious of French authorities' capacities, just as the Barings default undermined the reputation of the Bank of England. In the growing international global financial markets, the banks carry the reputation of France as a major player. For all these reasons they appear to be protected. Hostile measures taken against the banks would need a very good reason and strong political support.

At the same time it is clear that their conservatism raises difficulties and creates social and economic problems which the government has to solve. As has been shown in this chapter this is particularly due to their organizational conservatism which prevents supervisory authorities from intervening. The authorities are only able to insist upon certain external forms of control but internally the banks continue to act in the old ways which are unsuitable for the era of deregulation. Furthermore because the banks are so central to so many aspects of the economy (for example, financing firms and holding and developing the savings and loans of individuals as well as supporting the state's macroeconomic and welfare policy) any action to control them may have unexpected and dramatic consequences on the financial system as a whole. Public action in the banking sector is therefore a mixture of rules, negotiations, persuasions and exhortations, influence, and circumvention. In this respect, the close link at the level of senior management between the banks and the administration is particularly important. Generally the top managers in large banks are nominated from the ranks of the civil service and in particular the Treasury (Thoenig, 1987; Bauer and Bertin-Mourot, 1987). The nominated manager therefore feels that he or she is still part of the administration in some way and thereby becomes a carrier of public banking policy, at the same time as acting on behalf of the bank.

It is likely that it will be the effects of competition rather than regulation which will change the behaviour of the banks. In particular, the process of privatization will create new conditions of competition for the banks. The banks will have to reach international standards in terms of their profitability and return on assets if they are going to be able to finance their activities either through the stock markets or the wholesale funding markets at a rate which is competitive with other international banks. Moreover, it has become progressively more difficult for the state to intervene to support the banks as one after the other have become privatized (Société Générale in 1986 and BNP in 1993). These privatized banks have strongly criticized the state's efforts to support Crédit Lyonnais, arguing that the official policy is to create a level playing field for competition and therefore any aid to an ailing institution, even a nationalized one, is unfair. However, it appears that the intention of the state is to support Crédit Lyonnais for the moment, partly because it is 'too big to fail', and then to clear its major losses before it is privatized. In this sense, privatization is not so much a liberal inspiration to create a competitive market as a means whereby the French government can push the large and protected French banks into the international competitive arena and thereby force them to change their behaviour. In itself, this does not solve the question of the potential over-capacity of the French banking system (see Dietsch, 1993), nor does it overcome its severe organizational deficiencies (profitability is low compared with other countries), or the defensive game in which the universal banks are involved, or the exclusionary effects its development has for some customers.

CONCLUSION: AN ON-GOING AND PROBLEMATIC TRANSFORMATION

Whatever the country, the transformation of the banking sector is not an easy question and it implies bankruptcies, crises, and losses that are significant for the rest of the economy and the clients of the banks. Actions to reduce risk at the balance sheet level (through, for example, the Basel Committee's recommendations on capital – asset ratios which are supported by the Commission Bancaire in France) can only be one part of the solution. These ratios are only one part of the whole complex set of relationships which constitute a banking system. These relationships are embedded in specific local contexts which generate particular levels of risk whatever is being monitored by the regulators. The nature of regulation and supervision in a particular society, attitudes towards money, debt and credit, links between banking institutions, the role of the legal system in handling debts and bankruptcies: these are but a few of the phenomena which create a particular domestic environment, inimitable from one country to another.

On the other hand, there do exist factors which point towards convergence, standardization and even homogeneity in banking activity from one country to another. It is certain that the cooperation between states, governments and central banks, as well as the European Union, is key in this respect. It is most probable that at least for certain aspects of the globalization of financial exchanges, this will increase. That is why deregulation, or rather the multiple aspects that the opening of frontiers and the partial harmonization of the basic rules of the collective game take on, is inevitable whatever one's ideological view. To ask whether deregulation is positive or negative, or if it can, as such, be applied from one country to another, when the various financial systems are organized so differently, is probably putting the question in the wrong way. It is more interesting to consider how states have initiated or participated in this move towards deregulation since it has become a major decision for any administration. What appears to be most common and has been shown in the case under consideration is that partial deregulation is brought in which has unexpected consequences. There has been no global, overall approach; instead deregulation has occurred sector by sector. The result is that those who are severely dizadvantaged by deregulation, as in the case of the consumer credit crisis, turn the issue into a political problem. Thus deregulation becomes entangled with a wider range of issues and the process itself is opened out to include clients, judges, and civil servants. The way in which these groups interact is based on the specific social context in which

152 *Transformation of the Banking Sector in France*

they are located. The result is a specifically French construction of deregulation that is different from elsewhere even if the underlying trends are common to other European countries.

Note

1. Commercial banks are represented by the Association Française des Banques (AFB); all the Caisses of Crédit Agricole are represented by the Caisse Nationale de Crédit Agricole; Banques Populaires are represented by the Chambre Syndicale des Banques Populaires; all the Caisses of Crédit Mutuel are represented by the Confédération Nationale du Crédit Mutuel; the Caisse centrale de crédit coopératif represents the cooperative banks and the financial affiliate institutions; CENCEP represents the Caisses d'Epargne and their affiliates; Union Centrales des Caisses de crédit municipal represents the various Caisses de Crédit Municipal, Association Française des Sociétés Financières (ASF) represents all the financial firms, title houses, etc.; and Groupement des Institutions Financières Spécialisées represents the specialized financial institutions (such as Comptoir des Entrepreneurs).

References

P. Achard, Rapport au Ministre d'Etat, *Le marché unique de 1992: Perspectives pour les banques, les assurances et le système financier français*, Paris, Décembre (1987), Ministère de l'Economie des Finances et de la Privatisation.
M. Aglietta, 'Comportement bancaire et risque de système', *Revue d'Economie Financière, Numéro spécial: L'industrie bancaire*, 27, Winter (1993) pp. 439–663.
C. Andrieu, *Les banques sous l'occupation*. (Paris: Presses de la FNSP, 1992).
C. Andrieu, L. Le Van and A. Prost, *Les nationalisations de la Libération. De l'utopie au compromis*. (Paris: Presses de la FNSP: 1987).
M. Bauer and B. Bertin-Mourot, *Les 200. Comment devient-on un grand patron?* (Paris: Le Seuil, 1987).
M. Best, *The New Competition. Institutions of Industrial Restructuring*. (Cambridge: Polity Press and Basil Blackwell, 1990).
H. Bonin, *L'Argent en France Depuis 1880. Banquiers, Financiers, Epargnants*. (Paris: Masson, 1989).
J. Bouvier, 'Monnaie et Banque d'une après-guerre à l'autre', in F. Braudel and E. Labrousse (eds), *Histoire économique et sociale de la France, IV, 1–2, 1880–1950* and *IV, 3, 1950–1980*. (Paris: Quadrige-PUF, 1993).
R. Boyer and J.P. Durand, *L'après-fordisme, Alternatives économiques*. (Paris: Syros, 1993) pp. 236–239.
J.L. Butsch, 'Gestion de bilan et dispositions réglementaires', *La Revue Banque*, 514, March (1991) pp. 228–234.

P.H. Cassou, 'Les évolutions de la réglementation bancaire', *La Revue Banque*, 514, March (1991) pp. 228–234.

P.H. Cassou, 'L'adaptation de la profession bancaire aux exigences du marché unique', *La Revue Banque*, 524, February (1992) pp. 136–138.

M. Dietsch, 'Les surcapacités bancaires en France', *Revue d'Economie Financière, Numéro spécial: L'industrie bancaire*, 27, Winter (1993) pp. 169–198.

M. Douglas, *Risk Acceptability According to the Social Sciences*. (London: Routledge & Kegan Paul, 1986).

F.X. de Fournas, *Espèces de banquiers, Essai de management et de zoologie bancaire*. (Paris: Economica, 1993).

A. Gouldner, *Patterns of Industrial Bureaucracy. A Case Study of Modern Factory Administration*. (New York: Free Press Paperback, 1964).

A. Hahn, 'Introduction à la sociologie de Niklas Luhmann', *Sociétés*, 43, Paris (1994).

C. Huveneers and A. Steinherr, 'Economie industrielle des institutions bancaires, Réglementation, structure, performance', *Revue d'Economie Financière, Numéro spécial: L'industrie bancaire*, 27, Winter (1993) pp. 13–46.

N. Landau and R. Stout, 'To Manage is not to Control: Or the Folly of Type II Errors', *Public Administration Review*, 2, March/April (1979) pp. 148–156.

O. Pastré, *La modernisation des banques françaises, Collection des rapports officiels*. (Paris: La Documentation Française, 1985).

R. Raymond, 'Les difficultés des banques dans un milieu en rapide transformation', *La Revue Banque*, 519, September (1991).

R. Tainio, P.J. Korhonen and T.J. Santalainen 'In Search of Explanations for Bank Performance – Some Finnish Data', *Organization Studies*, 12, 3 (1991) pp. 425–450.

J.C. Thoenig, *L'ère des technocrates. Le cas des Ponts et Chaussées*. (Paris: L'Harmattan, 1987).

J.C. Thoenig and F. Dupuy, *La loi du marché. L'électroménager en France aux Etats-Unis et au Japon*. (Paris: L'Harmattan, 1986).

F. Varela, *Autonomie et connaissance. Essai sur le vivant*. (Paris: La couleur des idées: Seuil, 1989).

A. Wildavsky, *Searching for Safety*. (New Brunswick: Transaction Books, 1988).

A. Wildavsky and M. Douglas, *Risk and Culture. An Essay on the Selection of Technical and Environmental Dangers*. (Berkeley: University of California Press, 1982).

M. Wright, 'De la nécessité de placer les réseaux de politique publique dans leur contexte au sein de l'analyse comparative des politiques industrielles', *Politiques et Management Public*, 8, 2, March (1990) pp. 1–33.

J. Zysman, *Governments, Markets, and Growth. Financial Systems and the Politics of Industrial Change*. (Oxford: Martin Robertson, 1983).

7 National Management Styles: A Comparative Study of the Strategy of *Bancassurance* in Britain and France

Andrew Sturdy, Glenn Morgan and
Jean-Pierre Daniel

INTRODUCTION

During the 1980s, many banking and financial institutions across Europe took up the strategy of *bancassurance* or *Allfinanz*. In broad terms, the strategy referred to the goal of selling both insurance and banking products through an integrated distribution system in which existing bank branch networks were crucial. There have been a number of studies by major consultancies evaluating the extent to which national financial systems have adjusted to this model. Most of these studies take the notion of a *bancassurance* strategy for granted. They assume that within the confines of different regulatory systems, the goal of *bancassurance* is the same and therefore managerial practices and knowledge of the strategy itself and its implementation process can be transferred across national boundaries.

This chapter reports on research carried out between 1990 and 1994 on *bancassurance* within Britain and France (Daniel, 1992a and 1994; Sturdy and Morgan, 1993; Morgan *et al.*, 1994). The research was part of a wider and continuing project concerned with the development of national financial systems in a number of European countries. This focuses upon the historical linkages between financial institutions and patterns of public and private expenditure on consumption and welfare and how this affects the strategies, structures and competitive position of banks, insurance companies and other retail savings and lending institutions. From this perspective, the view of a common European strategy of *bancassurance* begins to look less tenable.

154

The chapter consists of the following sections. First, the nature of *bancassurance* and its growth within France and Britain is outlined. Second, our comparative research on the implementation of *bancassurance* in the two countries is briefly summarized. This enables the identification of key differences between this process in France and Britain. In the third section, we discuss the implications of these differences. Our argument is critical of the idea that there are general strategies such as *bancassurance* which can be applied in multiple national contexts. We argue that whilst consultants and senior managers may seek to transfer strategies and discourses such as *bancassurance* across national boundaries, the process of formulation and implementation is still shaped strongly by national and sectoral contexts.

BANCASSURANCE IN BRITAIN AND FRANCE

The breakdown of boundaries between banks and insurance companies since the mid-1980s has been part of a range of strategic changes in the organization of the financial services industry. Central to these changes has been the attempt to turn bank branches into 'one-stop' financial supermarkets. *Bancassurance* is the French term commonly used to describe an integrated approach to the sale of traditional banking products (such as money transmission, savings and loans) and insurance and investment products within a retail branch network. The strategic logic of such an approach is clearly understood. It is assumed that the bank (or insurer) thereby makes more intensive use of existing assets and resources, that is, its branches and people.

Since the mid-1980s, in Britain, France and most of Europe the financial services industry has been characterized by the breakdown of old demarcations between deposit-taking institutions such as banks and building societies and insurance providers (Salomon Bros, 1990; Thwaites, 1991; Ennew *et al.*, 1990; Coopers & Lybrand, 1993). It is increasingly the case that those institutions with extensive retail networks are using them to sell insurance and investment products (Howcroft, 1991; Stephenson and Kiely, 1991; Burton, 1991, 1993). This involves a major strategic change in the nature of these institutions. Until the 1980s, banks and building societies in the UK could rely on customers coming to them to open new accounts or to borrow money. In the 1980s, deregulation opened the way for many new entrants and weakened the ability of the existing institutions to operate quasi-cartel agreements. The expansion of lending and credit that fuelled the boom of the mid-1980s gave way in the late 1980s and early 1990s to huge burdens of unserviced debt and large losses for banks and building societies. In this context, the search for more profitable products and for more efficient use of existing resources became urgent. In addition, in some cases there was an increasing need for capital to support growth. Insurance and investment products (which were already being sold on a small scale in the banks and societies) came to be seen as one of the main areas in which new profits could be safely secured and increasingly sophisticated and 'mobile' customers could be 'courted' and retained (see Knights *et al.*, 1993).

In France, the reasons for the convergence of the two sectors are similar. Successive governments followed an albeit piecemeal and somewhat haphazard policy of liberalization and (de-)regulation (see Cerny, 1989; Sturdy and Morgan, 1993). For example, businesses were allowed to bypass banks and gain direct access to the financial markets. At the same time, banks were encouraged to be more commercially orientated with the setting up of new markets such as financial futures, the removal of credit controls and privatization and even reprivatization. Mergers and acquisitions were supported to help strengthen the position of French banks in Europe and tax incentives were provided for medium- to long-term savings.

Despite these changes the state still controls banking to an extent unseen in other Western European countries. It is the banks' largest customer and supplier of funds and, with privatization, direct state control was simply replaced by a strategy of coopting members of the financial establishment and the 'allocation of favours'. As a consequence, the banks have been protected from the costs of mismanagement with, for example, little evidence of cutting staff numbers (*The European*, 20–6 January 1995; see also O'Reilly, 1992).

Nevertheless, the impact of deregulation, privatization and increased competition cannot be ignored and it is clear that from the mid-1980s, the banking sector has been in a 'state of flux' (Rawsthorn, 1991; p. ii). It had become known in the press as the 'steel industry of tomorrow' because of its 'overstaffing' and stagnating profitability (*The Economist*, 1990). This assessment was a reflection of the changing ideological climate in terms of market competition. It also reflected the high labour costs of what was, in European terms, a very extensive branch network operating in a protected, but saturated, market (de Boisseau, 1990).[1] Bank management became increasingly concerned about profitability and became more market(ing)-orientated. As in the UK, it sought to diversify services from the branch network by developing new distribution channels. For example, travel insurance was introduced and, in the case of Crédit Agricole, a travel agency. However, the main shift was towards the increased selling of life assurance-related products, where margins remained wide and market share could be rapidly gained. As elsewhere in Western Europe, expansion of this business was seen as key to restoring profitability even if margins were placed 'under pressure' in the recession (Rawsthorn, 1991; AFB, 1991).

Alongside the motivating factors to strategy experienced on both sides of the Channel, an additional factor explains the dramatic expansion of *bancassurance* in France. As new entrants to the insurance market and apparently largely unconcerned about its complexities, French banks began by marketing products which were less heavily commission-based, more transparent and more flexible than those of traditional insurers. They therefore responded to the expectations of increasingly informed consumers who have, thanks partly to a particularly well-developed financial press in France, been critical of traditional life assurance contracts (especially endowments with their high commissions).

In this chapter, our concern is with *bancassurance* defined as the sale through the bank branch networks of life assurance and related investment products of a single insurer which is either owned or part-owned by the bank. In the UK, trends in the industry indicate that as far as life insurance and pensions are concerned all of the major banks and most of the major building societies are now 'backward integrated', that is, own their own life insurance company. Some retain the capacity to offer advice on the products of other companies but because of regulation this has to be strictly separated from the sale of their own products. In France also, most banks have created or bought a life assurance subsidiary which produces and manages the distributed products. For example: Crédit Lyonnais owns Assurances Fédérales; BNP owns Natiovie; Société Générale owns Sogecap, and Crédit Agricole owns Predica.[2]

The development of *bancassurance* can be seen from its continued expansion in the UK since the late 1980s.

The table outlines the market share of *bancassurance* for three product categories combined: unit-linked and non-linked (that is, with profits) life assurances and annuities and personal pensions business. The other main distribution channels are independent brokers and insurance company sales forces whose share of single premiums has changed from 43 to 39 per cent and 37 to 34 per cent respectively over the same period. Direct

Table 7.1   UK sources of premium income (life business)
(% market share of *bancassurance*)

	Independent		Agents		Total
	Banks	BS	Banks	BS	
New annual premiums					
1989	2	3	3	2	10
1993	1	1	6	4	12
New single premiums					
1989	3	1	5	*	9
1993	3	3	7	5	18

*Less than 0.5%.
Source: Association of British Insurence *Statistics Year Book 1983–1993*, pp. 88–9.

marketing has continued to represent 3 per cent of annual premiums and 1 per cent of single premiums.

The growth in market share is most pronounced with linked policies, especially single-premium products, where building societies (BS) have secured 14 per cent of the market (compared with 1 per cent in 1989) and banks 18 per cent (compared with 11 per cent in 1989). It has been claimed that the banks' market share of life assurance business has grown from 'next to nothing' to 13 per cent in seven years and may reach between 30 and 50 per cent of the retail financial services market by the end of the decade (*Independent*, 16 January 1994). The attraction of *bancassurance* is clear – it offers banks and building societies a major new source of profit at a time when traditional banking services, especially money transmission, are no longer profitable. Although exact figures are difficult to obtain, it was estimated that between one-fifth and one-third of pre-tax profits in banks and building societies derived from the sale of insurance products (Knights *et al.*, 1993).

In France, the figures are even more spectacular, with the *bancassurance* share of the life market rising from 17 per cent in 1980 to 39 per cent in 1990 (FFSA, 1991). More specifically, in 1985, bank branch networks, including those of the Caisse Nationale de Prévoyance (the Post

Office, the Public Treasury and the savings bank, Caisses d'Epargne de l'Ecureuil), collected 25 per cent of a 75 billion franc turnover in life business. In 1993, this income had grown to 52 per cent of the 332 billion franc turnover (Daniel, 1994). The distribution by banks of life assurance-related products was both the condition and the consequence of a dramatic development whereby the overall turnover of life assurance generally increased ninefold from 1980. For example, life business represented around 25 per cent of all insurance premiums between 1950 and 1980. By 1987, the share had risen to 42 per cent (see also Bouchaert and Schor, 1988). France had, for a long time, been 'underdeveloped' in terms of life assurance premiums per capita and this continued until recently, at least compared with other Northern European countries (Zajdlic, 1988; Ernst & Young, 1989). This requires more space than is available here to explain. Nevertheless, it can be argued that it relates to a predominantly Latin and Catholic culture with associated attitudes to risk, individual material security and fate (Daniel, 1992b). Also, as we shall see, most occupations had been covered since the war by a relatively generous 'pay as you go' pensions system (Baldwin, 1990) with consequent effects on people's interest in saving for old age through the medium of an investment-related insurance policy. However, the culture(s) and demographics of French society were changing (Mendras and Cole, 1991) and this provided fertile ground for the development of personal financial services generally and *bancassurance* in particular.

It is no exaggeration to say that, through *bancassurance*, the French discovered a new dimension to assurance in all its financial forms. If banks in particular have been so successful it is partly because the form of the life insurance-related products they sold was very close to that of their established savings and investment products (e.g. bonds) as well as conforming to the growing demand for medium- to long-term savings in an ageing population and, perhaps, more individualized culture (Sturdy and Morgan, 1993; Sturdy and Knights, 1996). In particular, the contracts promoted by the banks were much easier to understand than those of established life companies. The banks sold insurance linked to interest rates in the stock exchange index. These products were more transparent than the traditional endowment policies sold by insurance companies where annual and terminal bonuses were dependent on complex actuarial calculations. Essentially, they were promoted as a way of saving with a 'good' rate of interest and favourable fiscal treatment. This appealed to the growing population of people approaching or commencing retirement with a surplus to invest at a relatively low level of risk (Daniel, 1994).

BANCASSURANCE IN OPERATION

Our research is primarily based on a series of case studies of the implementation of *bancassurance* in the UK and France (three in each country). These case studies are written up in detail elsewhere (Morgan *et al.*, 1994). In this chapter, we simply wish to draw attention to the main points of comparison.

Common Problems of Implementation

As we have seen, at the broadest structural level, the dominant forms of *bancassurance* in both France and the UK are those of bank ownership of an insurer. The key problem which emerged in both countries concerned the relationship between the two parts of the organization – the bank and the insurer. This in turn can be analysed at two levels.

Intra-Managerial Conflict

In our cases, there was a common problem of conflict between the parent (the bank) and subsidiary (the insurer) which was resolved or addressed in similar ways. Whether acquired or newly formed, all the insurance subsidiaries tended in the first instance to have organizational cultures which were very different from that of their bank parents. These cultures tended to emphasize, and even celebrated, their separateness from the bank at both branch and senior management levels. This led to antagonism between the senior managements of the two parts of the organization and also undermined attempts at a coordinated system of *bancassurance* selling in local branches. Bank managements eventually utilized their more powerful position to enforce the secondary or subsidiary status of the insurer through three main mechanisms:

- personnel changes involving the installation of bank 'people'
- an explicit change of the subsidiary's corporate identity, for example, changing its name, moving its headquarters
- an incorporation of its management functions into the bank

These problems are familiar in corporate mergers and organizational structures generally. To a certain extent, they can be explored by reference to theories of group behaviour and conflict, functional differentiation and corporate culture and power (Morgan *et al.*, 1994). Nevertheless, the particular form of the 'cultural' difference relates to the broader changes which *bancassurance* requires.

Occupational Conflict

In a recent consultants' survey of *bancassurance* in Western Europe, one of the key implementation issues identified was that of 'bridging occupational, cultural and remuneration differences' between banks and insurance companies (for example, fixed salaries in banking or branches and sales commission in life assurance or direct sales forces). For example, it was claimed that one of the main reasons why some of the largest banks avoided acquisition and developed insurance business from 'scratch' was to minimize cultural differences. However, such differences were not seen by the management respondents as 'major obstacles' and the authors prescribed classic management techniques of incremental change and 'open communication' (Coopers & Lybrand, 1993 p. 24). Our case studies, particularly in the UK, and other commentators (Seys, 1992) suggest that this issue should not be so readily dismissed. In both countries, bank branch staff had to confront a shift away from a deposit-taking mentality. In some cases, this involved a retraining of existing bank employees to sell insurance; in others, it meant recruiting a new type of bank employee, specializing in insurance-selling and in still others it meant the implantation of an insurance company employee in the bank. Each of these strategies sometimes generated conflict primarily because of the differences between the occupational expectations of a bank employee and the role of an insurance salesperson.

   In both countries, banking and insurance have up until recently been very distinctive sectors. Banking has primarily revolved around providing security for money deposits, the provision of money transmission services and the maintenance of loan and credit facilities. Banking institutions have been large bureaucratic organizations offering well-paid, high-status, lifetime careers to their male employees, whilst utilizing a large pool of educated women workers to staff branch networks.[3] Mass banking was predicated on the customer's need for money transmission services. It has become increasingly difficult to participate in social life without a bank account. Indeed, in France, there is a strong preference for using cheques as a method of payment compared to other European countries and almost all households have at least one cheque account

(CREP, 1991). Employers must pay salaries and wages into bank accounts; creditors prefer to be paid directly out of bank accounts and more generally credit facilities are only granted if the individual is shown to be financially worthy which means that a bank account is a *sine qua non* of many economic transactions. Employees in banks have never had to go looking for customers; they have always had plenty. Whether they have had the 'right' customers from the bank's point of view (i.e. 'profitable' customers) is another question and has now become the point of competition as banks compete with each other and other financial institutions (Sturdy and Morgan, 1993). However, until the 1980s, employment in banking was a high-status occupation offering stability of employment and good salaries. Many of the banks' employees therefore entered with a view that what they wanted was a high-status stable career inside a bureaucracy where promotion was based on long service and qualifications.

The selling of insurance, particularly life insurance, requires a different orientation (Morgan and Knights, 1991; Seys, 1992). Whilst there are a number of organizational approaches to this problem, which relate amongst other things to national differences, in broad terms it can be asserted that life insurance sales people have to search out their customers much more actively than is the case with bank employees. This is traditionally associated with a form of payment which is based on commission rather than a fixed salary. Insurance selling *per se* does not therefore constitute part of a career. It tended to be an occupational role which individuals either passed through on their way to something completely different or stayed in for a long time. It was rarely a stepping point up a ladder within the insurance company since here different management and technical skills were required which few sales people had or desired. On the other hand, the 'good' salesperson was driven by monetary incentives to sell as many products as possible.

In broad terms, then, selling insurance products through bank branches risks mixing two very different phenomena; the career-oriented banker with a fixed salary and high status placed alongside the insurance salesperson pursuing customers ruthlessly in order to achieve high levels of commission. However, although these tensions were broadly common to France and Britain, their depth and importance differed considerably. In our case studies in France, they appear to have been more easy to resolve than in Britain. The ability of the French institutions to resolve this problem points to the different nature of the two financial systems in Britain and France.

Differences in Implementation

The key difference which we identified in our case studies was that French banks were able to achieve greater integration of banking and insurance selling than were their British counterparts. This in turn was partly because the insurance products which they sold were not as diverse or different from their banking products as was the case in Britain. Therefore, bank employees did not feel such a great disruption to their roles, skills and remuneration as has been the case in Britain.

In Britain, there appears to have been a two-stage evolution in the selling process. In the first stage, banks set up a specialist insurance sales force. This sales force worked off leads generated for it by bank employees. Sometimes, this sales force was directly located in bank branch offices; in other cases, it worked from its own separate set of offices but came into bank branches to deal with appointments. In all cases, however, the insurance sales force was under the control of a separate sales management team from that of branch employees. Often, sales people were recruited from outside the bank and were offered remuneration packages distinct from branch employees, including high levels of commission. Bank branch staff were deemed to be incapable of selling insurance products to the same level of productivity as would a specialist sales force.

The reasons for this lie in the strong differentiation which had arisen in the British context between banking and insurance products. Banking products until the 1980s primarily consisted of deposit and savings accounts which offered fixed rates of interest. Returns on bank savings were secure, if low. Insurance companies in the UK had however developed a wide range of products. From the late nineteenth century they were offering clients endowment products where savers could benefit from the investment management of their premiums through the receipt of guaranteed bonuses. From the 1960s, products were also developed which transferred the investment risk and gain entirely to the customer. Unit-linked insurance products effectively brought together unit trusts and a life insurance element; any gains or losses made on the units purchased on the client's behalf by the company were passed on to the client. Both endowment and unit-linked products became further differentiated in the 1970s as companies created specialist funds in which the policyholder could invest. Although this was often invisible to the policyholder, wide variations in risk between different types of policy existed on the market. Companies depended on specialist sales forces to sell these products. In theory, this was related to the degree of knowledge required to be familiar with all the different nuances but in practice, the specialist skill was more likely to be necessary because few people wanted to buy the products. A great deal of persistence and sheer selling skill was required to deal with the many rebuffs and low status which the life insurance salesperson had to endure. In order to compensate, companies designed products which would offer high levels of commission to each successful sale. Commissions paid per sale might equal the value of the whole of the first year's premium of a regular insurance policy.

When British banks moved into *bancassurance*, they took on board many of the characteristics which they saw in the existing insurance industry, that is specialist sales force, complex product range and high commissions. They transferred this model almost wholesale and tried to adapt it to working within a bank environment. However, this model creates major problems of coordination. Unlike in traditional insurance companies, where sales people had to find their own customers and were left alone to manage their relationship with the client, in the *bancassurance* model the insurance sales people are dependent on good relations with bank employees since it is from the branches that they get their contacts. Furthermore, relations with the client cannot be just managed by the insurance salesperson since the bank has a vital interest in what is happening to its customer. Yet because the old insurance model was transferred, the remuneration package, career prospects and overall style of approach of the insurance sales people was very different. Bank employees were often resentful of the high earnings and sometimes ostentatiously 'anti-bank' attitudes shown by the sales people. By tacitly withdrawing cooperation, they could effectively sabotage the efforts of sales people to meet customers. Senior bank management responded by tightening controls over bank employees, for example, by creating targets for the number of referrals to the insurance sales people and the amount of insurance business generated by individual branches but even this was not enough to resolve the conflicts.

Therefore, *bancassurance* in Britain appears to be evolving towards a second phase where the salary, status and career differences between bank employees and insurance sales people are reduced. This is part of a broader change in the notion of what a bank is. Increasingly, bank branches are being treated as retailing environments in which the key skill is that of selling to the customer. This has many implications for management and employees. On the remuneration side, and as part of a more general trend in 'human resource management', banks are building in more performance criteria as determinants of salary. Thus, it is not just job position which determines salary but also performance within the position. Relatedly, career advancement is more difficult as hierarchies are 'flattened'. Moreover, banks are no longer able to offer men careers in the expectation that women will effectively 'voluntarily' stand aside when they decide to start a family. Thus competition over careers is increasing and mere seniority is no longer as relevant. Furthermore, the attainment of traditional banking qualifications is no guarantee of advancement. Of increasing importance, here, is the general pressure on costs which all the banks are currently exerting. Closure of uneconomic branches, the switches towards telephone banking and the introduction of more sophisticated ATMs all have implications for the number of employees in branches, the number of hours worked and the type of work undertaken. In sum, expectations of career advancement, lifetime employment and fixed salary levels are all being disrupted. Employees unwilling to work under these conditions are being squeezed out both as a result of the general shrinkage of employment in the banks and as a result of early retirement and voluntary redundancies. Those who are left are being pushed to consider themselves more as part of a retail, selling environment – from a 'teller' to a 'seller' (Burton, 1993). In this sense, they are moving closer towards the insurance salesperson model.

However, from the other direction, the UK banks have learnt some of the lessons of maintaining a strong distinction between insurance sales people and bank branch staff. Most banks are moving away from salaries based entirely on commissions towards a system of salaries plus commission for their sales force. They are also encouraging more career mobility from the bank into the sales force and vice versa. Sales people located in branches are also encouraged to participate more widely in the work of the branch when required. Liaison between branch management and sales force management is also increasing. Sales forces are also becoming better trained as a result of regulatory change and adverse publicity. Regulation also makes it more difficult for sales forces to become entirely focused on sales; duties of 'best advice' and 'know your customer' which are now laid on all sales people in the field of insurance and investment and which have been reinforced by the Training and Competence Initiative imposed by the regulators since 1990 are gradually curbing the worst excesses of high-pressure selling. In this second phase of *bancassurance* in the UK, then, considerable efforts are being made to overcome problems of integration and conflict by bringing bank and insurance staff together.

On the other hand, the British model is still built on the complex differentiation of products, the maintenance of high levels of commission and the general belief in the need for a highly skilled sales force to sell the products. Our French cases, however, suggest another route towards *bancassurance*. Here, the initial impetus towards *bancassurance* was much less disruptive because insurance products have from the start been much more closely integrated into the range of investment and savings products available within the French banking system. There is less 'technical' (i.e., 'banking' or 'insurance') distinction made in the promotion or distribution of products – 'insurance' products tend to be presented and sold as part of the range of savings and investment services, albeit sometimes differentiated in terms of customer groups or segments (Sturdy and Morgan, 1993). Similarly in most cases, the structure and, in particular, the remuneration of sales staff is not strongly differentiated, although separate training or legal authorization is provided for.

The apparent relative ease with which new products were introduced into French bank branches can also be linked to the greater job variety already experienced by staff. In a comparative study of labour flexibility strategies in retail banking, O'Reilly (1992) shows how French branch staff were more 'polyvalent' than in the UK. For example, dealing with foreign exchange and especially large sums of money were not specialized tasks. This difference is explained by reference to the different countries' institutions and business systems. More specifically however, branches in France have emerged as smaller (and more numerous) than in the UK and, since the 1970s, with better security for all cashiers. In addition, staff are generally better educated and have better access to customer data through IT. It is shown how these conditions facilitated the shift towards a more pronounced functional flexibility in France which was part of the state-supported 'commercialization' of the sector and organizational strategies of developing a more integrated service policy (i.e. *bancassurance*) with fewer and more flexible staff (O'Reilly, 1992, p. 230). Thus, as in the UK, *bancassurance* is linked to wider and more general employment practices and strategies.

Notwithstanding the peculiarities of the organization of financial services in both countries, similar occupational culture differences are apparent in France and in the UK. For example, Seys describes the relatively frequent yet impersonal or bureaucratic nature of staff relations with clients and the more numerous, transparent and standardized products in banking which are often 'free' or, at least priced similarly between companies. He contrasts this with the traditional life assurance channels where products were more complex and relations with clients more individualized (Seys, 1992).[4]

Seys documents the problems that integrating such cultures can present and how some banks, such as Crédit Mutuel, initially had a separate insurance counter in the branch. He also noted that there is less potential for resistance from bank branch staff when products are simple and easy to sell (e.g. single premiums). This is borne out in our case studies. Here, in one company an attempt to adopt forms of life assurance practices (e.g. sales commission on insurance products) was reversed with the director responsible subsequently leaving the company. Overall, the remuneration of staff (based primarily or exclusively on a fixed salary) was not linked to an insurance–banking product distinction. Rather, even in one case where sales staff were differentiated by client groups or market segments (and therefore also product types), products were integrated into a range and, for the branch counter staff, were deliberately kept simple in form and training requirements. Whilst there was some evidence of resistance to the change from 'teller to seller', in another case, staff apparently welcomed the opportunity to sell new products as partial relief from existing routines.

It appears then that the French banks have been reluctant to follow traditional insurance sales and marketing approaches, particularly in terms of remuneration. They developed products which competed directly with, but also complemented, those sold by the insurance companies and their agents by offering a simpler and cheaper range of insurance. Their existing bank staff were also more polyvalent and better educated and therefore more able to absorb these new products with little change to their conditions of work. The pricing structure of these products reflected the advantages of mass distribution outlets through branch networks. Thus, they were able to differentiate themselves on price from the products of most of the traditional French insurance companies and certainly the 'rigid and costly' network of tied agents (KPMG, 1989; Zajdlic, 1988).

In Britain on the other hand, the banks have developed a range of products which are indistinguishable from those of the insurance companies. There is no evidence that bank products are any cheaper than those of the insurance companies or that their performance is significantly better (Knights *et al.*, 1993; Morgan, 1994). Rather, bancassurers in Britain simply aim to be average performers, confident that they can attract new customers primarily on the basis of their brand name and their already existing close contact with and information about their clients. On the other hand, the banks have a different cost structure to the insurance companies even though they use the same pricing parameters. The banks have an existing set of resources – their employees and their branch network – which they can now utilize more intensively in order to sell insurance products on a mass basis. Insurance companies have to employ specialist sales people at high levels of commission. The result is that costs per product are likely to be much higher for insurance companies with their own sales force than for banks. Therefore, being an average performer from the point of view of the consumer can conceal the fact that *bancassurance* is a highly profitable operation in Britain.

In conclusion, our case studies identified that whilst there was a common logic to the strategy of *bancassurance*, as well as a range of common problems in Britain and France, there was also an underlying crucial difference. At the level of products and the sales process itself, French *bancassurance* shows a greater integration and stability than is the case in Britain. By developing products more closely related to bank products, the French bancassurers have avoided the worst conflicts which arose in some of our British cases. They differentiated themselves much more clearly from existing insurance practice, often creating new simpler products that could be integrated more quickly into their existing product range with far less disruptive effects on their existing employees.

We would argue that these two routes to *bancassurance* offer distinctive models. In the final section, we consider the implications of this argument.

ACCOUNTING FOR THE DIFFERENCES

Our argument is that the strategy of *bancassurance* cannot be understood simply as a universally applicable model with certain national variations. Instead, we wish to argue that how financial systems develop is integrally related to the business system in which they are located. *Bancassurance* may be a Europe-wide discourse but how it develops and is implemented is shaped by its location within national business systems. Our research is currently concerned with investigating this relationship.

In this chapter, we highlight one core aspect which we believe has been under-represented in these discussions and that is the role which the state and its welfare policies play in the construction of financial institutions. It is well-recognized that through its regulatory role often mediated by semi-independent central bank institutions, the state shapes the development of financial institutions. However, our argument is broader than this in that we believe the way in which specific strategies such as *bancassurance* develop can often be explained, in part at least, by reference to the development of state policies.

To summarize our previous arguments, *bancassurance* in Britain took over the model which had been established in the insurance industry in terms of the range and nature of products and the way in which they should be distributed and sold. Thus the evolution within the UK has been towards trying to create organizational structures and strategies that bridge the divide between banking and insurance. In France, on the other hand, banks developed their own products that could be more easily sold through their existing workforce. The traditional products and distribution channels of French insurance companies were not emulated.

What explains this difference? This is an ongoing question for our research but our general argument would be that this cannot be explained simply at the level of the firm. In other words, we cannot understand these differences solely by examining how managers formulate strategy. Instead, we have to examine the conditions and context of this process of strategy formulation. In particular, the explosion of *bancassurance* in the French case was associated with the attempt of the French state to meet its growing fiscal crisis in the sphere of pension provision. The state sought to stimulate rapid and extensive personal savings. Traditional insurance companies were for a variety of reasons less capable of achieving this whereas banks took the opportunity to move into this market very quickly. In Britain, on the other hand, the insurance companies had long been active in pension schemes. They adapted rapidly to the new challenges and banks followed using very similar products and pricing methods.

The development of *bancassurance* in France since the early 1980s has been almost exclusively based on savings/retirement-based products rather than protection products[5] (for example 59 per cent compared to 2–3 percent of life assurance respectively in 1987) (Bouchaert and Schor, 1988) and is marketed as such. Indeed, capitalization is the second most important type of 'life business' (18 per cent of premium income in 1990) and is classed as insurance, but is a savings plan with no benefit payable on death (Lindisfarne, 1992). Moreover, even today, some banks do not sell any term insurance (i.e. protection-only products) and it is estimated that 95 per cent of *bancassurance* turnover consists of savings-oriented 'insurance policies' (Daniel, 1994). The growing demand for medium- to long-term savings and governments' promotion of these products are associated with the growing ageing population and the associated and increasingly public 'crisis' in the 'pay-as-you-go' pension system which reached a peak with recent reforms. In other words, the government had an urgent need for the expansion of insurance products which could act as means of saving for old age to supplement other benefits. Insurance companies appeared slow to respond, whereas banks, who enjoyed a more positive public image (KPMG, 1989; CREP, 1991) seized the opportunity to develop simple products that could respond to the new opportunities being opened up by the state. It was on the back of these changes that *bancassurance* in France really took off. Clearly, this crisis in funding welfare also existed in Britain (and elsewhere) as did the prescription for its solution, that is, a move towards 'privatization' or individualization of welfare. However, the response in Britain was different as was its impact on the emergence of *bancassurance*. In order to understand this, it is necessary to briefly examine the funding of the welfare state (and in particular, the old age pension system) in both societies (see Morgan *et al.*, 1993, for further discussion of this).

To the outsider at least, the French social welfare system is extremely complex – 'a monumental social labrynth' (Saint-Jours, 1982; p. 142) wherein the precise role of the state is often 'indecipherable' (Ashford, 1982; p. 229). Consequently, our necessarily brief account here of the pensions arrangements and recent reforms is a simplification.

Most of the system is organized around the once fully independent occupational schemes and their, for the most part compulsory, wage-related contributions.[6] These schemes were administered by the 'social partners' of employers and employees (i.e. unions) at regional and national levels. In addition to these contributor representatives, other consultative members were often involved. For example, insurance companies and Friendly Societies might act as advisers or even managers of the funds. The system was based on the 'pay-as-you-go' principle whereby employees' (and employers') contributions were paid more or less directly to the group's retired population rather than invested for the future on their behalf (a 'funded' scheme). This meant that as individual occupations declined in numbers, financing benefits became difficult. As a result, the state became intricately involved in the restructuring or combining of pensions in the postwar period – arranging transfers between funds and acting as a direct provider in some cases (Baldwin, 1990). For example, in 1980, working farmers contributed only 18 per cent of benefits paid (Hantrais, 1982). With the relatively generous levels of payments compared to other countries (for example, up to 70 per cent of final salary: OECD, 1990), the role and financial commitments of the state increased. For example, pensions benefits rose from 6 per cent to 12 per cent of GDP between 1960 and 1988 (*Données Sociales*, 1990).

Perceptions of an impending 'crisis' were augmented by the prediction that the growth of an ageing population would reduce the ratio of contributors to pensioners from 3:1 in 1970 to 2:1 in 2010 (*Libération*, 25 April 1991). Other factors such as increasing early retirement and reducing the retirement age in 1983 exacerbated the situation. Some attempts were made by the government to reduce the costs of pensions. For example, early retirement was discouraged and benefits were offered to employers to recruit older employees. However, significant reform to the pension system itself was a highly sensitive political issue, not least because of the levels of benefits enjoyed. As in other countries, there is a strong public commitment to the social security system overall. For example, in opinion surveys pensions are seen as a basic right (*Libération*, 25 April 1991) and attempts to reform health care have resulted in demonstrations and strong political opposition (*Le Monde*, 13 June 1991). A White Paper was produced in 1991 calling for a year of debate about pension reform and outlining possibilities such as the creation of group funds (company or occupation) based on the 'funded' approach which would complement and perhaps eventually replace existing compulsory and supplementary schemes (*Risques*, 1991). The debate continued into the mid 1990s with banks and insurers in dispute over whether benefits should be in the form of capital or annuities (i.e. payments until death) respectively.

The White Paper also discussed the further promotion of personal savings and pensions through tax incentives. Indeed, given the caution over direct pension scheme reform, this has been the most visible of state actions to reduce its financial commitments. Of course, there is nothing new about a government encouraging savings as part of its economic management. Indeed, this was evident in the mid-1970s and 1980s, with share ownership also being a focus in the latter case. However, of concern here was the removal of tax (5 per cent) on life assurance premiums (and individual pensions) in 1990 although pension benefits remained taxable. Also, and with more impact, the state authorized and gave tax incentives for a 'pension savings plan' (PER) in 1987/8 with multiple or, more often, single premiums for 6–10 years. This was heralded by insurers at the time as a key product in a market lost to them since the (postwar) development of social security (Ruffat *et al.*, 1990). However, this promise was not fulfilled as banks developed a 'near monopoly' (KPMG, 1989) in its distribution. The PER was replaced in 1990 by the 'popular savings plan' (PEP) which was even more successful and marked a shift away from the once dominant 'capitalization' market in life business (FFSA, 1991). The PEP was classified into insurance and financial (no insurance element) forms, both of which were, once again, strongly marketed and adapted by the banks (FFSA, 1991; Sturdy and Morgan, 1993).

It appears then, that the banks have been more successful in taking advantage of the state's encouragement of saving for old age. Given the insurance element of such products, this success has contributed to the growth of *bancassurance*. The reasons for this disparity between institutions are multifarious and require further exploration. Nevertheless, the apparent reluctance or hesitation of the state in directly reforming pensions seems to be significant. While motivated by the pensions 'crisis', the state has encouraged savings rather than pensions or even life assurance specifically. The banks, already experienced and seen as suppliers in this field, have taken advantage of this along with their branch networks and a new 'marketing' approach. They are still reluctant to become involved, or associated with pensions as such. Indeed, given that the savings ratio in France declined between 1977 and 1987 and has only increased 'slightly' since then, it could be argued that the massive growth in life assurance as a percentage of household savings[7] largely reflects a simple substitution in the form of savings amongst the relatively well-off (FFSA, 1991; Bouchaert and Schor, 1988). While it has been estimated from surveys that 40 per cent of life and capitalization contracts are purchased for supplementary retirement income (25 per cent of all life premiums in 1990), historical figures are unavailable and for most people, pensions continue to be associated with the social insurance regimes and, for some, the small number of supplementary 'firm' retirement schemes marketed by insurers (6 per cent of life premiums in 1990: FFSA, 1991).

In Britain, on the other hand, insurance companies had long been more directly involved in the provision of pension schemes. The British welfare state had in some respects a simpler structure than that in France. A state pension was available for all those who had been in paid employment. However, the state pension in the British case was relatively low. In France, the system of pensions consisted of many different mutual funds, backed by the state. Each fund sought to pay a pension commensurate with the employed wage and status of its membership. Thus there was not the same sense of egalitarianism in the French system but rather a communitarianism based on shared occupation and status.

The British system however became hierarchically divided as groups sought to lever themselves above the miserly level of the state pension. For management and white-collar workers, this was achieved through the creation and expansion of company pension schemes (Hannah, 1986). For the self-employed, private pension schemes were developed. In all of these movements, insurance companies played a central role. They calculated the level of contributions necessary and administered the whole system, including the investment management of the funds and the payments to pensioners. Compared to their French counterparts, British insurers were already well-established as the dominant provider in the sphere of pensions when the Conservative government indicated its intention to press for a major expansion of the private pensions system from 1988.

In order to share in the potential bonanza of private pensions, therefore, the British banks had to catch up with the insurers which had, for many years, cooperated closely with the state in providing extra occupational pensions to the better-off. Furthermore, the rules of competition of this territory were already well laid out. In particular, products were designed so that substantial margins were built in. These margins allowed companies to pay their agents high levels of commission to sell products and yet still retain substantial profits. Banks saw no reason to disrupt this system as it offered high profits which were very necessary at this time in order to overcome the massive losses which they had incurred on bad lending. Thus they took on the model of the existing insurance companies and developed their distinctive form of *bancassurance*.

In conclusion, we would argue that it is impossible to understand the differences between the two types of *bancassurance* without understanding their historical and national contexts. French *bancassurance* developed in a particular way because of the apparent weakness of the existing insurers' image and distribution channels, the impetus from the state towards the development of new pensions relaved savings products and of a more market/profit-orientated financial services sector and the nature of the existing bank branch network and labour force. In Britain, *bancassurance* sought to emulate existing insurance companies. In doing so, it generated many problems and conflicts. However, this was all in the context of its ability to grow rapidly and work profitably for the banks.

CONCLUSIONS

It is now very common to identify convergence trends in strategy and structure that are creating European if not global institutions which share many features. Key terms in strategic discourse are readily transferred across national boundaries by many actors, for example, academics, consultants, senior managers and journalists. It is possible to identify many concepts which have gained a worldwide currency as though they can be picked up and utilized by managers wherever they work. In general management theory, terms such as just-in-time, total quality management and business process reengineering are only three of the more recent vogue phrases. The same process goes on at a sector level. Solutions to particular problems become repeated across the world as though they offer a generalized strategic recipe.

These homogenizing tendencies are not to be dismissed as entirely the figments of our imagination but the use of a common language can inhibit as well as enhance understanding. Our research on *bancassurance* leads us to be sceptical of the notion that this is a generic strategy which can be followed in any particular country. On the contrary, our investigation of France and Britain suggests that we can understand far more about these phenomena by investigating their conditions and contexts in more detail. States have shaped financial institutions in order to further their own policy goals, whether these consist of acquiring cheap funds for state ventures or offering safe havens for money and wealth or providing the means for the construction and reconstruction of a system of social welfare. If we wish to understand how strategies evolve in this sector, we need to understand how the state and the social context influences and shapes the choices which senior management takes. Management strategy in *bancassurance* is shaped by its context. Questions of transferring this strategy across different national contexts are more complex than is often assumed. Until more is known about national contexts, any such transfers indicate a naive faith in universalistic prescriptions which is not justified by the evidence.

Notes

1. According to de Boisseau, there were 1524 inhabitants per branch in France compared to 2283 in the UK in the mid-1980s (1990, p. 193).
2. In addition to these major banks, there are several networks of medium-sized banks which are legally autonomous but federated by a central body. There are examples of insurance companies associated with these networks but the regional banks are under no obligation to deal with them. The clearest example is that of Fructivie which works with the Banques Populaires. There is also the particular case of an insurance company, GAN, owning a bank, Crédit Industriel et Commercial (CIC) which is in fact made up of 14 independent regional banks. Our study concentrates on the large national banks and their move into *bancassurance*.
3. The historical evolution of the gender composition of bank labour forces has been extensively studied (see, for example, O'Reilly, 1992).

4. In 1990, these channels accounted for 55 per cent of life assurance business – 25 per cent from company sales forces, 18 per cent from self-employed tied agents and 11 per cent from non-tied brokers (FFSA, 1991).
5. Protection products are those which only pay out on the death of the policy-holder. There is no savings element involved.
6. The role of private pensions has traditionally been very limited in France. Similarly social assistance provided directly by the state out of taxation has had limited importance.
7. It rose from 9.8 per cent in 1980 to 46.2 per cent in 1990 with both liquid assets and shares and bonds declining accordingly. However, this dominance is predicted to decline with the growth of non-insurance PEPs and unit trusts ('UCITS') (FFSA, 1991).

References

AFB, *L'Europe en Vue – Rapport Annuel*. (Paris: Association Française des Banques, 1991).

D.E. Ashford, *Policy and Politics in France: Living With Uncertainty*. (Philadelphia Pennsylvania: Temple University Press, 1982).

P. Baldwin, *The Politics of Social Solidarity*. (Cambridge: Cambridge University Press, 1990).

C. de Boisseau, 'The French Banking Sector in the Light of European Financial Integration', in J. Dermine (ed.), *European Banking in the 1990s*. (Oxford: Blackwell, 1990).

H. Bouchaert and A.D. Schor, *'Les Sociétés d'Assurance en France'*, No. 4875. (Paris: La Documentation Française, 1988).

D. Burton, 'Tellers into Sellers?', *International Journal of Bank Marketing*, 9, 6 (1991) pp. 25–9.

D. Burton, *Financial Services and the Consumer*. (London: Routledge, 1993).

P.G. Cerny, 'From Dirigisme to Deregulation? The Case of Financial Markets', in P. Godt (ed.) *Policy Making in France*. (London: Pinter, 1989).

Coopers & Lybrand, *Making Bancassurance Work*. (London: Coopers & Lybrand, 1993).

Centre de Recheche d'Epargne, *Money As They Like It – Europeans' View of Financial Products*. (Paris: CREP.OPENERS SECODIP, 1991).

J.-P. Daniel, *La Bancassurance*. (Paris: Editions de Verneuil, 1992a).

J.-P. Daniel, 'Boudda et Confucius – Même Combat Contre Sainte Barbe?', *Directions*, 12, June (1992b) pp. 24–5.

J.-P. Daniel, *Les Enjeux de la Bancassurance*. (Paris: Editions de Verneuil, 1994).

Données Sociales (Paris: INSEE, 1990).

Economist, The Economist Guides – France. (London: The Economist, 1990).

C. Ennew, T. Watkins and M. Wright, 'The New Competition in Financial Services', *Long Range Planning*, 23, 6 (1990) pp. 80–90.

Ernst & Young, *Insurance in the EC – An Industry Overview*, 2nd edn. (London: Ernst & Young, 1989).

FFSA, *French Insurance in 1990* (English translation). (Paris: Fédération Française des Sociétés d'Assurances, 1991).

L. Hannah, *Inventing Retirement*. (London: Macmillan, 1986).

L. Hantrais, *Contemporary French Society*. (London: Macmillan, 1982).

B. Howcroft, 'Increased Marketing Orientation: UK Bank Branch Networks', *International Journal of Bank Marketing*, 9, 4 (1991) pp. 3–9.

D. Knights, G. Morgan and A. Sturdy, 'Quality for the Consumer in Bancassurance?', *Consumer Policy Review*, 3, 4 (1993) pp. 232–40.

KPMG, *Deadline 1992: France*. (London: KPMG, 1989).

I. Lindisfarne, 'C'est La Vie', *Post Magazine*, 15 October (1992) pp. 26–9.

H. Mendras and A. Cole, *Social Change in Modern France*. (Cambridge: CUP, 1991).

G. Morgan, 'Regulation in Personal Financial Services', mimeo, Manchester Business School (1994).

G. Morgan and D. Knights, 'Gendering Jobs: Corporate Strategy, Managerial Control and the Dynamics of Job Segregation', *Work, Employment and Society*, 5, 2 (1991) pp. 181–200.

G. Morgan, A. Sturdy and D. Knights, 'Business Systems and the Welfare State: The Provision of Old Age Pensions', paper presented to European Business Systems Group, Helsinki, March (1993).

G. Morgan, A. Sturdy, J.-P. Daniel and D. Knights, 'Bancassurance in Britain and France: Innovating Strategies in the Financial Services', *The Geneva Papers on Risk and Insurance*, 71, April (1994) pp. 178–95.

OECD, *OECD Economic Surveys – France*. (Paris: OECD, 1990).

J. O'Reilly, 'The Societal Construction of Labour Flexibility – Employment Strategies in Retail Banking in Britain and France', in R.D. Whitley (ed.), *European Business Systems*. (London: Sage, 1992).

A. Rawsthorn, 'Debate Over Role Models', *Financial Times, European Finance and Investment, France Supplement*, 12 December (1991).

Risques, 'Assurer L'Avenir des Retraites', special issue, May (1991).

M. Ruffat, E.-V. Caloni and B. Laguerre, *L'UAP et l'Histoire de L'Assurance*. (Paris: Maison des Sciences de l'Homme, 1990).

Y. Saint-Jours, 'France', in P.A. Köhler and H.F. Zacher (eds), *The Evolution of Social Insurance 1881–1981*. (London: Frances Pinter, 1982).

Salomon Bros, *Multinational Money Center Banking: The Evolution of a Single European Banking Market*. (London: Salomon Bros, 1990).

J.-C. Seys, 'Comment Surmonter les différences culturelles entre les deux professions?', in EFMA conference proceedings Banque–Assurance–Après les Illusions, Les Vraies Synergies, (Paris: EFMA/CAPA, 1992).

B. Stephenson and J. Kiely, 'Success in Selling The Current Challenge in Banking', *International Journal of Bank Marketing*, 9, 2 (1991) pp. 30–8.

A. Sturdy and D. Knights, 'The Subjectivity of Segmentation and the Segmentation of Subjectivity', in S.R. Clegg and G. Palmer (eds), *Constituting Management: Markets Meanings and Identities*. (Berlin: DeGruyter, 1996).

A. Sturdy and G. Morgan, 'Segmenting the Market: A Review of Marketing Trends in French Retail Banking', *International Journal of Bank Marketing*, 11, 7 (1993) pp. 11–19.

D. Thwaites, 'Forces at Work: The Market for Personal Financial Services', *International Journal of Bank Marketing*, 9, 6 (1991) pp. 30–5.

W. Zajdlic, *Longman International Insurance Reports: France*. (Harlow: Longman, 1988).

8 The Swedish Banking Crisis: The Invisible Hand Shaking the Visible Hand

Lars Engwall

INTRODUCTION

In many countries the 1980s brought radical changes to the banking industry in two ways that affected working conditions: (1) the development of computer and communication technology, and (2) deregulation. Whereas the first of these can be described as a rapid but fairly continuous process, the second was more in the nature of a single episode. In a sense it can be seen as a huge field experiment, in which the basic rules of the game were suddenly switched from one system to another. Speaking in metaphors we could say that the invisible hand, introduced into economic theory in 1776 by Adam Smith in the *Wealth of Nations*, had long been pinioned but was suddenly released. This in turn put considerable pressure on bank managers to adapt to the new conditions. Extending the metaphor we could then say that the visible hand, Alfred D. Chandler's term for management (Chandler, 1977), has been shaken by the invisible hand.

However, it cannot be claimed that the invisible hand has immediately led the Swedish financial market towards a new market equilibrium. Instead the market found itself in a very delicate situation, which meant that in the early 1990s many banks found themselves in great difficulties and the whole system was close to collapse. This in turn has led some observers to ask how such a thing could happen. Several explanations have also been provided. One refers to developments on the property market, to the speculative turn which this market took, and to the sudden dramatic decline in inflation (see, for example, Hjalmarsson, 1993). A second invokes the bad timing of the deregulation in relation to the Swedish tax reform. A third, often voiced in the media, places the whole responsibility on the banks' top managers. But, although it would have seemed fairly natural, few have adopted an organizational approach to analysing the Swedish banking crisis. Such a route will therefore be taken in the present chapter. In order to set the scene the following section will briefly describe the regulatory system and the changes which have been made to it. Then, following a summary of the structure of the industry, explanations of the crisis will be sought in data on the overall employment structure of the industry and the formal organization of the main actors. This evidence will then be used as a basis for some general conclusions.

RESTRICTIONS ON THE INVISIBLE HAND

Legislation

The development of the Swedish banking industry has been governed by legislation which has varied in character over time. Swedish banking legislation, like that of other countries, such as the United States (see Sinkey, 1986, p. 143), has thus exhibited patterns of 'regulation cycles'. This in turn can be seen as a good illustration of the point made in Cyert and March (1963) that organizations operate according to the principles of a fire brigade, that is, that they only act in response to arising problems. Throughout its history the Swedish banking system can be said to have experienced regulated entries into and exits out of the industry.

The first banking law appeared in 1824, and regulated the conditions under which joint stock banks with unlimited liability could be founded.[1] After legislation regarding the foundation of joint stock bank companies (1848) and branch banks (1851), opportunities were created by the Bank Reform Act of 1863 for a free market for capital within the banking system.[2] By 1869 there were 38 banks in Sweden, and the number continued to rise successively under this liberal system to 83 in 1909. However, in 1911 a stricter banking law was introduced, aimed at *promoting the concentration* of the banking industry. As a result the number of commercial banks in Sweden declined quite dramatically: by the end of the 1910s the number was down to 43 and by the end of the 1920s to 30, respectively. As a result new legislation was introduced in 1919, now with a view to *impeding the concentration* of the Swedish banking industry. However, the world economic crisis of 1929–32 also reached Sweden, where its most dramatic effect was the crash of a conglomerate created by Ivar Kreuger around Swedish Match. The financial turmoil following this event led to legislation in the early 1930s imposing new restrictions on the banks. This legislation has by and large governed the Swedish banking market ever since. Later changes included a new banking law in 1987, which was less specific on the rights to delegate decisions to lower levels within the banks. As regards entry into the industry, the main change involved permission for foreign banks to open subsidiaries in Sweden (1985), and later for them to open branches (1990).

Regulation

In addition to the legislation described above, the Swedish banks have also been governed by a number of other measures restricting their operations: liquidity quotas, interest controls, credit limits and currency controls. All this meant that many strategic decisions were not taken by the banks themselves, but by the Ministry of Finance or the Central Bank. The leaders of the Central Bank in particular seem to have imposed a strict regime on the banks' top managers, quite often treating them like a group of pupils up before the headmaster (see Jonung, 1993).

In the late 1970s and during the 1980s the international wave of deregulation, which emanated largely from the United States (see, for example, Carlson, 1990), also reached Sweden. Measures affecting banking activities included the removal of interest rate controls on deposit accounts in 1978, of liquidity quotas in 1983, of interest rate controls on loans and limits on SEK lending in 1985, and of currency controls in 1989 (Lybeck, 1992, p. 191).

This gradual process does not seem to have been politically controversial to any noticeable extent. There were some critical comments from the Federation of Labour (Hadenius and Söderhjelm, 1994, p. 32), but the overall impression is that these deregulation measures, introduced by a Social Democratic government, were generally accepted as unavoidable.

Of the deregulation measures, those introduced in the mid-1980s were probably the most important. The removal of limits on lending was particularly significant. As a result the volume of lending grew rapidly in the late 1980s from 80 per cent of GNP in 1985 to 140 per cent in 1990 (Bankstödsnämnden, 1994, p. 4).[3] To a significant degree this expansion took place outside the banks, by way of loans from other credit institutions. However, on average the credit volume of the Swedish banks in the period 1985–9 grew by about 17 per cent annually (Pettersson, 1993, p. 199).

Supervision

Until 1907 the operations of the Swedish banks were supervised by the Ministry of Finance through the agency of a special office. Following a parliamentary initiative in 1905, the tasks of this office were taken over by a new independent body, the Royal Bank Inspection Board (Kungl. Bankinspektionen).[4] This board was merged in the 1960s with the corresponding body inspecting the savings banks (Sparbanksinspektionen). In 1991 with reference to the deregulated environment an integrated financial supervisory authority (Finansinspektionen) was created through still another merger, this time between the Bank Inspection Board and the corresponding body supervising insurance companies (Försäkringsinspektionen).

Needless to say the power of the bank inspectors seems to have been related to the intentions of the current legislation. In restrictive times their authority appears to have been stronger than during periods of more liberal legislation, and vice versa. However, under all circumstances the board has been in a difficult position. In relatively problem-free periods the board has been criticized for intervening too much, but when the problems pile up it has been accused of not doing enough.[5]

During the 1980s the Bank Inspection Board was first headed by a Director General, a lawyer who had been in office since 1971. He had been quite active in his role as bank supervisor, and had several times questioned moves made by the banks. In mid-1986, when the deregulation process was in full swing, he retired and was succeeded by another lawyer. The new DG, a highly trusted civil servant with three earlier appointments as Director General, did not however have any previous banking experience – a fact which led some bankers to feel that the government did not take the problems of the banking industry seriously. His tenure, which lasted until 1990, was dominated by a focus on ethical issues such as tax evasion and insider trading, and fees for banking services. This orientation did not find favour with his successor, who came from a post as Deputy Director of the Swedish Central Bank. Rather, in March 1990 he called attention to the risks involved in the failure of a bank or a finance company. Eight months later his fears were confirmed as a large finance company crashed. This was only the beginning of the financial crisis in Sweden.[6] However, before turning to this subject, we should first take a closer look at the industry and its actors.

THE VISIBLE HANDS

In 1990 the banking structure resulting from the framework described above included eleven commercial banks, which could be divided in principle into four groups (see, for example, Pettersson, 1993, p. 199): three large nationally operating banks (SE-Banken, Svenska Handelsbanken and PK-Banken), two medium-sized banks (*Gotabanken* and *Nordbanken*), four provincial banks (Skånska Banken, Skaraborgsbanken, Wermlands-banken and Östgöta Enskilda Bank) and two small 'niche' banks (Bohusbanken and JP Bank). In the period 1990–94, further consolidation has taken place.

The largest in the first group was the Wallenberg bank *SE-banken* (SEB), created by a merger in 1972 between Stockholms Enskilda Bank (founded in 1856) and Skandinaviska Banken (founded in 1864). It has long-standing relations with the major Swedish corporations.[7]

Second to SEB in size, but for many years more profitable than its larger competitor, was Svenska Handelsbanken (SHB). This bank was founded in 1871 by some directors leaving Stockholms Enskilda Bank. Like SEB it has gradually extended its presence throughout the country during the present century by acquiring local banks (see Hildebrand, 1971). The latest acquisition, in 1991, was one of the few then remaining regional banks, Skånska Banken. SHB also maintains close relations with a number of large Swedish industrial companies.

The third of the banks operating nationally was·PK-banken (PKB), created in 1949 after a parliamentary decision aimed at providing a state-owned alternative to the private banks. In 1972 this bank also came to include the banking operations of the Swedish Post Office, thus generating the name PK-banken (i.e. Post and Credit Bank). In 1990 this bank expanded further by acquiring one of the medium-sized banks, Nord-banken, which was itself the result of a merger in 1986 between two regional banks (Sundsvallsbanken and Uplandsbanken). The new bank even took over the name of the bank it had acquired.

The other medium-sized bank, Götabanken, also eventually became part of a bigger actor, the Gota Group, after merging with two regional banks, Wermlandsbanken and Skaraborgsbanken, in 1990. This deal was part of a project for creating a 'strong financial organization suited to meeting changes that have occurred and continue to occur on the financial markets' (*Annual Report of Skaraborgsbanken 1989*, p. 4, my translation). In addition to these three banks, the group included a finance company and a stockbroker. As a result of the Gota deal and the above-mentioned SHB acquisition of Skånska banken, only one of the regional banks, Östgöta Enskilda Bank, still exists as such in 1994. Similarly, the two small 'niche' banks were acquired in the early 1990s.

In addition to the Swedish commercial banks mentioned above, a dozen foreign banks established subsidiaries in the country in 1986 as the barriers to entry were lifted. In the late 1980s five of these withdrew and one other entered the Swedish market, thus leaving eight foreign banks in 1990. Their significance in the Swedish banking market has so far been limited. At the end of 1987 they accounted for only 3 per cent of the total assets in the industry (Johnsen, 1990, p. 99).[8] Another feature of the Swedish banking system is the large number of savings banks (116 in 1987: Thunholm, 1989, p. 108), and rural credit associations (388 in 1987: Thunholm, 1989, p. 121). Originally locally established, they have undergone a merger process similar to that of the commercial banks, albeit later. For the savings banks this culminated in the merger of eleven of the largest savings banks to create Sparbanken Sverige (Savings Bank Sweden) in 1992.[9] A similar restructuring also occurred among the rural credit associations, which were merged into Sveriges Föreningsbank in 1991. A year later this bank changed from cooperative ownership to become a joint stock company.[10]

SHAKING HANDS

For a long time Swedish banks had had very limited credit losses, and had even been accused of too great an aversion to risk. However, an increase in the losses from SEK 21 million in 1974 to SEK 1.6 billion in 1984 (*Veckans affärer*, 17 October 1985) silenced that criticism. It has now also become apparent that the losses of the 1980s were not the end of their troubles. In 1992 all Swedish banks showed deficits, while their joint reserves against credit losses had grown from SEK 12 billion in 1990 and SEK 36 billion in 1991 to SEK 74 billion in 1992 (Dahlheim, Lind and Nedersjö, 1993, pp. 25–6). A similar pattern was exhibited by unsettled credits, which almost doubled during 1992 from SEK 100 billion to SEK 197 billion (ibid., p. 29).

The foundations of these credit losses seem to have been laid in the later 1980s, when the above-mentioned credit expansion occurred. It can also be noted that some of the banks were more expansive than others; the most expansive increased its credit volume by 38 per cent per year. As can be seen from Figure 8.1, this credit growth left most of the expanding banks with customers who turned out to be the cause of losses.[11]

The patterns obtaining in the late 1980s persisted in the early 1990s. If losses are related to total loans, we find in principle three groups: Svenska Handelsbanken and SE-Banken in a lower group, Föreningsbanken and Sparbanken Sverige in a medium group, and Nordbanken and Gota Bank in a high-loss group (Table 8.1). In terms of the sources of the losses it is clear that the dominant part of the losses came from corporate lending. Only about one-tenth of the losses thus had its origin among household customers. Among the corporate customers it was particularly companies

Figure 8.1　Credit losses as a function of credit expansion in Swedish banks, 1985–9

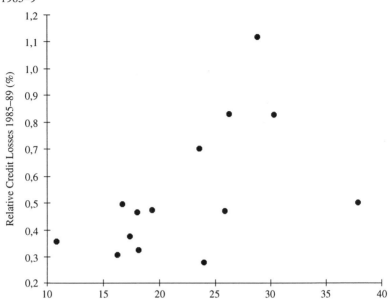

Source:　Data from Pettersson (1993, p. 199).

associated with financing and the building industry which turned out to be bad risks. Some few very large business failures were especially important for the development of the Swedish banking crisis.[12]

As a result of the credit losses all the big banks except one (SHB) started negotiations with the Ministry of Finance in order to secure their long-term survival. A special government body (Bankstödsnämnden) was created to provide state support for the troubled banks, and thus to guarantee the Swedish banking system. Several of the banks were by then under new managements, which were working on programmes of restructuring; among other things these included the creation of 'bad banks', that is, banks to which all the bad loans of the parent bank are transferred. These measures, in combination with a dramatic decline in interest rates during 1993, eventually improved the situation of the banks, and market solutions were found for the long-term financing of the troubled banks.

Table 8.1   Credit losses in the largest Swedish banks, 1991 and 1992

	Credit losses (SEK billion)		Loans (SEK billion)		Losses in per cent of loans	
Year	1991	1992	1991	1992	1991	1992
SHB	3.2	8.0	264.0	266.2	1.2	3.0
SEB	4.8	11.2	314.7	328.7	1.5	3.4
FB	2.8	3.5	97.3	85.1	2.9	4.1
SB	10.2	18.5	417.4	410.0	2.4	4.5
NB	10.5	19.3	246.0	249.0	4.3	7.8
GB	3.7	12.5	74.0	78.1	5.0	16.0
Summa	35.2	73.0	1413.4	1417.1	2.5	5.2

Source: Data from Finansinspektionen reported in Larsson (1993).

THE STRUCTURE OF THE VISIBLE HANDS

The Overall Employment Structure

A first natural step in analysing the development of the banks is to look at the employment structure of the industry as a whole.[13] In the case of the Swedish banks this is quite possible, since salary statistics include information about type of job, job requirements, education, and so on. Since the principles for these statistics were changed in 1983, the analysis has been limited to the period 1983–90. From this material we can see that the total number of bank employees increased by 29 per cent in the relevant period, from 40 685 to 52 621. A particularly marked increase by more than 7 per cent occurred after the deregulation, that is, between 1986 and 1987 (Figure 8.2).

An examination of the four main groups of Swedish bank employees – Commercial, Administrative, Accounting and Miscellaneous – for the period 1983–90 shows that these account for 75 per cent, 10 per cent, 10 per cent and 5 per cent respectively. The largest of the four groups, *Commercial*, has grown at about the same rate as the total population of bank employees (29 per cent). However, in connection with the banking

Figure 8.2   Total number of bank employees, 1983–90

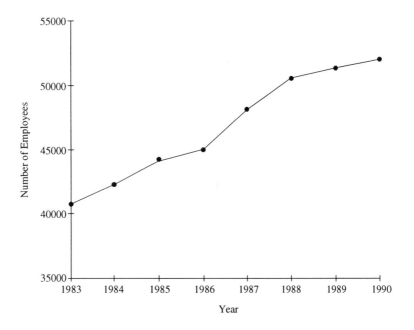

Source: Löner för banktjänstemän. Gemensam Lönestatistik, 1983–90.

crisis one feature in particular should be mentioned. Two subgroups, marketing and advertising, increased at a much faster rate, that is, 65 and 118 per cent respectively.

Although the number employed in these two categories is relatively small, the growth in their numbers is nevertheless interesting, since through their positions at head office they may have had considerable influence on the thinking in the banks. While noting this, it should also be pointed out that during the 1980s marketing efforts took a new turn. Although marketing was not new to the banks (see Persson, 1994), earlier efforts had been directed mainly at depositors. During the 1980s, on the other hand, banks were eager to attract borrowers.

Even in the second group, *Administration*, an increase in one particular group, computer-related activities, can be noted. This is of course a natural result of the development of modern computer and communication technology, and of the banks' efforts to exploit these tools.

Figure 8.3   Number of bank employees involved in marketing and auditing, 1983–90

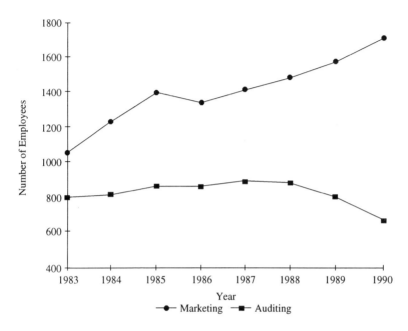

Source: Löner för banktjänstemän. Gemensam Lönestatistik, 1983–90.

In the third group, *Accounting*, a decrease in one subgroup is worth noting, namely a drop of 12 per cent in the number of people working in auditing and reviews. This is particularly interesting in relation to the above-mentioned increase in marketing activities, and it nicely illustrates the change in mood in the Swedish banking industry. As shown in Figure 8.3, the gap between the groups increased considerably in the late 1980s. In 1983 the number of people involved in marketing was 30 per cent higher than the number in auditing. In 1990 the corresponding figure was 150 per cent.

Of course it can be argued that banks tended to use outsiders and computer systems to an increasing extent to handle auditing. However, it should also be remembered that the volumes requiring audit increased dramatically in the late 1980s, something which should have called for more people in auditing. Support for such a view is also provided by a report from the Financial Inspection Board in February 1994, which points at 'serious breaches of the authority granted by authorities in credit instructions and deficiencies in the internal control regarding decision procedures, risk handling and follow-up' (Finansinspektionen, 15 February 1994).

Finally, in the fourth relatively limited group, *Miscellaneous*, the increase in the number of employees involved in educational activities in connection with the deregulation is specially interesting. This group increased by 38 per cent, again particularly between 1986 and 1987 when there was a 10.2 per cent rise, compared to the average of 3.8 per cent.

These changes in employment structure were associated with a move upwards in the average qualification level, from 6.0 in 1983 to 5.7 in 1990.[14] Behind this change we may note a growing share of employees working with more general handling rules (level 5 and 6) instead of standardized rules (level 7). This in turn can be seen as a result of the banks' ambition to entrust routine transactions to customers, and to let employees do more work on the consultation side.[15]

The above-mentioned changes in employee structure and in qualification requirements are of course closely related to the banks' recruitment policies. And, in this connection, it may be noted that banks have traditionally tended to recruit their employees young, and then to increase their competence successively by on-the-job training and internal education (see, for example, Hildebrandt, 1993; McMurry, 1958; and Remitz, 1960).

In the new climate the banks may well have asked themselves whether this would still be an appropriate strategy in the future. One reaction has been to increase internal education, something to which the increasing number of employees involved in such activities already bears witness (see above).[16] However, they may also have asked themselves whether this was enough. For it can be argued (1) that education takes time, particularly when long-time employees are expected to learn new behaviour, and (2) that it interferes with day-to-day business operations. An alternative reaction then is to recruit better-educated people. This creates another problem, however, that such recruits are not sufficiently familiar with banking.

A study of the educational background of Swedish bank employees also supports the supposition that more employees with a longer education behind them were actually taken on. Between 1983 and 1990 the share of employees with academic degrees thus increased from 10 to 15 per cent, and the share who had spent three years at grammar school rose from 31 to 36 per cent. This in turn implied that the average educational level had gone up, particularly during the period of deregulation, from 2.34 in 1983 to 2.50 in 1990.[17] It has also resulted in a rise in the median age from 38 to 40 years in the period studied.

All in all we have thus observed a number of features which may be interpreted as responses to the changing working conditions in the banks, and which may be connected with the banking crisis. We have noted a greater number of employees involved in marketing activities and computer support, while the number involved in internal auditing has declined. We have also seen a rise in educational activities and a tendency to recruit employees with a higher level of education than before. These figures are of course no proofs of a direct link between recruitment policy and corporate performance. However, it does not seem unlikely that the increased emphasis on marketing, the deemphasis of control and the hiring of people without banking experience provided prerequisites for a less traditional banking behaviour.

Formal Organization

A second step in our analysis is to look at the formal organizational design of the major actors. Here we find that a dominant organizational principle has been that of geographical differentiation. This has been most consistently developed in SHB, which since the early 1970s has been operating through eight regional banks within a decentralized structure. Its main competitor, SEB, has traditionally worked with three different head offices in the three largest Swedish cities – Stockholm, Gothenburg and Malmö – each one with its own president. During the 1980s these were augmented by certain other functions. After the crisis of the early 1990s the number of presidents was reduced to one.

The third of the large banks (PKB/NB) also entered the 1980s with an organization based on regions. However, in 1986, in the wake of the various deregulations, the bank chose a product-based divisionalization structure instead. There was one division for private customers and another for corporate customers, each with its own president. However, this type of organization, which had been used earlier by Citicorp in the United States and had probably been introduced into Sweden by consultants, turned out to have general drawbacks. A study of PKB/NB found that this type of organization led to a lack of community between the divisions, which was bad for the bank as a whole. It pointed out in particular that the selling culture which dominated the Private Division was transferred to the Corporate Division, 'where the incorrect "sale" of a credit may cause a loss of several million' (Rydbeck, 1993, pp. 113–14, my translation).

Tendencies similar to those observed in PKB/NB seem to have appeared in GB,the fourth of the Swedish commercial banking groups, as well. In this case, too, aggressive marketing seems to have been a significant factor behind the bank's problems. For instance, in 1988 one of the banks in the merger, Götabanken, launched a campaign called 'The Big Lift', with a view to attracting medium-sized firms as customers. However, the bank's subsequent credit losses seem to suggest that these new customers should rather have been labelled 'The Big Load': in the 1990s over 90 per cent of the large credit losses (see Table 8.1) came from the business segment of the bank's operations.

Turning to the savings banks, we find that a number of the bad loans had been given by the individual banks before the creation of Sparbanken Sverige. However, it seems that many of these were the result of trying to expand outside the traditional customer groups. This applied particularly to Första Sparbanken, which had been created by a merger between two savings banks in Stockholm and one in Gothenburg. Interestingly enough this bank, in addition to having one president in Stockholm and another in Gothenburg, also happened to choose the product-based divisionalized structure like the one adopted by PKB/NB. This also seems to have had the same negative effect in Första Sparbanken as in PKB/NB.[18]

As far as Föreningsbanken is concerned, the merger of the 331 local rural credit associations in 1991 involved heavy centralization, which meant that the bank came to resemble the commercial banks more closely, with among other things a joint balance sheet. Like the savings banks it also suffered from growing credit losses as a result of expanding into new customer segments. Thus the traditional customers of the bank, that is, farmers, did not account for any great part of the credit losses. Instead a considerable share of the losses came from loans granted to companies in the construction and real estate industries.[19]

Thus an examination of the formal organization of the banks reveals evidence that their activities were governed by marketing efforts and competition between different units. They all seem to have had decentralized structures, developed to a greater or lesser extent. One of the maxims in Peters and Waterman (1982) – about getting close to the customer – thus seems to have been taken to heart by the main actors. They even appear to have mimicked each other to no small extent.

However, if they all had decentralized structures, it seems appropriate to ask why some of them performed better than others. Looking at the two extreme cases in Table 8.1 above, PKB/NB and GB, we note first of all that these two banks were the result of mergers of considerable magnitude. Needless to say such a background is likely to have created special difficulties when it came to controlling operations.[20] Second, both were very aggressive in their marketing, eager to become major players on a par with SEB and SHB. This in turn seems to have contributed to certain deficiencies in the internal control procedures. Studies of the two banks made by a lawyer (Rydbeck, 1993, 1994) suggest that these procedures left much to be desired. In the case of PKB/NB, Rydbeck notes that the members of the credit committee and the board had very limited material on which to base their decisions. The credits which were later the cause of great problems to the banks had often not been discussed at board meetings until the problems had become obvious (Rydbeck, 1993, pp. 39–40). It is also evident that the decentralization of decision-making was going too far, giving too much power to the heads of the regional banks. Further, there was heavy emphasis on selling with the use of 'revenue–cost ratios'. The intention was to keep these ratios as high as possible, that is, to achieve high revenues at low cost. However, it turned out that the numerator and denominator were both far from certain. The revenues from many deals shrank as interests remained unpaid, while the costs grew as credit losses loomed.

In GB the problems seem to have been even worse, due to the custom of providing notification to customers in advance, based on a joint decision of the Chairman of the Board, the President and the heads of the regions. In 1990 as much as two-thirds of the limit increases of a total of SEK 33 billion were of this kind (Rydbeck, 1994, p. 22). This type of behaviour was part of a general corporate culture, which according to the American consultancy firm Arthur Andersen (1992, p. 7) contained the following themes:

- focus on growth, profitability and cost reduction
- inappropriate and inadequate consideration of risk
- motivation through sales promotions and personnel incentives
- decentralization and regional autonomy
- deemphasis of documentation and control
- belief in continued property value increases

The same source particularly emphasizes the weaknesses of the internal control system, which in turn was reinforced, among other things, by a 'lack of adequately skilled and trained personnel' and the fact that 'internal audit were not allowed access to the overall group, nor did internal audit feel that appropriate action was taken to correct the problems noted' (ibid., p. 8).

We can thus conclude that in terms of formal structure, too, there were signs similar to those observed in connection with the employment structure, namely a shift from control to marketing and selling. The idea of the ancient banking institutions becoming modern and resembling industrial corporations more closely seems to have made a deep impact. How this came about will be the subject of the following section.

THE SOCIALLY CONSTRUCTED INVISIBLE HAND

A basic idea behind the deregulation of the Swedish banking industry was that competition would increase efficiency in the system. Lending rates would come down and projects which had previously been refused financing would be given a chance to get off the ground. The Visible Hand of the regulators would be replaced by the Invisible Hand of the market. However, this whole idea was based on a few assumptions which turned out not to have been appropriate.

First of all, even after deregulation the Swedish banking industry was a far from perfect market. As we have seen, it consisted of a small number of identifiable units, whose managements were able to watch each other's behaviour. And, in an uncertain situation such as a period of deregulation when it is particularly difficult to grasp cause-and-effect relationships, it is very natural to do what your competitors do. Thus, following Berger and Luckmann (1966), we can say that the invisible hand was socially constructed by interactions between the main actors. We could even argue that the organizational field of Swedish banking was governed by something that could be termed *organizational stress*, that is, the managements of the different organizations were unable to maintain a cool attitude to events, but were drawn into a speculative mode by watching their competitors. This seems to have been the case, to a greater or lesser extent, at all levels in the banks, that is, at the local, the regional and the national level. Bank managers saw their colleagues chasing customers and felt forced to do likewise. And any sceptics, on the boards for instance, had difficulty in getting support (see, for example, Rydbeck, 1993, p. 112).

This copy-cat behaviour also appears to have been reinforced by the very people who were supposed to provide a critical scrutiny, namely the journalists. Thus Hadenius and Söderhjelm (1994) analysed the coverage of the banking industry in the Stockholm dailies and three business newspapers between 1984 and 1990, and provided evidence that similar mimetic behaviour does occur in the media. To a considerable extent journalists have followed one another, uncritically permitting the actors in the financial service industry to tell their own story. This coverage was then read by bank managers and bank employees, who found in it confirmation of their socially constructed view of the invisible hand.

And the source of this copy-cat behaviour was the same in the media as in the banking system: in concentrated markets actors feel compelled to watch each other and to match each other's actions. This conclusion is consistent with the findings of other studies of newspaper markets (see Engwall, 1981, 1986), which point to the fact that even as regards the choice of news to be covered, newspapers tend to follow one another. In the banking crisis this was especially noticeable in connection with the top managers of the banks, particularly the two expansive banks PKB/NB and GB, who were presented in a heroic light. Comprehensive critical analysis was rare.[21]

Second, the advocates of deregulation seem to have overlooked a special feature of banking, namely its technology and in particular the liquid character of its product. The assumption seems to have been that the selling of a loan has the same characteristics as the selling of a consumer good such as a vacuum cleaner. However, there is one important difference between the two activities. While the vendor of a vacuum cleaner does not usually see the product again after the sale, the banker is supposed to get his product back again after an agreed time. This calls for quite a different approach to the screening of customers, in order to find out whether this will in fact happen. And here the banker faces what economists usually refer to as asymmetric information (see, for example, Akerlof, 1970), that is, that the borrower knows more about his own situation than the lender does. Needless to say this is also one explanation of the tradition of long-term relationships in banking (Engwall and Johanson, 1990), since such relations tend to create trust and to reduce considerably the asymmetry of information.[22]

Third, the deregulators seem to have overlooked research findings from the time of March and Simon (1958), Cyert and March (1963) and March and Olsen (1976) onwards, which have highlighted the importance of bounded rationality in decision-making. This is a valid point in the case of individuals in relatively stable situations, and it becomes even more potent when groups of actors have to interact and the context for their interaction is undergoing radical change. This was the situation during the period of deregulation, and weaknesses on two fronts appeared: the learning of new behaviour was too hasty, and employees with too little experience of banking were being taken on. In other words older employees had to unlearn control and adopt a focus on marketing, while new recruits were trained in marketing but knew little about control.

Our limited human ability to handle information adequately is well-illustrated by Swedish banking history, in that this latest crisis was not the first one. Much earlier evidence was available. In Sweden there had been similar crises at the beginning of the century and again in the 1930s (see Benckert, 1911; and Thunholm, 1991), while there had been bank crashes in the United States as recently as the 1970s (Franklin National Bank) and the 1980s (Penn Square Bank). There had also been problems in a number of other big banks in the United States, such as the Bank of America, Bankers Trust, Citicorp and Chase Manhattan. And there was other even more recent evidence closer to home, Norway. The crisis started there in 1987, but few foresaw anything similar happening in Sweden. However, with hindsight we can see a number of lessons that could have been learnt from Sweden's neighbour (see, for example, Reve, 1990; and Johnsen *et al.*, 1992).[23]

IMPLICATIONS

The events of the Swedish banking crisis have a number of implications for *organization theory*, for policy-makers and for managers. In terms of *organization theory* they have underlined the importance of focusing on fields of organizations, and especially on their mimetic behaviour. A particularly interesting feature in this context is that organizational stress tends to be an important factor in the hampering of organizational rationality. Further research into this type of stress therefore seems highly desirable.

For *policy-makers* the banking crisis has shown that it may be unwise to apply standard solutions to all industries; moreover it is important to consider the specific conditions of individual industries, when the rules of their game are changing. The banking crisis has also provided clear evidence that organizational learning and unlearning are rather difficult and time-consuming processes. This could mean in turn that incremental changes are to be preferred to giant leaps. The crisis can thus be said to have provided further support for the position adopted by Charles Lindblom in his classic article 'The Science of Muddling Through' (Lindblom, 1959), where he advocates making decisions and taking action in small steps.

In the same vein the crisis has demonstrated to *managers* that strategic moves into new markets are likely to be dangerous. Solid knowledge of markets and customers appears to be a basic prerequisite for successful operations. Long-term customer relationships have their advantages in the same way as relative stability in management and organizational structures. And stable relations with customers are probably particularly important when, as was the case in the banking industry, working conditions are undergoing radical change and the main product has a highly liquid character.

Notes

1. This paragraph is based on Bergström, Engwall and Wallerstedt (1994, pp. 34–6). For further discussions of the development of Swedish banking legislation, see Fritz (1988), Larsson (1989) and Sandberg (1978).
2. The joint stock banks with unlimited liability were allowed to issue paper bills, while this was not true for joint stock bank companies and branch banks. The joint stock bank companies were characterized by the limited responsibility of the owners, while branch banks were provincial banks closely connected to the Bank of Sweden.
3. Measured at fixed 1980 prices, the lending increased from about SEK 250 billion in 1985 to almost 450 billion in 1990 (Boksjö, Ingelsson and Jakobsson, 1993, p. 3).
4. For a description of the creation of the Bank Inspection Board, see the foreword by Ernst Söderlund in Benckert (1911). In its main text this book reports on the experiences of this board during the first years in operation.
5. For historical evidence of this last, see Benckert (1911, pp. 133–40 in the 1993 edition). For more recent examples, see Hadenius and Söderhjelm (1994, pp. 147–64).
6. For a review of the work of the Bank Inspection Board in the period 1984–90, see Hadenius and Söderhjelm (1994, pp. 147–64).
7. On the historical development of Stockholms Enskilda Bank, see Gasslander (1956 and 1959), Lindgren (1987) and Olsson (1986). On Svenska Handelsbanken, see Hildebrand (1971), and on Skandinaviska Banken Söderlund (1964 and 1978). Summaries of the development of the banking system are provided by Nygren (1985) and Thunholm (1989) among others.
8. As is shown in Johnsen (1990), the foreign banks experienced considerable difficulties in entering the Swedish market, just as Swedish banks met with problems abroad (Marquardt, 1994).
9. Quite a few small local banks resisted the accusation of being too conservative and decided to stay outside. During the crisis they also happened to show low credit losses. For an analysis of the merger process, see Bjerke Jaccard (1992).
10. See *Inbjudan till teckning av aktier i Föreningsbanken AB* (1993, pp. 44–5).
11. The rank correlation between the two variables is 0.48. It may of course seem questionable that data from the same period have been used for the two variables. However, using data for the four largest commercial banks and relating the credit expansion in 1985–9 to credit losses in 1992 provides a similar picture.

12. For statistical evidence, see *Bankkrisen* (1994) and *Bankerna under krisen* (1995), particularly Wallander (1994) and Edin, Englund and Ekman (1995).
13. For a more elaborate discussion, see Engwall (1995).
14. A low value implies a high qualification level and vice versa.
15. Further evidence of this is provided by the results reported in Eriksson and Marquardt (1989) regarding the utilization of office space in a selection of Swedish banks. The authors show that between 1974 and 1985 the share of space employed for customer contacts and consultation increased by 50 per cent, while the space for cashiers' desks decreased by a third.
16. Further evidence can be provided by data from Götabanken, for instance, where the number of days spent on education in the bank increased from 6500 in 1982 to 10 300 in 1988 (Annual Reports, Götabanken, 1982–8).
17. The average figures are based on a calculation using the following scale: pre-grammar school = 1, two years of grammar school = 2, three years of grammar school = 3, and post-grammar school = 4.
18. For an analysis of the organization structure in Första Sparbanken, see Eriksson (1994).
19. See *Inbjudan till teckning av aktier i Föreningsbanken AB* (1993, pp. 32–3 and 44–5).
20. For a discussion of problems in connection to bank mergers, see Jungerhem (1992).
21. An exception was the *Financial Times*, which was probably able to maintain a more balanced view, since its coverage of the Swedish financial market was not subject to any corresponding competitive pressure from other newsrooms.
22. That this is not only true for financial input but also for other types of input as well is shown in research in the area of industrial marketing and purchasing (see, for example, Håkansson, 1982 and 1989; and Ford, 1990).
23. The development in Finland was more parallel to that in Sweden. Needless to say the development there exhibited similarities to that in Sweden (see Chapter 9 in the present volume by Risto Tainio, Kari Lilja and Timo Santalainen).

References

G. Akerlof, 'The Market for "Lemons": Qualitative Uncertainty and the Market Mechanism', *Quarterly Journal of Economics*, 84, 3 (1970) pp. 488–500.

A. Andersen, 'Review of Gota Bank: 1986–1992', *Executive Summary of Findings*, 14 December 1992.

Annual Reports from Götabanken and Gota Bank.

Bankerna under krisen (The Banks During the Crisis). (Stockholm: Fritzes, 1995).

Bankkrisen (The Banking Crisis). (Stockholm: Fritzes, 1994).

Bankstödsnämnden, 'Värdering av fastigheter i bankstödsprocessen' (The Evaluation of Real Estate in the Bank Support Process), Valuation Board, Final Report, 16 March (1994).

R. Benckert (1911) *Benckerts testamente. Konfidentiella anteckningar (Benckert's Will. Confidential Notes)*. (Stockholm: Fischer and Co., 1993). (Earlier published by Kungl. Samfundet för utgivande av handskrifter rörande Skandinaviens historia, Handlingar del 4, Stockholm, 1976).

P.L. Berger and T. Luckmann, *The Social Construction of Reality: A Treatise in the Sociology of Knowledge*. (Garden City, NY: Doubleday, 1966).

R. Bergström, L. Engwall and E. Wallerstedt, 'Organizational Foundations and Closures in a Regulated Environment: Swedish Commercial Banks 1831–1990', *Scandinavian Journal of Management*, 10, 1 (1994) pp. 29–48.

M. Bjerke Jaccard, 'Liten. Men Stor. Är detta verkligen förenligt?' (Little. But Large. Are They Really Compatible?), Seminar Paper, Linjen för personal och arbetslivsfrågor, Uppsala universitet (mimeo) (1992).

A. Boksjö, M. Ingelsson and J. Jakobsson, 'Från kreditexpansion till kreditförluster – en studie av bankkrisens bakgrund' (From Credit Expansion to Credit Losses – A Study of the Background of the Banking Crisis), Memo, spring semester 1993, Department of Economics, Uppsala University.

B. Carlson, *Den amerikanska avregleringsvågen (The American Wave of Deregulation)*. (Stockholm: SNS, 1990).

A.D. Chandler Jr, *The Visible Hand*. (Cambridge, Mass.: The Belknap Press, 1977).

R.M. Cyert and J.G. March, *A Behavioral Theory of the Firm*. (Englewood Cliffs, NJ: Prentice-Hall, 1963).

B. Dahlheim, G. Lind and A.-K. Nedersjö, 'Utvecklingen i banksektorn 1992' (The Development in the Banking Sector 1992), *Penning – valutapolitik*, 2 (1993) pp. 24–37.

P.-A. Edin, P. Englund and E. Ekman, 'Avregleringen och hushållens skulder' (The Deregulation and the Debts of the Households), in: *Bankerna under krisen (The Banks During the Crisis)*. (Stockholm: Fritzes, 1995) pp. 73–129.

L. Engwall, 'Newspaper Competition: A Case for Theories of Oligopoly', *Scandinavian Economic History Review*, 29, 2 (1981) pp. 145–54.

L. Engwall, 'Newspaper Adaptation to a Changing Social Environment: A Case Study of Organizational Drift as a Response to Resource Dependence', *European Journal of Communication*, 1, September (1986) pp. 327–341.

L. Engwall, 'Bankkris och bankorganization' (Banking Crisis and Banking Organization), in *Bankerna under krisen (The Banks During the Crisis)*. (Stockholm: Fritzes) 1995 pp. 131–206.

L. Engwall and J. Johanson, 'Banks in Industrial Networks', *Scandinavian Journal of Management*, 6, 3 (1990) pp. 231–44.

K. Eriksson, *The Interrelatedness of Environment, Technology and Structure. A Study of Differentiation and Integration in Banking*, Doctoral Dissertation, Department of Business Studies, Uppsala University (1994).

K. Eriksson and R. Marquardt, 'Banker i förvandling' (Banks in Transformation), Seminar Paper, Department of Business Studies, Uppsala University (1989).

Finansinspektionen, 'Intern kontroll och internrevision i bankerna' (Internal Control and Internal Auditing in the Banks), Memorandum, 15 February 1994.

D. Ford (ed.), *Understanding Business Markets. Interaction, Relationships and Networks*. (London: Academic Press, 1990).

S. Fritz, 'Bankväsen och banklagstiftning i de nordiska länderna ca 1880–1920' (Banking and Bank Regulation in the Nordic Countries 1880–1920), paper presented at the Second International Workshop on Bank–Industry Relations in Interwar Europe: Austria, Hungary and Sweden, mimeo (1988).

O. Gasslander, *Bank och industriellt genombrott. Stockholms Enskilda Bank kring sekelskiftet 1900. I–II (Bank and Industrial Revolution. Stockholms Enskilda at the Turn of the Century 1900. I–II).* (Stockholm: Esselte, 1956 and 1959).

S. Hadenius and T. Söderhjelm, *Bankerna i pressen (The Banks in the Press)*, Appendix to the Commission on the Banking Crisis. (Stockholm: Fritzes, 1994).

H. Håkansson (ed.), *International Marketing and Purchasing of Industrial Goods – An Interaction Approach.* (Chichester: Wiley, 1982).

H. Håkansson, *Corporate Technological Behaviour. Cooperation and Networks.* (London: Routledge, 1989).

K.-G. Hildebrand, *I omvandlingens tjänst (In the Service of Change).* (Stockholm: Seelig, 1971).

S. Hildebrandt, 'Berufsbildung und Beschäftigung in französichen Kreditinstituten. Ein institutionelles Beziehungsgeflecht im Wandel', Discussion Paper FS I 93–101, Wissenschaftszentrum Berlin (1993).

L. Hjalmarsson, 'Nationalekonomins olika ansikten' (The Different Faces of Economics), in *Tvivlet på nationalekonomin. Fyra ekonomer diskuterar vetenskapen och verkligheten (The Doubts on Economics. Four Economists Discuss Science and Reality)*, Källa/40, Forskningsrådsnämnden, Stockholm (1993) pp. 16–37.

Inbjudan till teckning av aktier i Föreningsbanken AB (Invitation for Subscription of Shares in Föreningsbanken). (Stockholm, 1993).

G.E. Johnsen, 'De utländska bankerna' (The Foreign Banks), in C.G. Thunman and K. Eriksson, (eds), *Bankmarknader i förvandling* (Bank Markets in Transition). (Lund: Studentlitteratur, 1990) pp. 99–110.

T. Johnsen, 'Bankkrisen i Norge' (The Banking Crisis in Norway), *SNF-rapport 29/93* (Bergen: Stiftelsen for samfunns- og næringslivsforskning, 1992).

L. Jonung, 'Riksbankens politik 1945–1990' (The Policy of the Swedish Central Bank), in: L. Werin (ed.), *Från räntereglering till inflationsnorm. Det finansiella systemet och riksbankens politik 1945–1990 (From Interest Control to Inflationary Norm. The Financial System and the Policy of the the Swedish Central Bank 1945–1990).* (Stockholm: SNS, 1993) pp. 288–419.

S. Jungerhem, *Banker i fusion (Banks in Merger)*, Doctoral Dissertation, Department of Business Studies, Uppsala University (1992).

M. Larsson, 'Svensk affärsbankslagstiftning 1910–1970' (Swedish Bank Legislation 1910–1970), Working Paper, Department of Economic History, Uppsala University (mimeo) (1989).

C.E. Lindblom, 'The Science of Muddling Through', *Public Administrative Review*, 19, Spring (1959) pp. 79–88.

H. Lindgren, *Bank, investmentbolag, bankirfirma. Stockholms Enskilda Bank 1924–1945 (Commercial Bank, Investment Company, Accepting House).* (Stockholm: Institutet för Ekonomisk Historisk Forskning (EHF) vid Handelshögskolan i Stockholm, 1987).

J. Lybeck, *Finansiella kriser förr och nu (Financial Crises Earlier and Now).* (Stockholm: SNS, 1992).

J.G. March and J.P. Olsen, *Ambiguity and Choice in Organizations.* (Oslo: Universitetsforlaget, 1976).

J.G. March and H.A. Simon, *Organizations.* (New York: Wiley, 1958).

R. Marquardt, *Banketableringar i främmande länder (Bank Establishments in Foreign Countries).* (Department of Business Studies, Uppsala University, 1994).

R.N. McMurry, 'Recruitment, Dependency, and Morale in the Banking Industry', *Administrative Science Quarterly,* 3, 1 (1958) pp. 87–117.

I. Nygren, *Från Stockholm Banco till Citibank. Svensk kreditmarknad under 325 år (From Stockholm Banco to Citibank. The Swedish Credit Market During 325 Years).* (Stockholm: Liber, 1985).

U. Olsson, *Bank, familj och företagande. Stockholms Enskilda Bank 1946–1971 (Bank, Family and Entrepreneurship. Stockholms Enskilda Bank 1946–1971).* (Stockholm: EHF, 1986).

J.-E. Persson, 'Sundsvallsbanken 1955–1970. En longitudinell fallstudie av förändringar i marknadsföringspolitiken och effekterna av dessa i en affärs-/provinsbank' (Sundsvallsbanken 1955–70. A Longitudinal Case Study of the Changes in Marketing Policy and the Effects thereof in a Provincial Commercial Bank), Examination paper, Department of Business Studies, Uppsala University (1994).

T.J. Peters and R.H. Waterman Jr, *In Search of Excellence: Lessons from American Best-Run Companies.* (New York: Harper & Row, 1982).

K.-H. Pettersson, *Bankkrisen inifrån (The Banking Crisis from the Inside).* (Stockholm: SNS, 1993).

U. Remitz, *Professional Satisfaction among Swedish Bank Employees.* (Copenhagen: Munkgaard, 1960).

T. Reve, 'Bankkrisen: Hva gikk galt?' (The Banking Crisis: What Went Wrong?), *Rapport, 3'90,* Senter for anvendt forskning, Norges Handelshøyskole–Sosialøkonomisk institutt, Universitetet i Oslo (1990).

O. Rydbeck, *Om styrelseansvar m.m. Slutrapport om ansvar för Nordbankens styrelse avseende bankens kreditgivning främst under tidsperioden 1988–1990 (On the Responsibility of Board Members. Final Report on the Responsibility of the Board of Nordbanken Regarding the Lending of the Bank Primarily in the Period 1988–1990).* (Stockholm: Setterwalls, 1993).

O. Rydbeck, *Ang. mål nr T 2–2374–93; Gota Bank ./. Per-Olof Sjöberg och Gabriel Urwitz (Regarding Case T–2–2374–93: Gota Bank vs. Per-Olof Sjöberg and Gabriel Urwitz),* Inlaga till Stockholms tingsrätt, Avdelning 2 (Memorial to the Stockholm Court), May (1994).

L.G. Sandberg, 'Banking and Economic Growth in Sweden before World War I', *Journal of Economic History,* 18, (1978) pp. 650–80.

J.F. Sinkey Jr, *Commercial Bank Management in the Financial Services Industry.* (New York: Macmillan, 2nd edn 1986, 1st edn 1983).

A. Smith, *An Inquiry into the Nature and Causes of the Wealth of Nations.* (London, 1776).

E. Söderlund, *Skandinaviska Banken i det svenska bankväsendets historia 1864–1914 (Skandinaviska Banken in the History of Swedish Banking 1864–1914).* (Göteborg: Skandinaviska Banken, 1964).

E. Söderlund, *Skandinaviska Banken i det svenska bankväsendets historia 1914–1939 (Skandinaviska Banken in the History of Swedish Banking 1914–1939).* (Uppsala: Almqvist & Wiksell, 1978).

L.-E., Thunholm, *Svenskt kreditväsen (The Swedish Credit System)*, 11th edition. (Stockholm: Rabén and Sjögren, 1989).

L.-E., Thunholm, *Oscar Rydbeck och hans tid (Oscar Rydbeck and His Time)*. (Stockholm: Fischer and Co., 1991).

Veckans affärer, 17 October 1985.

J. Wallander, 'Bankkrisen. Omfattning. Orsaker. Lärdomar'. (The Banking Crisis. Scope. Causes. Lessons), in *Bankkrisen (The Banking Crisis)*. (Stockholm: Fritzes, 1994) pp. 67–180.

9 Changing Managerial Competitive Practices in the Context of Growth and Decline in the Finnish Banking Sector

Risto Tainio, Kari Lilja and
Timo Santalainen

INTRODUCTION

In this chapter we examine changes in managerial competitive practices in Finnish banks during the period of deregulation in the 1980s and 1990s. 'Deregulation' here refers to the process of removing various institutional barriers, namely protective banking regulations.

In Finland it is widely argued that 'deregulation increased banking competition' during the 1980s. Although it is not quite clear what 'increased competition' means, it seems evident that the removal of institutional barriers extended competitive space and created a new type of competitive practice. This change coincided with an unusually strong economic boom of long duration in Finland during the 1980s.

In late 1989 banking competition changed again. The Finnish economy plunged into a deep recession, now under the conditions of deregulated financial markets and liberalized exchange controls. For banking, this meant the start of an intense struggle for survival.

This chapter explores these changes in managerial competitive practices. Previously they have been explained mainly from the perspective of external forces and processes. For example, the emergence of new competitive practices in the mid-1980s period of growth has usually been explained in terms of the impact of deregulation. The destructive consequences in the Finnish banking sector in the 1990s and the related competitive practices have, on the other hand, been explained mainly by the economic recession, decreased demand, persistence of the overvalued mark, high interest rates, and other macroeconomic indicators.

These explanations are powerful and obvious, and they demonstrate important insights into the competitive dynamics of the Finnish banking sector. However, they have their limitations. Especially the role of the banks themselves in the changing nature of competition needs more attention and elaboration. This may be described as an internal perspective.

From this internal perspective it can be shown that the changes of competitive practices in the period of growth were not, in fact, activated by major institutional reforms, but rather by the banks' own initiatives and small-scale experiments with new businesses. The banks altered the nature of competition between themselves by engaging in new activities, which were later on accentuated by new institutional rules and structures, that is, 'deregulation'.

The managerial struggles to find a new paradigm of competitive practices encouraged mimetic behaviour, and resulted in 'managerial traps'. These traps locked managers into certain practices which made it difficult for them to adapt and change when the Finnish banking sector moved from growth to decline.

COMPETITIVE PRACTICES

In the previous literature the most common view of competitive practices is a 'stylized' one. Competitive action is described as intentional, rational moves and countermoves by major actors in existing market structures. In general, these moves and countermoves are hypothesized to follow a certain behavioral principle. Both contemporary neoclassical analyses and early visions of strategic management were built upon 'calculated rationality' in order to exploit competitive advantages and opportunities (Levinthal and March, 1993).

More recent strategic management literature increasingly views competitive practices from the perspective of intentional, offensive action. Attention focuses mainly on 'creative' competitive management, where management develops its capabilities and competences to create new sources of competitive advantage. By learning from experience, management improves its competitive strategies and their implementation and is therefore able to dominate other players and affect the institutional rules of the competitive game. This 'offensive approach' mostly assumes a strong 'agency' perspective on management; management is a self-sufficient strategic agent in national and international competitive arenas (Ansoff, 1991). Competitors are mostly seen as 'opponents', and the major managerial challenge is to dominate these opponents in the markets with distinct competitive strategies (Porter, 1980) and related resources and competences (for example, Bourgeois and Brodwin, 1984).

Another equally important but often neglected side of competitive practice is that of defence. Intentional efforts to avoid losses and failures become the central focus of the description. Attention turns to the ways management can renew and strengthen its agency character under deteriorating conditions (Weitzel and Jonsson, 1989). Management seeks to identify ways out of crisis and to change its organization and often management itself in order to effect a turnaround. In reality, these defensive practices exist simultaneously with offensive ones in the same competitive arenas.

Both of these characterizations of competitive practices build heavily on the intentional side of managerial action. They pay little attention to the unintentional aspects of competitive dynamics and practice. These 'irrational' features, or unanticipated outcomes, of competition include phenomena like vicious and virtuous circles, unpredictable side-effects (i.e. surprises), and contradictory tendencies producing outcomes that are not intended by anyone (for example, March, 1981; Masuch, 1985). These unintentional appearances and outcomes seem, however, to be inherent in any competitive dynamics.

Managerial practices are:

on the one hand, a result of a piece of past history and, on the other hand, an attempt to deal with a situation that is sure to change presently – an attempt by those firms to keep on their feet, on ground that is slipping away under them. (Schumpeter, 1942, p. 84)

In this chapter, we do not discuss the notion of rationality, but we do deal with the intentional and unintentional, as well as the offensive and defensive aspects of competitive practices. We examine how competition as 'creative destruction' actually occurs in the Finnish banking context. How does the institutional environment make new managerial practices possible and how do these new competitive practices further activate possible changes in institutional structures?

FINNISH FINANCIAL SYSTEM AND ITS INSTITUTIONAL DEVELOPMENT

The Finnish financial system can be characterized as predominantly credit-based (Zysman, 1983). Bank credit plays a central role in social and economic development. The banks pool resources from the public and allocate these resources to firms on a long-term basis. Since most investment credit is provided by banks, firms tend to become dependent on particular banks, and the banks tend to become dependent on the success of their major borrowers. Thus the industrial firms and bank groups in Finland are firmly interlinked on a long-term basis as are their counterparts in Germany. A credit-based system also enables state agencies to play a major role in controlling the allocation of financial resources and in directing firms' choices (Whitley, 1992). In Finland the major state institutions controlling and coordinating financial operations have long been the Bank of Finland and Bank Inspection.

Until the 1980s the Finnish banking sector consisted of six major banks: two large commercial banks (KOP and SYP), one medium-sized commercial bank (HOP), the state-owned Postipankki Ltd, OKOBANK Group (cooperative banks), and SKOPBANK Group (savings banks). All these major Finnish banks have their own historical roots and customer groups. The closest rivals have traditionally been the two major commercial banks KOP and SYP. They form the hard core of 'Finnish' and 'Swedish-speaking' industrial groups in the country. OKO and SKOP-BANK have been another competitive pair. They have specialized in retail banking and have been dominant in the rural areas of the country. In the mid-1980s, SYP took over HOP. In 1993, most of the savings banks were split and liquidated by the four other banks, and finally in 1995 SYP and KOP were merged. In 1995 there were three major financial blocs to the Finnish economy; the commercial bank bloc, the agricapital bloc, and the state bloc.

For over 60 years, until the mid-1980s, the Finnish banking sector had been sheltered by several protective and regulatory barriers. Bank competition in interest rates was eliminated already in Finland in the early 1930s by the Bank of Finland under the Tax Relief Act. Deposits obtained tax-exempt status as a condition for a uniform deposit rate. The Bank of Finland also imposed strict regulations on lending. The banks borrowed money from the Bank of Finland, which determined their lending rates. Foreign financing was also subject to the Bank of Finland's prior approval. Regulated interest rates provided the banks with moderate but steady margins and 'automatic' profits. Under these regulated conditions there was also a constant excess demand for credit in the economy. This made the small number of banks powerful organizations, as their customers became dependent on them for credit.

Under these conditions, the competitive leverage of the banks was a direct function of their market shares. They offered products and services on almost identical terms. The competition between banks was largely

superficial. Competitive practices appeared mainly in building up dense
branch office networks to reach new depositors, in careful rationing and
monitoring loans in order to minimize losses, and in improving the internal efficiency of bank organizations.

From 1970, new trends emerged which changed the nature of competition. In 1970 new banking legislation was passed under which all the
banks received equal rights to operate and compete in consumer, commercial, and investment banking. In the late 1970s and early 1980s, short-term
interfirm money markets emerged in Finland. The biggest corporations
started to lend their excess cash to each other at daily rates. These 'grey
markets' were to a large extent due to the increased financial operations
and high share of exports of the largest Finnish companies. Also the
favourable prepayments obtained from the bilateral trade between Finland
and the Soviet Union catalysed this stage of development in the Finnish
financial markets.

The emergence of the disintermediation and new 'industrial bankers'
created pressure to reform the financial system. Banks became worried
about their future role when the largest companies could lend and
borrow directly from the money markets. The Bank of Finland became
concerned about the functioning of two separate and simultaneous
markets. Gradually steps were taken to remove some of the protective
barriers in the 'official' banking system and at the same time to allow
banks to compete more effectively in the new arenas. The first foreign
banks started operations in Finland in 1982, and two years later Finnish
banks were allowed to establish foreign subsidiaries. In 1984, remaining
foreign exchange controls were liberalized, and Finnish banks started to
operate in international credit markets. New investment companies and
other financial service firms entered the financial markets. The major
step in deregulation occurred, however, in 1986. The Bank of Finland
stopped regulating loan rates. Now banks had abundant domestic and
foreign funding sources. Interest rates started to balance demand and
supply in the banks' loan markets. There was a shift away from competition for depositors, which was a consequence of interest rate regulation,
towards competition in interest rates and in the pricing of services.
Markets for certificates of deposit were created rapidly in the same year,
and short-term interbank markets emerged and became institutionalized.
In 1987, stock options and futures markets were created and they
expanded rapidly. In 1989, a new stock exchange law adjusting Finnish
practice to international norms and legislation was passed. However, no
compulsory debt to equity ratios were applied to money markets at that
time.

The impact of deregulation on the Finnish banking sector, especially after 1986, was strong and indisputable. Old bank competition, based on regulated pricing and homogeneous 'products', gave way to new dynamic forms of competition based on more flexible manoeuvring in the loan market. The formerly stable and bureaucratic bank organizations rapidly became competitive agents with an aggressive market approach with no restraints as to their equity requirements. Similar changes and tendencies in the 1980s have also been observed in Norway and Sweden (cf. Reve, 1990; Engwall, 1994; and Chapter 8, this volume).

CHANGE IN COMPETITIVE PRACTICES: THE EXTENDED COMPETITION

Viewed from the banks themselves, the new era in Finnish banking competition had in fact already started in 1985, before the major deregulation steps in 1986. The change culminated in a battle over HOP, the medium-sized commercial bank (Saari, 1992; Repo, 1992; Lassila, 1993; Hakkarainen, 1993). The impact of this battle on competitive relations and practices in Finnish banks was immediate and far-reaching.

The instigator of that battle was SKOPBANK, which had just obtained a new, young, and ambitious board in late 1984.

In the beginning of 1985 SKOPBANK and one of the new venture capital companies began gradually acquiring HOP shares, which looked cheap considering their substance value. In the spring of 1985 rumours spread that HOP had made a 50 mFIN loss on its currency business. More and more HOP shares came onto the market. In October the two big commercial banks saw the real danger in SKOPBANK's takeover attempt; the emergence of a new, sizeable merchant bank in Finland. During the last week of October the battle became fierce. The prices of HOP stocks skyrocketed, when SYP and KOP also started buying them. During the last days of October KOP abandoned the struggle, and SKOPBANK sold its shares to SYP. The President of SYP described the deal as 'historical'. (Saari, 1992)

The old system of bank competition was soon left behind by these events and a new competitive game was opened. Formerly bureaucratic banks, which were used to following rules and regulations, suddenly started to act in new ways. Stability was further undermined as competition shifted to the spheres of investment banking and corporate finance, where speculative and risky activities abounded. Competition in these spheres started to dominate overall bank competition and to affect both the structure of the banks and their institutional context. The HOP battle was fought with relatively small stakes, but when the flows of funds were really opened in the summer of 1986 the scale of competitive operations increased rapidly. All the major banks started to compete openly in developing their securities business, expanding their international activities, engaging in corporate takeovers and venture capital operations, and in reorganizing the whole industrial structure of Finland. Institutional control of these operations was difficult because there were only a few laws and regulations to follow and those that existed were easy to elude or reinterpret. A good example was the law that banks can own only 10 per cent of the shares of industrial companies. This was easily circumvented by establishing subsidiaries, using 'loyal' companies of the finance group, or, as in the case of SKOP-BANK, with the help of hundreds of independent savings banks. In some new business areas there was simply no legislation. In securitization, for example, norms and behavioral principles were created through practice. Although the legislation implemented later on is commonly related to the process of 'deregulation' it would be more appropriate to link it to 'regulation'. It finally brought practices which had previously been unregulated and uncontrolled in Finland under internationally established regulations and standards (for example, in the sphere of insider trading).

From the bank perspective it can therefore be argued that change in the competitive practices of the Finnish banking sector was not activated by major institutional reforms, but rather by small-scale experiments with new businesses. The banks altered their competition themselves by engaging in new activities, which were eventually accentuated by 'deregulation'. New competitive practices quickly created their own morals and ethics, generating tension between new and old bankers, and between new bankers and state authorities. This created pressure to bring these new, secret, and speculative practices under institutional control.

The battle for HOP had permanently transformed the competitive scene in banking (Lassila, 1993). It was not only that competition was extended by the emergence of new forms and arenas of competition. The results of the battle also activated other processes which diffused new practices rapidly and eventually changed the competitive positions of the banks.

First, the results of the HOP battle unintentionally trapped managers into new ways of acting. The most notable example of this is the emergence of what may be termed a 'competence trap'. The process can, to some extent, be identified in all Finnish banks in the late 1980s, but was especially obvious in SKOPBANK. The competence trap occurs when favourable performance in one domain is rewarding in the short run. Management accumulates experience from this and the organization learns to specialize in niches where its competencies yield immediate advantage (Levitt and March, 1988).

In this case, the HOP takeover operation proved highly profitable for SKOPBANK, despite the fact that it did not achieve its ostensible object of taking over HOP (Saari, 1992). The bank had played aggressively. Although it did not have the strength for the final victory it was able to retreat and collect – much to its surprise and avid plaudits for its efforts – large profits. This whole process raised expectations of fast profits and new business opportunities in the SKOPBANK board. The chief executive officer became convinced that this was the way they would have to operate in the future. 'Strike unexpectedly, stay calm, capitalize, and withdraw' (Saari, 1992, p. 72). The success of this strategy occurred during his first year in office, and it was his first major personal accomplishment. The same type of manoeuvring continued, and was generally a success. During 1987–8 SKOPBANK's profits from investment banking were five times bigger than its net interest income. The facts seemed to support the contention that the 'success recipe' was working. This, together with public praise, created a strong atmosphere of self-sufficiency and complacency in the SKOPBANK board. As the CEO expressed it, 'Our competence had produced exceptional success, and that competence is a longlasting property' (Saari, 1992). The bank had also become a long-lasting prisoner of that competence.

This process is a classical example of the ways in which learning is self-limiting. The effectiveness of learning in the short run and from current experience interferes with learning in the long run and at a distance (Levinthal and March, 1993). The management of SKOPBANK experienced its first takeover attempt as a success and sought to repeat this success specializing in this type of manoeuvre. In doing so it standardized and routinized its actions. Management became increasingly removed from other bases of experience and strategy, and unconsciously 'trapped' in the existing routines. When the environment changed, as it did eventually in Finland, the trap became obvious to management, but by this time its successes had driven the bank 'beyond the limits of return'. It was too strongly committed to its own view of its competence to be able to adapt and change in different circumstances. Some other banks (for example, Postipankki Ltd and OKOBANK) avoided this trap by experiencing losses early enough in the period and therefore did not commit themselves in the way SKOPBANK did.

The emergence of success-related competence traps does not prevent but instead accelerates diffusion of new competitive practices. The 'winner' sets the standards of performance and becomes an example of how to achieve them. This tends to force competitors to follow, and, despite possible doubts, to further imitation. The major Finnish banks responded to deregulation – new business opportunities and increased funding possibilities – with similar strategies. They diversified their business operations and extended their presence in investment banking, international businesses, and corporate banking and consulting. They decentralized their organizations and decision-making to become more 'market-' or 'consumer-oriented', and started to rationalize their dense branch networks and cut their operating costs.

Second, the battle over HOP also raised and personalized bank competition to the highest level of top management – managing directors and their key investment bankers. In former times competition was mainly a matter for a bank's branch offices. Now it became significant for the entire organization. Critical to this extension of competition was how the final result of the HOP battle was interpreted. In public SYP was declared the winner. It won openly with the help of SKOPBANK. This changed the balance of power between SYP and KOP and became especially obvious in some of their jointly governed financial organizations. It created mistrust and cooled personal relations between the leaders of SYP and KOP (Lassila, 1993). When cooperation between SYP and SKOPBANK in investment banking continued, the mistrust between SYP and KOP deepened. This led to increased suspicions of each other's moves and to a need for self-protective measures. The time of gentlemen's agreements at the top level of Finnish banking was over and the competition became aggressive in spirit: 'the end justifies the means'. This meant that even deceptive strategies were acceptable, if circumstances so required. The two leading banks became worried about their own independence, their very existence. They attempted to take each other over. These secret takeover attempts came to light in 1988. Fights over bank ownership were also extended to battles over their major industrial customers.

The aggressive destruction of HOP had therefore activated another process, where resources were exhausted to guarantee the independence of the major banks. The independence meant, however, isolation, from which it was not easy to break out. Structures are usually easier to build up than to break down and therefore they have more far-reaching and long-term consequences than initially thought. In this case the ownership arrangements were protective moves which 'froze' the new banking reality.

The new businesses had resulted in great losses, but there was no return to the old banking practices. The way out could instead be expected to lie in these new practices, new competences and the insights provided by them. Thus it can be claimed that under extended competition the new competitive fields and new practices rapidly destroyed the old competition. The first offensive moves were initiated from within and accentuated by institutional reforms. New practices had unexpected and unhealthy consequences, which activated reregulation of these new practices. Extended competition tends to create internally generated processes which overheat development. Short-term success accelerates the destruction of old practices and institutional control; in the long run this tends to lead to self-isolating or even self-destroying effects.

CHANGE IN COMPETITIVE PRACTICES: THE RETRENCHED COMPETITION

The banks' new and expansive competitive practices together with the state's expansive fiscal and monetary policy overheated the Finnish economy by 1989. The Bank of Finland tried to cool the economy by imposing credit regulations on the banks, but was not entirely successful any more. In 1990, the Finnish economy entered a recession. This was due to both external and internal factors. The simultaneous slowdown in Western economies and the collapse of the Soviet Union were the major external factors. The Soviet trade, which had at best accounted for about 25 per cent of Finnish exports, practically disappeared. The decreased demand, the persistence of the overvalued Finnish mark, and the related high interest rates created a wave of corporate bankruptcies. The Helsinki Stock Exchange became sluggish. The property markets fell and interest rates stayed high. The whole banking sector drifted into a deep crisis. All the major banks started to fight for survival under these deteriorating conditions. The banks desperately sought leeway for their organizations, to identify their own solutions to problems, and to find new ways to exploit their remaining competitive resources.

In this new phase the banks found that they had trapped themselves into practices which were no longer relevant. When the external conditions changed, these traps became visible and 'real'. 'Success breeds failure', as organizational life has widely shown. Breaking out of these success traps became a major managerial challenge and the seed for a new set of competitive practices. In addition to springing internally generated traps, externally generated traps also emerged as economic conditions changed. What previously appeared as 'new' and 'successful' managerial practices now become increasingly problematic and questionable. Moreover, what had been earlier labelled 'old' suddenly became more respected and desired again.

In the late 1980s Finnish banks were slow to recognize the existence of internally generated traps, but they were quick to experience and respond to the unfavourable external conditions and their imprisoning nature. A good example of this kind of externally generated trap is the 'interest rate trap'. The removal of interest rate regulation did not have an equal impact on the lending and funding sides of banking operations. Most lending, especially long-term housing loans, was still tied to the low base rate which remained regulated. In contrast, the rates for funds acquired on the markets were unregulated and were increasingly expensive. This 'twin interest rate' problem eroded the profitability of all the banks since they had to lend at low rates whilst borrowing at high rates.

The difference between the market rate and the base rate exceeded 10 per cent in 1989–90 for several months. The banks tried jointly to persuade the Bank of Finland to raise the base rate, but Parliament, which determines the level of the base rate, refused. The losses sustained by the banks at that time were estimated at 4–5 bFIN a year (Lassila, 1993).

The interest rate trap can be described as external but unintentional. It was not 'planned' by anyone; it merely emerged as a result of the different rates of fluidity in various parts of the financial system and the different prospects and 'rhythms' of reforms made in them. At the outset this external trap was experienced as a common threat by the banks. It therefore encouraged them to increase their cooperation, but when these joint efforts were not successful, even more intense competition arose. This competition strikingly favoured the financially strongest banks. They could best resist the strain of the trap and the related problems.

In the phase of retrenched competition it is not only that 'the fittest survive', but that under these conditions the fittest are able to build on their existing advantage. The contracting economic space leads to intentional competitive manoeuvring to take advantage of the situation. This is where relative strength and resources matter most. Opportunities to capitalize on the relative weaknesses of competitors arise frequently, and various intentional efforts to trap weaker players are also likely to occur. In this case too, the strongest banks started to take advantage of the deteriorating position of the weakest in the early 1990s. Especially illustrative in this respect are the last years of SKOPBANK.

Competitors knew about SKOPBANK's emerging problems by late 1989. Its major venture capital company went bankrupt in June. It did not obey the orders of the Bank of Finland to limit lending in August. Its Managing Director committed suicide in December. All this spread rumours and mistrust about SKOPBANK's performance, but competitors did not take any action until early 1990. The other banks refused to buy SKOPBANK's certificates of deposit, or did so at a high price, thereby creating acute funding problems for SKOPBANK. Its overnight debt increased to almost 5 bFINs and also created problems in international funding (Saari, 1992, p. 200). At SKOPBANK this was interpreted as revenge for their earlier successes and undeniably arrogant behaviour. In the other banks all this could be regarded as normal, cautious business operations. The competitors also became active in spreading rumours about the critical situation of SKOPBANK once its survival was openly threatened. This eroded the public image of SKOPBANK and made it look like a failure well before the final disaster had actually occurred. The board had to use its time and energy in combating negative publicity. 'A retreating competitor can really be tortured', was how the Chief Executive Officer of SKOPBANK later summarized his experience.

In the light of our evidence, retrenched competition can be characterized as the simultaneous presence of externally and internally generated traps; it is characterized by a fierce struggle for survival and well-designed competitive moves by the strongest. The failure of the weaker players can be aggravated by the small, even unnoticeable moves of competitors, which facilitate entrapment or at least hinder escape. It is very difficult to distinguish condition-driven entrapment from competitor-driven entrapment in retrenched competition. Both processes work in the same direction. Their combined effect, however, is clear. They tend to lead towards an endless cycle of loss and failure in the weakest, often the trapped, organization. These failures escalate pressure to withdraw from the 'new' banking areas and tighten institutional control. SKOPBANK was brought under the control of the Bank of Finland in the autumn of 1990. A stabilization programme was proposed and accepted by the authorities, who monitored its implementation closely. The authorities were worried not only about SKOPBANK, but also about the Finnish banking system as a whole, especially its international reputation.

In 1991 the Bank of Finland had to take over SKOPBANK. As there was a danger that the Finnish banks would drop below minimum statutory capital-adequacy standards, the government was forced to give equity injections and state guarantees to all banks. A new agency, the State Guarantee Fund, was established to support the whole Finnish financial system. In 1992 the biggest savings banks merged and formed the Savings

Bank of Finland. In October 1993 this bank was split and liquidated by the four other major banks. Retrenched competition tends to create externally generated traps which 'freeze' development and encourage exploitation of known alternatives, recruitment of risk-avoiders, and other conservative practices. This leads, however, to a paradox, since the new structures remain. Banking still takes place in the deregulated environment. The global financial markets, liberalized exchange controls, and the internationalization of corporations create continuous pressure in the opposite direction; a search for new fields of specialization, new combinations of services, and new forms of competitive alliances between banks across national borders.

CONCLUSIONS

There is an obvious asymmetry in how management practices evolve in extended and retrenched competition. During extended competition 'new practices seem to destroy old ones' and 'new organizations arise to challenge old institutions and institutional structures'. During retrenched competition, on the other hand, 'old practices seem to destroy new ones' and 'old institutions, with some new elements, seem to modify what used to be "new" managerial practices' (March 1991). During the extended competitiveness phase, emphasis is mainly on the exploration of new possibilities, and during the contracting phase on the exploitation of old certainties. In the extended competition period bank initiatives, combined with old and weak institutions, catalysed the emergence of new competitive practices. These were diffused by institutional reforms and self-reinforcing business practices until the disturbances required new regulations and gradual institutional restructuring.

In the period of retrenched competition reduced demand alone was not decisive in changing managerial practices, but together with inherited success traps, it had the consequence of shaking out competitors. This shake-out of the whole banking sector activated new reforms in the institutions, that is, building up rescue structures and new control procedures. The changes in the competitive practices in the Finnish banking sector were indisputable and clear under regulation, deregulated growth, and deregulated decline.

Our examination suggests that internal impulses are significant in understanding these changes in competitive practices. These impulses are constantly 'testing' the strength of institutional regulations. If regulations are relatively weak they are not destroyed, but left intact until the tensions

Table 9.1   Types of managerial traps in the Finnish banking sector

	Internally produced	Externally produced
Unintentional	i.e. competence trap	i.e. interest rate trap
Intentional	i.e. trap of self-isolation	i.e. competitors' trap

and paradoxes created by new practices initiate institutional renewal processes. If regulations are relatively strong, exploitation of old certainties prevail or impulses are modified.

The interplay between external and internal developments and their relative strengths is conceptualized here by the various forms of managerial traps and their generative processes. The following types of traps could be identified from the development of the Finnish banking sector in the 1980s and 1990s.

The traps illustrate the limits of managerial action and the turning points in the competitive dynamics. During extended competition internally generated traps are likely to occur. Experimentation with new competitive practices dominates and successes lead to entrapment, which further diffuses new practices. The longer this lasts the more vulnerable the winners become and the more drastic the changes that can be expected in competitive positions if the environment changes. In retrenched competition, on the other hand, externally generated traps become more likely and the pressures to return to the old competitive practices increase. The formation of external traps tends to change the relative positions of competitors in favour of the financially strongest. This change is easily extended to intentional 'failure traps', to vicious circles where deteriorating conditions are aggravated by the intentional efforts of competitors to tighten the trap and to propel the victims towards failure. The formation of these traps sets the tone and rhythm for the institutional renewal of the Finnish banking sector. Institutional reforms dealt primarily with the consequences of earlier managerial practices. They regulated 'history', while the managerial practices moulded the 'present'.

EPILOGUE

After the full circle, boom and recession, who were the winners and losers in the Finnish banking competition? In public the losers seem to be the original innovators, and the 'winners' those who remained conservative.

From our perspective, however, the competitive victory went to those who balanced the 'creative' and 'conservative' competitive practices appropriately, and matched their changes to the pace of change in the wider social context. The losers were those who concentrated either mainly on the exploration of new possibilities or mainly on the exploitation of old certainties. And our guess is that this will happen again when the next boom occurs. Attraction to 'one truth', which 'fits' the conditions, may again prevent management from creating a balance between exploration and exploitation. It is difficult to create synthesis, if antithesis is absent, and if managerial learning itself contributes to this absence.

References

H.I. Ansoff, 'Strategic Management in a Historical Perspective', *International Review of Strategic Management*, 2 (1991) pp. 3–69.

L.J. Bourgeois and D.R. Brodwin, 'Strategic Implementation: Five Approaches to Elusive Phenomena', *Strategic Management Journal*, 5 (1984) pp. 241–64.

L. Engwall, 'Bridge, Poker and Banking', in D. Fair and R. Raymond (eds), *The Competitiveness of Financial Institutions and Centers in Europe*. (Amsterdam: Kluwer, 1994).

N. Hakkarainen, *Oravanpyörässä*. (Juva: WSOY, 1993).

J. Lassila, *Markka ja ääni*. (Hämeenlinna: Kirjayhtymä, 1993).

D.A. Levinthal and J.G. March, 'The Myopia of Learning', *Strategic Management Journal*, 14 (1993) pp. 95–112.

B. Levitt and J.G. March, 'Organizational Learning', *Annual Review of Sociology*, 14 (1988) pp. 319–40.

J.G. March, 'Footnotes to Organizational Change', *Administrative Science Quarterly* 26 (1981) pp. 563–77.

J.G. March, 'Exploration and Exploitation in Organizational Learning', *Organization Science*, 2 (1991) pp. 71–87.

M. Masuch, 'Vicious Circles in Organizations', *Administrative Science Quarterly*, 30 (1985) pp. 14–33.

M. Porter, *Competitive Strategy*. (New York: Free Press, 1980).

E. Repo, *Vallan havittelijat*. (Jyväskylä: Gummerus, 1992).

T. Reve, 'Mimetic Strategic Behavior in Banking', Working Paper, 48, Norwegian School of Economics and Business Administration, Bergen (1990).

M. Saari, *Minä, Christopher Wegelius*. (Jyväskylä: Gummerus, 1992).

J.A. Schumpeter, *Capitalism, Socialism and Democracy*. (New York: Harper & Brothers, 1942).

W. Weitzel and E. Jonsson, 'Decline in Organizations: A Literature Integration and Extension', *Administrative Science Quarterly*, 34 (1989) pp. 91–109.

R. Whitley, 'Societies, Firms and Markets: The Social Structuring of Business Systems', in R. Whitley (ed.), *European Business Systems: Firms and Their Markets in Their National Context*. (London: Sage, 1992).

J. Zysman, *Governments, Markets and Growth: Financial Systems and the Politics of Industrial Change*. (Ithaca, NY: Cornell University Press, 1983).

10 Governmentality and Financial Services: Welfare Crises and the Financially Self-Disciplined Subject

David Knights

INTRODUCTION

European financial services have experienced a dramatic change since the mid-1980s. The specific details of this change vary from country to country but the general thrust and direction of its impact are similar, taking the form of intensified competition of both a local and global nature. Much of this new competitive climate reflects global developments that, in part, may be attributed to floating currencies, the relaxation of exchange controls, and a proliferation of new more flexible financial instruments such as Eurobonds, futures, and derivatives (see Morgan, Chapter 1 in this volume). These developments in wholesale financial markets have established a trend that has found its counterpart in the retail sector of financial services across Europe, and indeed the rest of the world.

As a result of the New Right politics and neo-liberal economics of Margaret Thatcher, the UK experienced this clamour for economic de-regulation ahead of other European countries. Until the 1970s, UK financial services had enjoyed a comparatively comfortable, steadily growing market in which the different sectors such as banking and insurance and the different types of institutions within each sector had their own distinct set of customers, marketing/distribution systems, management skills, and regulatory procedures. Although there was overlap, for example, bankers offered advice on insurance and insurance companies used banker's orders and later direct debits as ways of collecting premiums, there was very little direct competition or cooperation between the different sectors and types of institution. Thus the term 'financial services' only became a meaningful label to describe all the different sectors and firms as competition and deregulation broke down these barriers and established a single market with distinct segments rather than completely different market-places.

These changes took place against a background of increasing government concern about the growing costs of welfare and especially index-linked state pensions. From the early 1980s, the Conservative government indicated its belief that personal provision for pensions, home ownership and welfare more generally was more preferable and practical than continued state funding. It created various incentives to encourage this saving and also used privatization as a means of spreading share ownership more widely. Around the same time, it also created new regulations in the Financial Services Act to protect investors against fraud and poor selling.

All these changes resulted in a proliferation of commercial, media, and regulatory discourse surrounding the financial services. One effect of this was to promote a greater public interest in savings and investment products and a recognition of the need for 'financial self-discipline' (Knights, 1988). This development does not occur smoothly and without interruption or disruption but the trend amongst the employed population is in the direction of seeking financial security and planning ahead to avoid the risk of future financial insecurity. After the event, these various interventions in the financial services market-place may appear as if they were the product of a coherent and coordinated government plan. However, this is far from the case and, as will be demonstrated, these are distinct, incremental interventions dealing with discrete sets of problems. Nonetheless, their aggregated impact on consumers is positive from the point of view of the goal of creating financial self-discipline and shifting from a welfare state model of provision to a model of private provision. This chapter examines the process of change in UK financial services and demonstrates that the shift towards financial self-discipline is complex and contradictory.

FINANCIAL SERVICES TRANSFORMATIONS IN THE UK

Deregulation in UK retail financial services first began in 1967 when the UK Prices and Incomes Board Report on Bank Charges forced the banks to begin competing with each other (Knights and Morgan, 1995, p. 199). Previously, interest rates on accounts and charges for bank services had been agreed by a cartel arrangement amongst the banks. Gradually competition entered the market and speeded up when building societies began to extend their activities into operating new forms of accounts. Competition over interest rates and charges led in to broader forms of competition as banks fought back against building societies by starting to offer mortgages. Both banks and building societies saw the chance to improve their overall margins by systematizing their approach to insurance-selling, where products had definite synergies with their own core offerings. The result was that competition spilled over from traditional banking functions into insurance, thus beginning to create the sense of a single 'financial services' industry.

This type of competition was also stimulated by the government's willingness to loosen credit controls for both personal and corporate customers, in turn consequent upon the extension of global financial markets during the 1970s. A greater availability of credit meant that new entrants could offer loans and mortgages to personal customers. Banks and building societies lobbied the government to remove restrictions on their activities in order that they could compete more strongly against each other as well as against new entrants. The Building Societies Act (1986) and subsequent further relaxations on the money market borrowing of building societies gave an enormous boost to their competitive challenge to traditional banks, as well as encouraging their developments into insurance, merger activity and, in some cases, demutualization. Credit expansion was complemented by an expansion in the sorts of savings products available for personal customers as privatization, unit-linked investment vehicles and new tax efficient ways of saving (such as personal equity plans and Tax Exempt Savings Schemes – PEPs and TESSAs) were established.

Because of the dangers inherent in this sweeping aside of traditional controls in financial markets and the expansion in the complexity and numbers of investment products, there has been some consumer protection legislation. The Financial Services Act (FSA) of 1986 attempts to protect the investor from both fraudulent and 'unprofessional' financial intermediaries and sales staff. While financial scandals have continued and even increased since the Act, many of them are a product of the industry failing to comply fully with the legislation and would not probably have been exposed prior to the legislation. These scandals, however, certainly demonstrate that new regulations are needed where financial markets have been otherwise deregulated or liberalized. The FSA has generated a framework of regulation that is in a continuous state of development and modification, intended to restrain competitive strategies from stepping beyond the boundaries of an ethical code of some minimal protection for the consumer.

In the same year of 1986, against the background of government anxieties about the impact of demographic changes on the future cost of state pensions, the Social Security Act (SSA) stimulated considerable financial services business activity. Alongside other fiscal stimulants to savings and investments, the SSA partially privatized pensions by offering individuals a government incentive to contract out of the index-linked state earnings-related pension scheme (SERPS) in favour of private personal pensions arrangements.

These changes in financial services have been part of a broader political commitment to extend the boundaries of the so-called 'property-owning' democracy beyond mere home ownership. Government has, thereby, sought to encourage a wider ownership of financial securities. As part of its populist appeal to the electorate, the radical right sought to ensure that every citizen had a financial stake in the economy through becoming a 'home-owner, share-owner, portable pension owner and stakeholder in local services' (Jessop and Stones, 1992, p. 176) whilst rolling back the socialist state that was believed to encourage welfare dependence (Knights and Willmott, 1993).

Whether this concern was connected with other neo-liberal economic policies to remove restrictive practices from the financial services through deregulation is doubtful. However, there was more than a semblance of compatibility between the two, for shaking the financial services out of their self-satisfied and inefficient complacency would make them more capable of delivering on Thatcher's dream of social integration through individual or collective 'financial self-discipline' (Knights, 1988). This is not to argue that government policies have been devised directly with this intention. Usually, as, for example, with the involvement of the general public in purchasing shares in the case of privatization, this has been subsidiary or supplementary to other governmental objectives. As has already been indicated, the revolution in financial services (Hamilton, 1986) was simply part of a trend to liberalize markets on a global scale. Indeed, as the engine room of international trade in an increasingly global economy, the financial markets had to be a central dynamic in the neo-liberal economics that was beginning to grip Western economies in the 1970s and 1980s.

Financial self-discipline is not then a direct policy objective but an indirect outcome of an intensification of activity in financial services that arises from both the deregulation of markets and the reregulation of transactions (in order to offer higher standards of consumer protection). Indeed, the very term 'financial services' may be seen as indicative of the way in which banking, insurance, credit and the vast range of financial institutions (for example, stock market, foreign exchange agencies, money markets) associated with the management of money are in a process of transformation. While there remain disputes about where to draw lines around different activities and divergent financial instruments, the 'packaging' of the major financial institutions within the broad category of financial services cannot be seen as merely a verbal convenience (Knights, forthcoming). It reflects and reproduces a discursive formation which has certain effects upon the construction and development of contemporary social relations. Combined with other social dynamics, the proliferation of discourse surrounding the regulatory and deregulatory changes in banking, credit and insurance has been to encourage a greater personal involvement of consumers in savings and investment.

This process is not continuous and unproblematic. For example, the large underclass of permanently unemployed or low wage-earners are in no position to fund their own pensions. Even those in better jobs find that growing insecurity of employment makes permanent saving and investment extremely difficult. Furthermore, in the light of falls in the housing market and the uncertainties in the stock market (which are periodically brought home by large falls in value), consumers may no longer feel as confident about saving and investing as they did during the boom years of the 1980s, particularly when they see major financial institutions collapsing (such as Barings Bank) or being sanctioned by the regulators (as has happened to many companies which sold personal pensions inappropriately). There is then an intricate and complex relationship between government policies which expand financial self-discipline and those which inhibit such an expansion. This can be seen through focusing in more detail on the crisis of welfare.

THE CRISIS OF WELFARE

The public's interest in saving and investment has been particularly stimulated by the 'crisis talk' surrounding welfare and especially the provision of state pensions and long-term care. The urgency of the welfare problem reflects not just the current but the extrapolated future discrepancy between effective demand and supply of welfare, which is predicted on the basis of changes in the demographic profile of populations in Western Europe (see Knights and Odih, 1995, and Odih, 1995, for further details of this argument). In 1993, for example, 15.8 per cent of the UK population were 65 and over and this proportion is projected to rise to 19.4 per cent by the year 2011 and 24 per cent by 2041. By this time the over-80s will represent almost 10 per cent of the population. When illustrated in terms of actual numbers, the figures look even more dramatic. While currently there are 9 million retired people against a formally working population of around 24 million, by 2031 the retired population is expected to rise to 14 million, possibly against an even smaller number in paid employment. The dependency ratio (that is, the numbers of working-age people in relation to those in dependent roles) is expected to fall from its 1991 level of 3.3:1 to 2.1:1 by 2050 and the over-80 age group is predicted to rise from under 4 per cent to almost 9 per cent over the same period. According to the UK Goverment Actuary in 1990, the over-80 group consumes health and personal social services on average eight times as much as those under 64. An ageing population consumes welfare services far more heavily than a young population. Consequently, larger and larger numbers are expected to be demanding more and more welfare services at a time when other economic and political pressures are weakening the lobby for increased public spending. The social security budget in the UK has risen from 9.5 per cent of GDP in 1979 to over 12 per cent in 1994–5, partly because of these changes in the demographic composition of the population. Since much of the funding for this increased expenditure effectively means an intergenerational redistribution of income, at a time when the working population is diminishing relative to the dependent population of the elderly, the young and the unemployed, it becomes both economically and politically problematic.

This is not unique to the UK; it is a problem in most highly developed democratic Western countries, for example, Italy (Knights *et al.*, 1992), Germany (*Financial Times*, 29 November 1995, p. 3) and France (Sturdy *et al.*, chapter 7 in this volume). Indeed in some respects, the UK is better able to cope with these problems since it has a more developed private sector for pensions and has sought to privatize the index-linked parts of the state's responsibilities which is where the greatest liabilities prevail. Nevertheless, a climate of insecurity partly created by a perception that the government is withdrawing from welfare is highly conducive to private sector financial institutions offering private financial security products.

Is the government in the UK following a self-conscious, coherent and coordinated policy of privatizing welfare and instilling financial self-discipline on the population at large? Despite appearances, this is not necessarily the case for, as Jessop and Stones (1992) have argued, neo-liberal measures are often 'developed casually or through trial-and-error' and, only after the event, can be seen as interrelated and forming a coherent whole. Many of the government-induced changes that have occurred were responses to a particular problem such as the concern that the UK stock exchange was in danger of being totally eclipsed by other international exchanges because of its inflexibility, or the fear that the state would not be able to meet the costs of index-linked, state earnings-related pensions (SERPS) as the retired population was expanding so rapidly. Policies are often *ad hoc* and reactive with respect to specifically identified crises but because of a general ideological preoccupation with reduced public expenditure and the promotion of 'free' markets, have a direction that appears programmed and planned.

For underlying the policies of economic deregulation, political re-regulation, privatization and a fiscal encouragement for particular forms of private saving and investment is a general philosophy of 'rolling back the state' and reinforcing market competition (Knights and Willmott, 1993) that gives a sense of coherence to the whole enterprise. But this coherence should not be exaggerated or assumed to bring about the particular desired results. Take, for example, the preoccupation with reducing public expenditure. In real terms, the policy may be seen to have failed since the latter has risen steadily, largely due to unemployment and the increasing costs of social security. In effect, concerns to reduce the public sector deficit came into conflict with monetarist and competition policy which had the effect of shaking out labour markets and thus increasing the social security and welfare bill.

Also the policy of creating a level playing field in financial services, which was a clear element of the early competition policy, came into conflict with the concern to encourage savings and, perhaps, financial self-discipline by giving tax breaks. So, for example, while tax relief was removed from life assurance policies in the 1980s as part of creating the level playing field, new tax reliefs were created in the early 1990s to encourage private saving and investment. Paradoxically, the former removed a fiscal incentive to save long-term (minimum 10 years), whereas the new tax breaks were on short-term savings (TESSAS – 5 years) and PEPS, having instant withdrawal facilities. In some respects, this was not thereby encouraging new saving so much as simple transfers of existing building society and other low-interest savings into the new medium. It would seem then that these new incentives on saving not only contradicted the concept of a 'level playing field', but also the concern to shift responsibility for long-term security (for example, pensions, long-term care) from the state to the private citizen. These are just a few of the examples that show the incoherence and unplanned nature of much policy-making and the danger of interpreting a general mood in government circles concerning the management of the economy as identical to the details of specific policy intentions and their effects.

FINANCIAL SELF-DISCIPLINE

The crisis of welfare interacts with the transformation of financial institutions to produce particular effects on financial self-discipline. However, these effects are difficult to predict in advance and cannot be understood simply as a directly planned outcome of government policy. Nevertheless, the current conjuncture is perhaps best understood from a historical perspective which reveals that there have been frequent occasions where particular schemes of saving, insurance and investment have been implicated in attempts to render certain categories of social agent into new forms of financial self-discipline by restructuring their field of action. Thus existing financial institutions become enrolled in the broader task of governing and disciplining populations and subjects.

> Insurance and its associated knowledge practices come to stand at the intersection between concerns about individual and collective security and a variety of practical problems of liberal governance. (Knights and Vurdubakis, 1993, p. 759)

The idea of 'governmentality' (see Foucault, 1991; Miller and Rose, 1990) draws attention to what Foucault refers to as 'the art of government', 'the correct manner of managing individuals, goods and wealth' (Foucault, 1991, p. 92). Governmentality is not simply a synonym for government or the state; it refers to the broader relations between knowledge, power, populations and social institutions. Insurantial technologies are a crucial means whereby governmentality can be practised and projects for the control and disciplining of populations constituted and managed. Insurance and actuarial practices construct risks as phenomena that can be managed through the creation of risk profiles and institutions to protect the individual against loss or hardship. Insurance practices therefore are a key mechanism through which individuals and governments perceive and construct the value of not just material objects but human life itself. Insurance introduces financial calculations as part of the normal everyday activity of monitoring the self. Ewald, for example, states that

> the insurer's activity is not just a matter of passively registering the existence of risks, and then offering guarantees against them. He 'produces risks'; he makes risks appear where each person had hitherto felt obliged to submit resignedly to the blows of fortune...Insurance is the practice of a type of rationality potentially capable of transforming the life of individuals and that of a population. (Ewald, 1991, p. 200)

In this sense, insurance may be seen as one of the earliest practices linked to 'financial self-discipline' (Knights, 1988). It is a form of discipline grounded on a social ethic which has economic rationality, planning and foresight, prudence and social/moral responsibility among its cardinal virtues (Daston, 1987; Ewald, 1986).

From this point of view, the current moves to privatize forms of insurance and create a new form of governmentality based on actuarial calculations of risk in old age and so on necessitate a broad programme of restructuring of social institutions – the deregulation of the financial services companies, the reconstitution of the regulatory system, the dismantling of state welfare and the construction of tax incentives to invest and the promotion of ideals of self-help and self-discipline. Such a programme of reconstructing governmentality and financial self-discipline is not unique; it has been studied in previous eras, particularly the late nineteenth century when there was a similar coming together of private and public institutions of insurance to lay the basis for the mix of state welfare and private provision which has been institutionalized in different ways in most Western European societies since that period (see Morgan, 1996, for a discussion of these models; also Esping-Andersen, 1990, 1994). Insurance in both its private and public (for example, national insurance) forms has been an essential instrument of moral reform for a variety of social movements and political programmes since the nineteenth century (for example, Donzelot, 1980; Supple, 1974; Gosden, 1961, pp. 155–98; 1973). It promises economic security and stability in a precarious and uncertain world (Knights and Vurdubakis, 1993). The current period, however, can be interpreted as a new extension of the principle of financial self-discipline.

But it is not just a precarious and uncertain world that serves as the condition for increased financial self-discipline. Clearly medieval society could be seen as far more precarious and yet it was not so marked by financial self-discipline as the current day. Indeed it may be argued that the very depiction of a world as precarious and uncertain is a part of modern subjectivity where individuals are particularly insecure. In part, this derives from the creation of an individualistic form of society where it is appropriate to turn the self into an object to be managed (Foucault, 1979a, 1979b, 1980; Miller and Rose, 1990). In part, however, this very task of self-management and self-discipline is undermined because it is dependent on others and yet individuals in contemporary society are increasingly separated off from one another. Individuals are pushed back on themselves to develop a meaningful sense of their own identity (Foucault, 1982; Knights, 1992). Security therefore remains elusive, but in a materialistic society like our own, monetary wealth promises the security not available elsewhere. For it is not only a means of purchasing other goods that help to sustain life in the present but also it can be stored or invested to secure subjective well-being in the future. Consequently, financial self-discipline can be seen directly as an identity-securing practice as well as an indirect effect of particular exercises of power or transformations of the field of action of individuals. The pursuit of material wealth offers both security and self-autonomy simultaneously, since, in contrast to other practices, it promises social respect through conformity to the material and symbolic values of success at the same time as it frees individuals from dependence on others for their survival. For this reason, if no other, financial security is a condition and consequence of the discursive formation of the modern subject and the power relations in which subjectivity is embedded.

As a general point, therefore, the restructuring of financial institutions and state welfare provision in the 1980s and 1990s is best understood from a theoretical point of view as a reconstitution in the nature of financial self-discipline. As has been shown elsewhere (Knights and Vurdubakis, 1993; Donzelot, 1980; Ewald, 1986), there are many other examples of this process of reconstitution. Each example needs to be identified according to its own conditions of existence and unanticipated consequences. There is no simple evolutionary transition to a model 'financial self-discipline' which will characterize all societies. Rather specific discourses and practices are reshaped within specific contexts.

FINANCIAL SERVICES, CRISIS AND FINANCIAL SELF-DISCIPLINE

In the context of this theoretical discussion, the proliferation of financial discourses through the institutions of banks, insurance companies, government and the media since the mid-1980s has encouraged a self-discipline to enter the sphere of domestic or family finance on a much greater scale than previously imaginable. For example, between 1990 and 1994 total savings in the UK increased by 27 per cent to a total of £157 544 million which represented a growth rate of approximately twice that of inflation (Green *et al.*, 1996, p. 5). Since the 1970s in real terms total UK financial assets have risen much faster than the gross national product and an increasingly larger proportion of those assets are mediated through financial service institutions. For example, the share of assets managed by life assurance and pensions institutions increased from 11 per cent in 1960 to 30 per cent in 1994 (Green *et al.*, 1996). Most recently, discourses on financial services have proliferated as a result of a variety of regulatory and deregulatory legislation, and media attention on the scandals that are an outcome of the industry failing to conform adequately to the new regulatory regime.

In addition, the financial and money pages of most newspapers and radio and television programmes have expanded as they have found a popular market for generic advice as product diversification, tax concessions and new regulations make the financial services ever more complex. While containing a good deal of negative stereotyping, the overall impact of all this discourse is to make it difficult for the general public to avoid being confronted by what financial services are offering them as consumers. Against the background of a real or imagined steady withdrawal of the state from social security, pensions and welfare provision, this proliferation of discourses has a tendency to stimulate an interest in financial services products that perhaps only requires limited effort on the part of the sector to transform into financial self-discipline. These changes are a product of neo-liberal shifts in economic management that are in favour of 'free market' principles and a minimalist state. The consequence of this policy is that there is an ideological urge to reduce the state's involvement in welfare. The implication of this in a social and economic world that, it may be argued, exhibits increasing elements of uncertainty and insecurity is that those able to pay for private means of insuring welfare risks will do so. In this sense, the more the state withdraws from the provision of collective security, the more financially self-disciplined the population becomes.

There are, however, serious limits to this development which indicate the complex interactions involved in reconstituting financial self-discipline and therefore the indeterminate nature of the outcome of this process.

On the one hand, the Financial Services Act (FSA) was introduced in order to protect investors and could have provided the appropriate conditions in which to shift some welfare responsibilities from the state to the private sector by reassuring investors about their decisions. On the other hand, there was little coordination within government between the departments involved in privatizing pensions and those involved in introducing the Financial Services Act. As a result, the regulatory context was not in place prior to the decision to allow the financial services to sell personal pensions. Consequently, dramatic mis-selling of personal pensions by the private sector took place as unscrupulous sales staff, building on the government's exhortations to people to purchase personal pensions, encouraged consumers to contract out of their company or occupational pension schemes, a decision which has later been seen to be detrimental to the financial security of many customers. Government advertising about personal pensions as part of its campaign to offload as many government pensions contracts as possible provided a background of legitimacy for what was essentially bad advice since company pensions can rarely be bettered by personal schemes. Thus the government was not all-powerful or omniscient in achieving its goal. On the contrary, by poor timing, it has ultimately rendered its goal less achievable since the scandal over personal pension selling has made some people resistant to further inducements to shift into new forms of saving for retirement.

This reflects the more general point that FSA regulation has revealed more dramatically than ever before the nature of the practices being undertaken in the financial services industry. As these have been revealed, they have almost inevitably contributed further to the distrust which people feel for the industry. In the short term, the Financial Services Act has provided a standard against which journalists and consumer interests could measure the inadequate regulatory performance of firms and thereby sensationalize improprieties. Turning the breaches of the rules of the regulators into public scandals, the media have clearly reduced the public's confidence in financial institutions – the exact opposite of what was anticipated or desired by government. The FSA was expected to prevent fraudulent and immoral practices that were seen to be bringing the financial services and Britain's role as an international centre of finance into disrepute. As long as there was a sense of mistrust regarding distribution in financial services, it was unlikely that private savings and investment could be encouraged on the scale necessary for the state to withdraw from social security provision beyond a minimalist 'safety net'. Yet paradoxically, the FSA has actually created a situation where negative media attention has produced an even greater public distrust of, and disaffection with, financial services. It has in the short term affected the behaviour of investors so negatively as to obliterate many of the potentially positive effects that the regulations could have on consumption. In effect, it has undermined financial self-discipline by making people less interested and willing to look after their own financial affairs and more likely to look to the state.

Another aspect of regulation that could be seen as contradicting the concern of governments to render individuals more financially self-disciplined is the problem of 'moral hazard'. Some practitioners who believe that regulation has gone too far argue that the level of regulation on financial services and the protection offered to consumers in terms of compensation for companies that go into liquidation creates a moral hazard. Investors may just as well take the highest risks with their investments on the grounds that they stand to gain excessive returns but with no downside risk due to regulatory compensation. Thus, rather than enhancing financial self-discipline, regulation may undermine it by making investors careless in the belief that they cannot lose because they will be rescued by government. Investor carelessness in effect attracts companies into the market that do not take the conventional precautions in the knowledge that they can secure a lot of business by offering excessive returns. The flow of business to such a company then contributes directly to the event that triggers the compensation requirements since the size of the funds clearly increases the potential for losses in a venture that is not risk-averse (Heimer, 1985, p. 31). Moral hazard is a routine problem of insurance practices since the knowledge that a risk has been insured can readily reduce the care that individuals give to the object of insurance. In the case of investments (as against general insurance risks, for example, cars, houses, property and so on), the nature of the moral hazard is complex. Regulation may guarantee compensation in the case of fraud or bankruptcy. It may further reduce the likelihood of these events by monitoring and control through agencies like the Bank of England or the Department of Trade and Industry. The consumer may feel that all companies are equally safe and therefore there is no reason to search out one from the other, once again reducing financial self-discipline. However, investment returns vary between companies and regulation offers no redress to the investor who invests with a company that has low returns unless it can be shown that inappropriate advice was given. There is therefore an incentive to search out best performers though here the difficulty of predicting best performance over the long term is such as to make this task problematic. Thus regulation has a complex effect on calculations of moral hazard and through this on the incentives for the consumer to become more financially self-disciplined.

The Financial Services Act has also had other consequences which may be seen as contradictory to the government's concern to encourage self-help and financial self-discipline. The regulations have encouraged a big decline of organizations offering independent advice in financial services (that is, advising clients on products from a number of insurance companies rather than just their own). For example, all the banks and a majority of the building societies have tied to a single insurance provider for endowment savings and pension products, largely for reasons of the higher costs of independence in regulation and training but also because by owning their own insurance companies, profits are secured at the production as well as the distribution end of the business. The result is that most consumers who look for financial advice from their insurance companies, banks and building societies receive advice only about the products of that particular company and are deprived of independent advice. This deprivation is reinforced by the increasing costs of regulation, forcing the independent advisers to go up-market so as to retrieve their escalating costs through economies of scale provided by high net-worth clients. It is only at these higher levels of wealth where independent financial advice is cost-efficient both for provider and client. Once again, therefore, the effect is that most consumers are not encouraged to examine a range of products in detail. They are offered a ready-made package from their usual bank or building society. The level of active individual involvement in this process is low. The impact on financial self-discipline is complex as it is undoubtedly the case that the growth of *bancassurance* (that is, banks which distribute the full range of insurance and investment products through their branch systems) has provided a greater and more broad-ranging degree of access to financial services for customers. Every high street in the UK now has several long-standing financial institutions with good brands and reputations willing and able to advise customers on the full range of insurance and investment products. Whether this induces financial self-discipline or possibly complacency on the part of the customer is not yet clear.

It can also be argued that the dramatic fall in total (i.e. regular and single premium) life and pension sales of 10 per cent between 1993 and 1994 (Green *et al.*, 1996) and 18 per cent between 1994 and 1995 (Whittaker, 1995) would appear to have some connection with the introduction of new regulations under the FSA. There has been an enormous increase in administration as well as education and training for sales and support staff and these increased activities cannot have been undertaken without negatively affecting productivity. Whether commission and charges disclosure has also directly had a negative effect on sales cannot be ascertained but there is little doubt that, as a result of many companies (e.g. the bancassurers) reducing significantly, and in some cases removing, the commission element of their remuneration packages, sales productivity is likely to have declined. This could certainly account for the much greater decline in life and pensions business of 33 per cent in *bancassurance* compared to only 18 per cent in the market as a whole between 1994 and 1995 (Whittaker, 1995).

Regulation also has a differential impact on types of companies within the system and the consumers which they serve. This raises a particular issue in the case of services provided to the less affluent in society. In the British context, this group have traditionally not been entirely dependent on the state. Rather they have been served by a particular type of insurance company (known as the industrial life company or the home service company). These companies have operated under a special set of regulations which has created a specific structure of distribution and products. The companies rely on collectors calling directly on clients at least once a month (and often in the past more often).

This regular collection system is highly expensive as a form of distribution and these products have therefore tended to have high charges and low returns compared to others. However, regular collection and personal contact between the client and the collector has made this system into a form of financial self-discipline for people who could not or would not save in any other way. The collector also comes to act as a type of money-lender by encouraging clients to cash in their policies early if they need some cash and then opening up a new product. In current parlance, this would be seen as 'churning' the products; it is advantageous to the collector who receives more commission each time a new policy is taken out. From the point of view of the client, it is not strictly economically rational as each time a new policy is opened, a new set of initial charges is incurred. On the other hand, it reinforces the role of the collector as a financial adviser and provider to the client who would otherwise be disconnected from any form of financial institutions.

The current regulatory system is undermining the conditions of existence of this process. Churning is generally frowned on and the poor value of industrial life products (because of their high distribution costs) means that most people are better advised not to purchase them. This is causing some of the home service companies to consider withdrawing from the market. If they do so, many of the clients which they have served will not be willing or able to take out the higher-value policies offered by other distribution channels. In effect, their current level of financial self-discipline (limited though it is) may actually decline.

Finally, the attempt to create a new form of financial self-discipline may be undermined by the changing nature of work and families in contemporary society. Economic deregulation has resulted in the generation of employment instability and impermanence for more and more people and not just those at the bottom of the class structure. Contemporary work is much more precarious than previously, often based on short-term contracts or other forms of impermanence, and the growth of new information technologies is contributing to a dramatic shift in the culture of work based on 'old-fashioned jobs' to one based on a contingent, 'just in time' workforce (Odih, 1995). Bank managers and factory workers, clerical staff and professionals are all subject to labour market forces that may currently deny them continuous lifetime employment, thus generating an insecurity that has not been witnessed by these occupations since before the Second World War. For not insignificant proportions of people, these insecurities are exacerbated by negative equity in their homes as a result of recent falls in house prices at a time when domestic property ownership has been strongly encouraged by tax incentives, easier mortgages and a history of increasing property values.

In these precarious times, then, saving a substantial part of one's income when in employment has become more important in order to ensure the means of subsistence when out of work, whether this is the result of retirement, sickness or unemployment. This has become ever more important because of the lengthening of the economically inactive period of people's lives at a time when, as the extended family declines, the younger generations are increasingly reluctant to absorb elderly relatives into their own domestic arrangements.

For a majority of women who have often structured their formal work roles as far as possible around their domestic activities, this experience of discontinuous employment, temporary and part-time work is nothing new. Continuous lifetime employment was never a realistic possibility in a patriarchal society where women assumed the responsibility for child-rearing and management of the domestic household. In terms of financial security, the population of women has traditionally been neglected not only by the private sector but by the state as well largely because of traditional male bread-winner assumptions that no longer and maybe never did have much validity. Given the high rates of divorce (one in three marriages and higher in the more underprivileged sectors of society) and the large number of single-parent (usually mothers) families, it is important to ensure that women make provision for their own pensions rather than relying on a male partner. However, neither government policy nor the private sector make this provision at all easy for women or increasingly for those men who are today experiencing much more insecurity and pre-cariousness in the labour market.

Although financial services providers are aware of the changes in employment trends and perceptions of personal insecurity, long-term con-tractual savings products such as endowments or pensions fail sufficiently to reflect these changes. Long-term contractual products are incompatible with the savings potential of those consumers not in continuous lifetime employment or having access to resources from such persons. These developments in our contemporary culture of work accentuate the need for flexibly structured contractual products. For if the traditional model of continuous lifetime employment is no longer valid, neither are contractual products that penalize interruptions in the premium payments to pensions or other long-term savings.

In sum, the private sector of financial services continues to offer contracts that are tailored more to outdated assumptions about lifetime continuous careers than to the reality of job insecurity and discontinuous employment (Odih, 1995), and to male head-of-household, bread-winner assumptions about gender in the family. But the government also helps to sustain this outdated view because the rules surrounding pension products also discriminate against those not in continuous lifetime employment and especially women who have often moved in and out of the labour market depending on family circumstances.

SUMMARY AND CONCLUSION

This chapter has explored the interrelationship between financial institutions, the crisis of welfare and the development of financial self-discipline. Deregulation has promoted a more competitive market-place in which the range of firms and products available to the consumer have mushroomed. This fits well with the government's overall goal of dealing with the crisis of welfare through shifting the burden from the state on to private individuals and families. In order to achieve this, the government has promoted the values of financial self-discipline and sought to create a regulatory system in which the consumer has confidence in investment and saving.

In numerous ways the conditions are extremely appropriate for consumers to be persuaded to become more financially self-disciplined and there is much evidence to suggest that government acts positively not only to reproduce those conditions but also to make it easier to save and invest. So, for example, the economy and welfare system continue to be managed in such a way as to encourage the belief that self-help is the only alternative to a state system that either cannot or prefers not to fund social security and welfare beyond a minimal subsistence level. The government has also intervened heavily in forcing the financial services to become both more competitive and ethical, thus offering a more attractive, efficient and trustworthy service to consumers. Finally, the government has introduced many new fiscal incentives to encourage people to save and invest through the financial services either in the form of direct or indirect equities or tax-free savings accounts with building societies or banks.

However, the conclusions of this chapter are that considerable ambiguity and uncertainty prevail, undermining some of the intentions and interventions. First, some of these, such as the recent problem in the UK of negative equity in domestic housing as a result of the reverse of a long period of house price inflation, are simply an outcome of market forces combined with the effect of other public policies (e.g. the control of inflation) that have a higher priority than the encouragement of financial self-discipline. Others, such as the recent scandals over the mis-selling of pensions, are an unintended consequence of regulatory interventions that are otherwise essential for creating the appropriate climate of consumer confidence and trust. The failure of the sector to ensure compliance with the new regulations has had the opposite effect, giving the media and consumer associations considerable ammunition to criticize the industry, and resulting in a public mistrust that may for some time limit the impact of the efforts of both government and the financial services to generate financial self-discipline.

But second, many of the government's interventions may be seen as inconsistent and contradictory in their impact on consumers. For example, while encouraging saving in general through the introduction of tax efficient savings schemes such as TESSAs and PEPs, these tend to be short-term whereas the longer-term savings of life assurance endowments have been discouraged by the abolition of tax incentives that existed for several decades previously. Also the failure to change the tax legislation on pensions to allow those in discontinuous employment to maintain such savings during periods of unemployment sends exactly the opposite of a self-help message to consumers, as does the complex set of regulations surrounding pensions that place ridiculous administrative burdens on both consumers and producers if they are to opt out of either the state scheme or occupational scheme. Furthermore, there is a major problem in the way in which the industry is restructuring so as to exclude certain groups (the less affluent who might previously have relied on the now less acceptable home service products) and to limit the range of advice offered to others (by encouraging many high street banks to go over to selling only their own products and making independent financial advisers focus more on high net-worth clients). In all these ways, the impact of the move towards financial self-discipline becomes diluted. The private sector of financial services does not appear to be ready, willing or able to meet the challenge of the current welfare crisis in all its complexity. Nor is the government consistent and strategic in its management of the problem.

Having noted some of the ambiguities, conflicting messages and uncertainties surrounding the financial services, it is still the case that deregulation and reregulation of financial services has resulted in a proliferation of discourses that in the longer term are likely to be productive, rather than destructive, of financial self-discipline. Of course, if the industry does not get its house in order sooner rather than later it is possible that a state-enforced savings system (in which funds are managed by private institutions) may be developed. This would represent a halfway house between full privatization and state control that in the current UK climate of post-neoliberalism may be the only realistic compromise. But it would be another government-induced boost to the financial services that, in the recent climate of poor compliance, could be interpreted as a reward for failure.

In conclusion, the chapter has offered an approach to understanding how financial institutions are at the intersection of a number of phenomena. From the point of view of government, financial institutions offer the possibility of escaping from the welfare crisis. From the point of view of consumers, they offer the opportunity for self-control and identity to be secured at least temporarily through material savings. However, the degree to which all three of these (government, individuals, and financial institutions) can actually come together to create a consistent and coherent model of financial self-discipline is still unclear. History shows that there have been moments when such transitions have occurred (Knights and Vurdabakis, 1993; Ewald, 1986; Donzelot, 1980). Whether we are moving through such a transition to a new stable system will not be clear for some time.

References

G. Burchall, G. Gordon and P. Miller (eds), *The Foucault Effect: Studies in Governmentality*. (London: Harvester, 1991).

L. Daston, 'The Domestication of Risk: Mathematical Probability and Insurance 1650–1830', in *The Probabilistic Revolution, Vol. I*. (Cambridge, Mass.: Cambridge University Press 1987).

J. Donzelot, *The Policing of Families*. (London: Hutchinson, 1980).

G. Esping-Andersen, *The Three Worlds of Welfare Capitalism*. (Cambridge: Polity Press, 1990).

G. Esping-Andersen, 'Welfare States and the Economy', in N.J. Smelser and R. Swedberg, (eds), *The Handbook of Economic Sociology*. (Princeton, NJ: Princeton University Press, 1994) pp. 711–32.

F. Ewald, *L'Etat Providence*. (Paris: Grasset, 1986).

F. Ewald, 'Insurance and Risk', in Burchall et al. (eds) (1991) pp. 197–210.

M. Foucault, *The History of Sexuality, Vol I*. (London: Allen Lane, 1979a).

M. Foucault, *Discipline and Punish*. (Harmondsworth: Penguin, 1979b).

M. Foucault, *Power/Knowledge*, edited by C. Gordon. (Brighton: Harvester, 1980).

M. Foucault, 'The Subject and Power', an afterword in H.L. Dreyfus and P. Rabinow, *Beyond Structuralism and Hermeneutics*. (Brighton: Harvester, 1982).

M. Foucault, 'Governmentality', in Burchall *et al.* (eds) (1991) pp. 87–104.

P.H.J.H. Gosden, *The Friendly Societies in England 1815-75*. (Manchester: Manchester University Press, 1961).

P.H.J.H. Gosden, *Self-Help: Voluntary Associations in the 19th Century*. (London: Batsford, 1973).

C. Green, J. Philips and D. Knights, *Retirement Related Saving in the UK: Estimating Market Sizes*. (Manchester: Financial Services Research Centre, UMIST, 1996).

A. Hamilton, *The Financial Revolution*. (Harmondsworth: Penguin, 1986).

J. Heimer, *Reactive Risk and Rational Action: Managing Moral Hazard in Insurance Contracts*. (Berkeley: University of Californial Press, 1985).

B. Jessop and R. Stones, 'Old City and New Times: Economic and Political Aspects of Deregulation', in L. Budd and S. Wilminster (eds), *Global Finance and Urban Living*. (London: Routledge, 1992). .

D. Knights, 'Risk, Financial Self-Discipline and Commodity Relations', *Advances in Public Interest Accounting*, 2 (1988) pp. 47–69.

D. Knights, 'Changing Spaces: The Disruptive Power of Epistemological Location for the Management and Organisational Sciences', *Academy of Management Review*, 17, 3 (1992) pp. 514–36.

D. Knights, 'Introduction', in D. Knights and T. Tinker (eds) *Financial Services and Social Relations*. (London: Macmillan, 1996, (forthcoming).

D. Knights, G. Morgan and F. Murray, 'Business Systems, Consumption and Change', in R. Whitley (ed.), *European Business Systems*. (London; Sage, 1992) pp. 198–218.

D. Knights and T. Vurdubakis 'Calculations of Risk: Towards an Understanding of Insurance as a Moral and Political Technology', *Accounting, Organisations and Society*, 19, 7/8 (1993) pp. 729–64.

D. Knights and H. Willmott, 'A Very Foreign Discipline: The Genesis of Expenses Control in a Mutual Life Insurance Company', *British Journal of Management*, 4, 1 (1993) pp. 1–18.

D. Knights and G. Morgan, 'Strategy under the Microscope: Strategic Management and IT in Financial Services', *Journal of Management Studies*, 32, 2 (1995) pp. 191–214.

D. Knights and P. Odih, 'A Statistical Revolution', *Money Marketing*, 26 October (1995) p. 32.

P. Miller and N. Rose, 'Governing Economic Life', *Economy and Society*, 19, 1 (1990) pp. 1–31.

G. Morgan, 'The Impact of Forms of Financial Security on Relations Between Employers and Employees', paper presented at the ESF EMOT Workshop, Barcelona, 25–7 January (1996).

P. Odih, *Demographic Profiles of the Consumer Market*. (Manchester: Financial Services Research Centre, UMIST, 1995).

B. Supple, *Legislation and Virtue: An Essay on Working Class Self Help and the State*. (London: Europa, 1974).

P. Whittaker, 'Distribution in Life and Pensions', *Financial Adviser*, 28 September (1995) p. 46.

Index